Britain's Greatest Private Detective

Britain's Greatest Private Detective

The Rise and Fall of Henry Slater

Nell Darby

An imprint of
Pen & Sword Books Ltd
Yorkshire - Philadelphia

First published in Great Britain in 2024 by
Pen & Sword True Crime
An imprint of
Pen & Sword Books Ltd
Yorkshire - Philadelphia

Copyright © Nell Darby

ISBN 978 1 39903 957 4

The right of Nell Darby to be identified as the Author of this work has been asserted by her in accordance with the Copyright, Designs and Patents Act 1988.

A CIP catalogue record for this book is available from the British Library.

All rights reserved. No part of this book may be reproduced or transmitted in any form or by any means, electronic or mechanical, including photocopying, recording or by any information storage and retrieval system, without permission from the Publisher in writing.

Typeset in INDIA by IMPEC eSolutions
Printed and bound in England by CPI (UK) Ltd.

Pen & Sword Books Ltd. incorporates the Imprints of Pen & Sword Archaeology, Atlas, Aviation, Battleground, Discovery, Family History, History, Maritime, Military, Naval, Politics, Railways, Select, Transport, True Crime, Fiction, Frontline Books, Leo Cooper, Praetorian Press, Seaforth Publishing, Wharncliffe and White Owl.

For a complete list of Pen & Sword titles please contact

PEN & SWORD BOOKS LIMITED
47 Church Street, Barnsley, South Yorkshire, S70 2AS, England
E-mail: enquiries@pen-and-sword.co.uk
Website: www.pen-and-sword.co.uk

or

PEN AND SWORD BOOKS
1950 Lawrence Rd, Havertown, PA 19083, USA
E-mail: uspen-and-sword@casematepublishers.com
Website: www.penandswordbooks.com

"I am not Henry Slater outside this office;
I am Smith, or Brown, or anything rather than myself."
- *Interview with Henry Slater, 1893*[1]

Contents

Acknowledgements		viii
Introduction		x
Chapter 1	When Kate met Tom... and Hugh	1
Chapter 2	The World of the Private Detective	16
Chapter 3	The Office on Basinghall Street	28
Chapter 4	Changing Direction	39
Chapter 5	Finding Evidence	49
Chapter 6	The Honey Trap	58
Chapter 7	The Agency Burns	64
Chapter 8	At the Divorce Court	81
Chapter 9	Will the Real Henry Slater Please Stand Up?	90
Chapter 10	Dubious Tactics	105
Chapter 11	Before the Chief Magistrate	112
Chapter 12	Cartwright's Revenge	121
Chapter 13	Off to the Old Bailey	128
Chapter 14	A Very Peculiar-Looking Man	134
Chapter 15	Plymouth Girls and Private Detectives	143
Chapter 16	The Verdict	155
Chapter 17	A Final Identity	165
Bibliography		173
Notes		178
Index		222

Acknowledgements

Thanks are due, as always, to my husband John and children Jake and Eva for their love and support. Without them, this book would not have been written. Thanks also to Carolyn and Saranna for endless coffees and the occasional cake.

I'd also like to thank the friends who have been there for me while I was writing this book: in particular, Royston, Julie, and Andrew, but also the other members of my running club, Hook Norton Harriers, and the team at Chipping Norton School parkrun for their support.

NOTE:

For ease of reading, events have, in places, been simplified as newspaper reports on occasion confuse or duplicate dates, names and locations. Some of the detectives who feature in this book used pseudonyms for work and were referred to both by these names and, in some cases, even charged with offences under their pseudonyms. For consistency, I have used their real names throughout, while making clear their pseudonyms and how these were used.

The exception is Henry Slater, who was charged and tried under the name of Henry Scott - neither his usual pseudonym nor his real name. I have used Henry Slater where the courts referred to Henry Scott, unless it is important to the story.

Other names were frequently misspelled in newspaper reports and official documents, the key names being Samuel Marrison, frequently referred to as Morrison, and Frederick Davies, also referred to as Davis. I have gone with the former spellings of their surnames, as used in birth and death records. Similarly, John Pracy was recorded as both Pracy and Pracey; I have used the name his birth was recorded under - Pracy.

Introduction

Probate, Divorce and Admiralty Division, Royal Courts of Justice, London. 30 March 1904

He stood there, sweating. Feeling the perspiration seeping into his moustache, meandering down the back of his neck, as he stood there in the dock, he waited his turn before the prosecutor. He tried to focus on just that one individual, sensing, but trying to ignore, the other four men who would also be facing this stern questioner. He was used to adopting different personalities, pretending to be someone else, and he knew he should be taking on a new persona now - that of a calm, professional man eager to refute the allegations against him. But how could he do that when this was also a trial by media? Every step of the long-drawn out journey to trial had been eagerly covered by the newspapers; every aspect dwelt on lasciviously in numerous column inches in papers that covered every inch, it seemed, of the United Kingdom, from Scotland down to Cornwall. It wasn't over yet, either: the case would rumble on for months after this. It was a story that had started in the divorce court, would progress to the Bow Street Police Court, and would end, in ignominy, in the Central Criminal Court – more popularly known as the Old Bailey.

The man standing there was Henry Slater, the 55-year-old proprietor of London's, and arguably Britain's, most famous private detective agency. Certainly, he had spent the previous decade arguing that his was the best agency in the land. He had prepared himself carefully for this day, both physically and mentally. An imposing man, his hair was neatly brushed to one side, his face freshly shaved apart from the thick moustache that extended to either side of his pursed mouth. Clad in a pinstriped suit, complete with waistcoat, a thin tie and high-collared white shirt, he looked every inch the dapper, successful, professional man. He had gone into the Royal Courts of Justice, the home of the High Court, that morning, confident that this was a formality, and that he could breezily convince those inside that nothing was remiss. Once inside, however, he had rapidly realised that what had appeared to be simply an annoyance was far more serious, and it was going to focus on him as an individual. As soon as he realised this fact, the sweat started forming, and his hands became damp, much to his annoyance. Now, he stood there, conscious of pulling himself up to his full height to present an image of self-confidence. He was aware that this image was a sham, a front that hid a sweaty, increasingly nervous, individual. He had been in this building before, but only as a witness, there to tell the court the information he had assembled with the help of his team of staff. Now, all eyes were on him again, but for a wholly different reason.

The High Court of Justice had been established in 1875, following an act two years earlier that had merged eight existing courts into a supreme court consisting of the High Court and the Court of Appeal. One of the High Court's divisions was the Probate, Divorce and Admiralty Division - a cumbersome title and one that encompassed both the living and the dead. Prior to 1875, these had been separate courts: the High Court of Admiralty, the Court of Probate, and the Court for Divorce and Matrimonial Causes. Although divorce and probate might arguably have things in common, it's harder to see why the admiralty court - a court with jurisdiction over maritime contracts and offences - would be combined with the other, more personal, courts. Unsurprisingly, perhaps, the unwieldy name of the admiralty court was often informally replaced with a nickname: The Court of Wills, Wives and Wrecks.

The prior Court for Divorce and Matrimonial Causes had itself been short-lived. Prior to 1857, a divorce could only be obtained by means of a private act of parliament, and matrimonial issues had been the preserve of the ecclesiastical, or church, courts. Following the introduction of the Matrimonial Causes Act, however, jurisdiction for marriage matters was transferred from the church courts to a new Court for Divorce and Matrimonial Causes. Less than twenty years later, this court became part of the new Probate, Divorce and Admiralty Division. It was here where divorce petitions were presented, and evidence heard relating to why a marriage had irretrievably broken down.

From 1882, divorce cases were heard at the Royal Courts of Justice - a gothic, grandiose building that opened that year. It was, and is, located at the point where Fleet Street meets the Strand, a centre for lawyers for centuries, with four Inns of Court surrounding it. Although the Great Hall of the Royal Courts of Justice was intimidating, with its high vaulted ceilings, echoing tiled floor and austere character, the divorce court was somewhat different. Each individual court - and each had its own character, being designed by a different architect - was located off the Great Hall; once you had walked the gamut of the entrance, footsteps clattering along, you found yourself in a smaller, more familiar room.[2] It was familiar because it featured at the centre of most private detectives' working lives: it was their evidence that provided much information for the divorce petition, and they could be called on to give evidence in court as a result. It was also familiar to any churchgoer, for there was much resemblance to a church, with its rows of wooden pews, set back from a central table at which the main players would sit. Around the wood-panelled walls were framed painting of former judges, and at the sides, large bookcases. There was plenty of room for each of the participants - defendant, magistrate, and more - as well as for the public, eager to hear salacious tales of sex and intrigue. It was, in fact, a relatively informal space: wooden boxes and benches, but simple, with pale walls and less formality than some other places he could have been in. Despite the lack of formality in the room's appearance, however, Henry Slater was nervous, and defensive: he knew he was going to get asked questions that he didn't want to answer. If he answered them honestly, his responses would expose him and rip away the fabric of mystique that he had carefully draped around his identity, his finances, and his business.

Slater was at a hearing called by the King's Proctor, an individual who acted as the Crown solicitor, and who would intervene in divorce cases where it was suspected that information was being suppressed.[3] At this time, the King's Proctor was Hamilton Cuffe, the Earl of Desart. Slater's agency had been hired two years earlier to shadow an individual whose wife sought a divorce; she had duly petitioned for the divorce, and the case had been heard at the divorce court. The King's Proctor, however, had raised suspicions that the information found out by Slater's detectives, and presented as evidence, was not all it seemed. He was authorised to investigate, and so he had stopped the divorce proceedings. He called on Slater, as head of the detective agency, together with the staff who had been tasked with finding evidence for the divorce case, to explain their actions. Although this was not a trial in name, it felt like one. There was a special jury, and a solicitor opening the case on behalf of the King's Proctor; witnesses would be called, and the facts examined.

In addition, Slater's reputation was on the line, as it would be in a trial, just by the fact that he and his associates had been summoned to the High Court. The lives and careers of the other four men - his long-term associate Albert Osborn, a respected solicitor, and his manager, George Henry, among them - were, he felt, in his hands, too. He felt a mix of emotions: trepidation, anxiety, anger at being put in this position by his employees, and a rising fear that the self he had carefully created for himself over the previous decades was about to be exposed. He was right to fear what was about to happen, and yet it was perhaps inevitable. In charge of the cross-examination was the formidable Sir Edward Carson, the Dublin-born barrister, king's counsel, and solicitor-general who, nine years earlier, had led the defence against Oscar Wilde's action for criminal libel. He had been employed by the defendant, the Marquess of Queensberry, who had himself employed private detectives as part of his assembling of evidence relating to Wilde's lifestyle. In court, Carson's opening speech had led to Wilde abandoning the libel case, ruining himself in the process when he was ordered to pay Queensberry's legal and detective bills. Carson, a striking man with piercing blue eyes, was renowned for his brilliance and his second-to-none legal knowledge and ability; he was a superb speaker and made defendants quail. Although Henry Slater was himself a formidable man, and of similar age to Carson, his contemporary was more than a match for him, and he knew it.

The questions, when they finally came, came fast and furiously. How many names had he passed under in the course of his career? What was his name when he was a child? What was his first occupation? What was his next occupation? Had he been on the stage? Did he perform for pay? Had he been dismissed from a job? What did he do next? Under what name? So many questions: they kept coming and coming. As he struggled to answer, trying to get his facts straight, trying to remember, he heard a swell of noise in the court. What was that sound? It started as a gentle rumble, but grew in noise until it was almost a chorus of laughter. Everyone was laughing: the lawyers, the clerks, the public up there in the gallery. They were laughing at him.

His face grew hot, and he knew it would be red to observers. He felt the sweat seeping into his shirt collar. But still the questions kept coming: why had he taken another name? Had he ever been attacked in print? Had he acted against his accuser? Had he changed his name – again – because of those attacks on him?

One of the last questions was more of a statement. No: it was an accusation, one that sealed his status now as a laughable creature. Sir Edward Carson, with a barely imperceptible sneer, said: "You say you are the greatest detective of the age?"[4]

And to that, what else could he say but yes, as that is what he had been saying for years and years'? He was Henry Slater, head of Britain's most famous detective agency, and it was his reputation that he now needed to defend.

Chapter 1

When Kate met Tom... and Hugh

The events that led to the downfall of Henry Slater and his agency started on a summer's day back in 1891. The setting was Forest Gate; not, as it is now, a built-up district of London, sharply contrasting with the green space of Wanstead Flats at its northern boundary. In the late nineteenth century, this was a thriving area of Essex, with new villas being built to accommodate those with aspirations. People came to live in Forest Gate from across England, from Scotland and even further afield. They found work as leather sellers, sail makers, labourers; a clerk might be the neighbour of a butler, and have a confectioner living two doors away. It is difficult to pin Forest Gate down to a particular class of resident because it was so mixed, and its residents in many cases defy pigeon-holing. For every resident who had moved out from the urban east end, there were others who had moved in from rural areas. Dust sifters, bottle washers, and engine cleaners lived and worked alongside cowmen, dairymen and brickmakers, older occupations mixing with newer industrial ones in an area that was becoming assimilated with the metropolitan sprawl.

It was a time of change in Forest Gate, and the expanding population put pressure on the parish. Those who had first been tempted to the area by better transport, with the first train station opening at Forest Gate by 1841, would find themselves far better served from 1894, when the Tottenham and Forest Gate railway would open, offering a new route from Barking to St Pancras and on to the City.[5] This would be a sign of things to come, a closer connection between the area and the metropolis that would lead to its integration into Greater London. On 4 July 1891, a young woman from Forest Gate would set off from her family home and travel the short distance to All Saints Church in West Ham to marry her fiancé. This couple were in some ways typical of the local population. Neither was originally from the local area – one had moved into it with her family, and the other was only there for the purpose of the marriage. The wife-to-be was 19-year-old Kate Sampson, the youngest of seven children born to pastry cook and biscuit baker Henry Sampson and his wife Jane. Both were originally from the market town of Buntingford in Hertfordshire, but following their marriage – at Kennington in 1855 – they had moved around, as was fairly common for Victorians in search of work.[6] Jane, in among these moves, had a steady stream of children, starting in 1857, and ending in 1872 with the birth of Kate, her youngest child.

The birthplaces of the seven children, together with evidence from the censuses, show the mobility of the family, as they moved around the country. In London, they lived in Southwark, Mile End and Borough, all in south London; they also lived in Sussex, where Frank and Jessie, the nearest children in age to Kate, were born in Portslade.[7] Kate was then born in 1872, back in Southwark.[8] By the end of the 1870s, however, they had moved to west London, settling at 16 Fowell Street in North Kensington. The road no longer exists, having been demolished in the twentieth century as part of clearance works to construct a new housing estate.[9] However, it was a typical London street, lined either side with three-storey mid-nineteenth century terraces, each fronting onto the road, with a single, low front window from where friends and neighbours would walk past at the same level as residents inside.

The area has long housed residents of mixed fortunes; in the mid-nineteenth century, residents of Notting Dale – the part of North Kensington in which Fowell Street was situated – were drawn largely from the working classes, and many of the women who lived there worked as servants or laundresses. It was also home to substantial piggeries, and many families kept both pigs and other animals, such as chickens. Cholera found a home here, resulting in Charles Dickens referring to the area as a 'plague spot'.[10] However, the area was not regarded as a slum but more as a respectable working-class area, and by the 1890s, the area would improve when a park was created, and new houses started to be built.[11]

The Sampsons were certainly respectable people, but not well-off, and Henry's career was not secure, for by 1881, he was no longer baking but instead working as a basket-maker. Henry and Jane's daughters were educated at local schools, with Kate attending the St Francis Roman Catholic School before enrolling with her older sister Jessie at St Clement's Road School in Kensington and Chelsea, when she was 8 years old.[12] Then, when Kate was in her teens, her family made the decision to relocate from west London to the other side of the capital, settling in Forest Gate. Their new home was at 55 Ridley Road, a modern terraced house, but one the Sampsons shared with boarders – a valuable source of household income.[13]

Kate was ambitious and sociable, but she was not from a rich family, and she and her siblings had to work as soon as they left school. At the age of 20, Jessie was working as an assistant in a confectionery shop, while 18-year-old Kate was a cashier in a restaurant. She was also making plans to marry a man nearly twice her age – a man who had already been widowed and was already a father of one. She saw her intended spouse, Thomas Pollard, as her opportunity to progress out of North Kensington, and to provide her with some financial security – but unfortunately, her fiancé was not all he seemed.

Thomas Pollard, often known as Tom, had wooed her with tales of his wealth and his own career. He claimed to be a commercial agent, earning £1,000 a year in addition to a private income from property of £150 a year.[14] His father was a retired farmer, but who Thomas proudly listed as a 'gentleman' on his marriage certificate. This 36-year-old Cornishman appeared to be a good prospect: he would give Kate some financial security and the kudos of being a married woman. However, there were clear differences between the two as well, the difference in age being just one of them. Kate's fiancé had taken a succession of jobs over the previous few years, but had not succeeded in any of them. Back in 1887, he was working as a tea merchant, and was based in Fuzhou, China. Some of his business dealings were in the US, as at some point, Tom struck up a relationship with a young Baltimore girl named Leslie Hepburn Buckler. Leslie, born in 1861, was the daughter of a respected doctor, who had died when she was a baby. She had been brought up by her widowed mother Clara, in the household of her maternal grandfather, hardware merchant George Washington Ward. Leslie was perhaps rather spoiled as her mother's younger daughter, and although she had her grandfather living with her, she had no father to keep her on course. When she met the dapper English tea merchant, with his tales of an exotic life in the east, Leslie found it very easy to fall in love with him. In turn, Tom had his head turned by a woman who was regarded by her local community as 'one of the reigning belles' of Baltimore. The couple married at St Michael's and All Angels' Episcopal Church in Baltimore on 29 December 1887, but there were signs even at this point of Tom's unstable and unreliable character. He insisted on marrying in secrecy, not even letting Leslie's widowed mother know about the wedding. Afterwards, the newspapers wrote of how this had prevented Clara Buckler from objecting to the marriage, perhaps Tom's aim in the first place. The couple married by licence, in front of the Baltimore mayor and another society man, one Alexander Brown, and then immediately left the city for Washington. The speed of the marriage, and its secrecy, was viewed with suspicion by those who knew the Bucklers, and it was written about afterwards as both a mysterious and sensational affair. It was also commented on how Pollard was 'unknown' - nobody knew of his background, or his reputation.[15]

Tom had, by this point, taken his young American bride back to England, rather than China, with the couple settling at 9 Dorville

Road in Lee, Lewisham. Although the house no longer exists – the nineteenth-century housing on the road has been replaced with an estate of 1980s housing – the pretty Victorian villas of neighbouring roads such as Burnt Ash Road indicate how the road might have looked at the time the Pollards lived there. It was a pleasant area away from the dirt and bustle of central London. However, it was the bustle of the metropolis that Tom preferred, and so he left his wife to deal with life in an alien country, with no friends or family near her, and lived largely elsewhere, mainly in a lodging house in Bloomsbury. He was no longer a tea merchant, but had moved into insurance work. In late 1889, Leslie became pregnant, but she would not experience motherhood. On 3 July 1890, she gave birth to her only child, a son. Giving birth in Victorian times was fraught with danger, especially given that most women gave birth at home. Leslie, in common with many other women, developed an infection as a result of the birth, and this infection turned into puerperal septicaemia. Although this should have been a time of happiness, instead, Leslie was feverish and in pain. The infection was recognised as a risk of childbirth to the extent that many patients and doctors alike feared it; women knew that if they contracted it, it was likely to prove fatal. Therefore, when the warning signs emerged, which usually occurred three days after childbirth, with a headache, fever and abdominal pain that became increasingly severe, doctors knew that their patient was on borrowed time.[16]

She died nine days after her baby son's birth, aged just 26. On 14 July, Tom registered both the birth of his son and the death of his wife.[17] The baby, Leslie Buckler Pollard, was named after his mother, but would never know her. Tom, perhaps reluctantly, moved the baby into his Bloomsbury lodgings with him. It was possible that he hoped that marrying into a good Maryland family would give him financial security, although this proved not to be the case. His career in insurance, however, was shortlived, and his first wife's death seems to have effectively put an end to it.

Just a year after his wife's death and his son's birth, Tom was ready to marry again – this time to Kate Sampson. It was clear from the start that this was not a marriage of equals, nor of likeminded people. Not only was he old enough to be his new bride's father, he was also a widowed man in his thirties. She, though, was still in her teens, an independent single woman with different experiences of life to him, and different expectations. He had travelled to the US and to the East; he had experience of different cultures – he had also failed to find a job that he could make a long-term career out of, and was living off his first wife's money. The 1891 census – taken just four months before his wedding – records Thomas Pollard as a widower with no occupation, staying in a Bloomsbury lodging house with his 9-month-old son. He was now preparing to marry again, and to make Kate take on the role of mothering his child.

The marriage took place on American Independence Day, 1891. It was the day that Kate lost a lot of her own independence. The couple married at Kate's parish church – All Saints, West Ham. This had originally served the whole of West Ham, but by the middle of the nineteenth century, the parish had been carved up, and three years later, a new parish would be formed even closer to Kate's home – that of St Mark's in Forest Gate. But at this time, All Saints covered a fairly wide area, with its twelfth-century origins obscured by centuries of additions and extensions. The clock in the church tower, nearly half a century old at the time, was the prototype of Big Ben to the west; but otherwise, this was a church that summed up the increasing population of the local area, struggling to seat more than a small proportion of its parishioners. The Pollard marriage either 'was not attended' or 'would not have been attended' by any members of Thomas's family. This was not necessarily because of any concerns about the union, but simply because they lived too far away, and it would have been quite an undertaking to get from Cornwall to east London for the service. Therefore, the marriage was witnessed by Kate's mother Jane, and her sister Jessie.

It was not a happy marriage. Soon after the wedding, Kate realised that she had made a mistake. Her husband was not a hard-working professional man: he preferred to lounge around at home, or to head to a local inn to drink. He claimed to be disabled, suffering from paralysis, but could walk perfectly well when he wanted to go somewhere. He was not working, and Kate, instead of being able to act as housewife and domestic manager, had to continue working herself. She stayed in the restaurant trade, working her way up to become a restaurant manageress, earning fifteen shillings a week. Out of these wages, she gave money to her husband each week to 'maintain' himself. Kate Pollard was the only income earner in their relationship, so from the start, this was not a marriage of equals.

There must have been moments of conjugal toleration, at least, for in December 1892, Kate gave birth to the couple's only child - a son, Reginald Skerrett Pollard. The couple moved to Chippenham Road in Paddington, and on 4 January 1894, Reginald was baptised together with his half-brother Leslie, at St Peter's in Paddington.[18] In the 'father's occupation' box on both boys' baptism record was recorded 'wine merchant' - perhaps an angry joke from Kate, for Thomas Pollard was, by now, a drunkard - incapable, it seemed, of getting a job, let alone holding one down.[19] Shortly after the baptism, Leslie was sent, in the company of a female servant, to America. Little Leslie's family in Maryland was willing to get to know and care for this little boy. He would be brought up by his maternal grandmother and his aunt Bessie - his mother's older sister - and remain in the States for the rest of his life, dropping his Pollard surname and becoming known as a Buckler instead. Tom had been able to almost delete his first family from his consciousness, but he would also prove unable to look after his second.

Despite the reduction in her family responsibilities caused by little Leslie leaving England, Kate remained frustrated. She was an ambitious woman anxious to make something of her life. However, she was held back by a spouse who wanted to be looked after, and who did not want to contribute anything to the marriage, whether financially or emotionally. She was looking for more than this disappointing union, reluctant to believe that this was to be her lot in life. She continued to work, and to lead her own life, but there was only so long she could remain with Tom. She was young, and eager for the attention that her husband seemed incapable of giving her. Another man, a real man, surely, would appreciate her more than Tom did – she just needed to find him.

And so it proved, as 1894 showed itself to be a year of change. Not only had both Thomas's boys been baptised, and 3-year-old Leslie shipped off to the US, but back home in London, Kate was soon provided with a reason, and the help, to leave her marriage. She went shopping in west London one day, and on heading into a shop, she met a rather portly man in his late twenties. He was well dressed, had a small moustache and an eye glass, and stood with confidence. In turn, he was immediately struck by this young, confident lady with the strong features and fashionable dress. He introduced himself to her as Hugh Knowles.

As with many Londoners, his outer façade of well-to-do Englishman masked a more complex family background; Hugh's father, Charles Julius, was, in fact, a Russian émigré, and Hugh had been born with the more exotic family surname of Kino, his family only later changing their name to the more English Knowles. His father was a successful tailor and merchant, with bases both in central London and in the City. However, his parents were also keen art lovers and collectors, owning a collection of art that included works by Alphonse Legros and James McNeill Whistler.[20] Hugh had been born in Park Lane and brought up in Kensington, both his family and neighbouring households looked after by several servants. In 1881, the Knowles family – still then known as Kino – employed a governess, two housemaids, a cook, and a nurse.[21] Given the continued presence of a governess in the house up until he was of school leaving age, it seems that Hugh was educated at home with his siblings, unlike Kate.

Hugh was undoubtedly well off, and he carried himself in the manner of a gentleman. Kate was entranced by his attentions, and Thomas Pollard had the opportunity to notice this instant attraction. He had arrived at the shop shortly after Kate, and saw his wife deep in conversation with the stranger. He immediately headed over to introduce himself to the man as Mrs Pollard's husband, making clear his 'ownership' over his wife. Despite Tom Pollard's presence at their initial meeting, a friendship developed between Kate and Hugh.

Kate now had something else in her life apart from work, childcare, domestic arrangements, and tolerating a husband she saw as lazy and drunken. Hugh would take her for dinner, or for walks. He later denied having taken Kate to the theatre, but this was a denial for appearance's sake. Their friendship excluded Thomas. Hugh never came to the Pollards' house, claiming that Thomas's drunken behaviour made it impossible for Kate to receive guests there. Despite never going to Kate's house, for the next seven years, Hugh and Kate were regular confidantes. They insisted it was a friendship rather than a relationship, but their closeness would have raised eyebrows among their families. Hugh was clearly committed to Kate, and had the means to support her in a way that her husband had proved unable.

In February 1900, Hugh's father died. As a successful company owner, Charles Knowles left a substantial estate of well over a million pounds - nearly £80 million in today's money. Aside from the charitable donations he made to charity, servants and his 'poor relations', as he termed them in his will, he also left £10,000 to each of his children, in addition to trust funds for them from the remainder of his estate, after his bequests and payments to his widow had been made. Hugh now had even more money to spend on his married friend - and he earmarked some of it to be spent furthering his goal of freeing Kate Pollard from her wastrel husband.[22]

The 1901 census - recorded on the night of 31 March - showed Tom and Kate Pollard still living together. They were at 9 Thornfield Road, a small road set back from the busy Uxbridge Road in Shepherd's Bush. Thornfield Road was, and still is, dominated by three storeyed late Victorian or early Edwardian villas, in terraces, with big bay windows on the ground and first floors: living in one of these modern villas denoted a quiet, middle-class respectability. Yet even the census implies an unconventionality in this particular household. Thomas was listed as being a 47-year-old unemployed man; his young wife (incorrectly recorded as being 26, rather than 29) was still maintaining her husband through her work as a restaurant manageress. How must Kate have felt, working while her husband loafed around - as she saw it - in their terraced house in bustling Shepherd's Bush? She mentally compared him, and his life, with that of Hugh Knowles, who at this time was boarding in a similar-style house to Kate's. However, his lodgings were in Vincent Square, in the heart of Westminster and just a couple of minutes' walk from Westminster Cathedral to the west, St James's Park to the north and the river, the mighty Thames, to the east. He was in the heart of things, living off his family's property, and enjoying all the things that central London had to offer, while she was stuck with a husband she increasingly despised.

With her thirtieth birthday looming and a realisation that she could not continue with the status quo, Kate reconsidered her situation. She was the primary wage earner in her relationship - in fact, the only wage earner, given that Thomas was still refusing to get a job. The census gave his status in very clear terms: unemployed. He spent most of his time sprawled in bed, or out drinking, and showed no inclination to pull himself together and start maintaining his wife and son - let alone Leslie, his child by his first marriage, whose upkeep must have been largely, if not solely, paid for by his maternal family.

Initially, Kate played on traditional concepts of marital concern, expressing to Thomas that she was worried about his health; he looked peaky, it was no wonder that he could not work if he was unwell. Perhaps the air of London didn't suit him, as a Cornishman used to the sea air and countryside of the south-west? Thomas' parents had relocated to Plymouth in the 1890s, and so she encouraged him to take an extended vacation to Devon. She argued that by staying with his family, he would have no responsibilities, and the chance to take in the sea air and get well for his dependants. In return, she stated that she would continue to give him his weekly allowance of ten shillings from her wages.

Thomas needed little encouragement to undertake a holiday by the sea. Within a month of the census being recorded, in April 1901, he departed for Plymouth, and remained absent for the next year. Although ostensibly a short, health-related break, it was really the end of the Pollards' marriage, and the start of a separation that saw Thomas back in his parental home, doing what he wanted. Meanwhile, Kate remained in London, working - and maintaining her 'friendship' with Hugh Knowles. She decided, for propriety's sake, not to continue living in the Shepherd's Bush house on her own, but instead moved in with one of her sisters.

The three Sampson sisters were close. Jane, the eldest, was recorded in the census as Jane Sampson Dale, and was living with her daughters Janet and Evelina, then aged 14 and 10. The middle sister, Jessie, had been staying with Jane at her home in Forest Gate in March 1901.[23] However, when Kate told Tom to leave, she and Jessie then found lodgings together. Jessie was the obvious sister to choose. They were both independent working women with no children to care for. In addition, for a young woman with aspirations like Kate, living with Jane may not have been ideal. Although she claimed to be married, no marriage between Jane Sampson and a man named Dale can be found, and neither of her daughters had a father named on their birth certificates.[24] They were born as Sampsons, and the addition of Dale came later; despite Evelina claiming on her marriage to be the daughter of Henry Dale, gentleman, there is no evidence of him living with her mother, let alone being married to her.[25] Kate's unsuccessful marriage already made her suspicious in the eyes of a moralistic Victorian society; living with a sister who had had children out of wedlock would have made her even more so.

Although she had found a 'flatmate' and alternative accommodation, Kate did not want this situation to continue forever. It was not a satisfactory position for a still young woman who was frustrated by her husband's failures and who had an admirer who was willing to buy her expensive foods and drink, in a way that her husband never had. Hugh Knowles refused to buy Kate items such as jewellery – knowing they would cause suspicion – so instead gave her items such as salmon; items that she could explain away slightly easier. She consulted Hugh about what she could do. They both knew that in order to gain a divorce, Kate would need to prove that Thomas had both been cruel to her, and had committed adultery. The problem was that they had no proof that he had been unfaithful, and with his drinking habits, it seemed unlikely that he could be. Hugh knew that if Kate divorced Thomas, he could then marry her, and they could stop furtively scurrying around together under the guise of friendship. He had the means to help her, and a motive to do so, and so he did.

Hugh's suggestion was that he and Kate should engage the services of Britain's most famous detective agency, Slater's, to follow Thomas Pollard, and to uncover evidence of adultery. He also offered to pay whatever Slater's charged, becoming both Kate's benefactor and her protector. Slater's Detective Agency was duly commissioned by Hugh, and as he was paying a substantial amount of money for their services, he expected results. Nearly a year of undercover work, surveillance, and the passing of money in various directions passed – actions that would eventually bring the reputation not only of the

Pollards, but also of Slater's agency, particularly its boss, Henry Slater, into question. On 14 July 1902, though, on Kate's behalf, London solicitors Osborn and Osborn were able to file a petition for divorce. One half of Osborn and Osborn, Albert Osborn, was also Henry Slater's solicitor and long-time friend, and thus there was a ring of individuals intent on gaining Kate her divorce at any cost.

Kate's was one of over 700 divorces petitioned for in England between 1899 and 1903, and so she was just one of many men and women wanting to end their unhappy marriages.[26] Hers should have been like any others – a petition filed, a setting down of the cause of the marriage breakdown, a *decree nisi* issued, and, finally, the granting of a final decree. Divorces were good business both for lawyers and for private detectives, often employed by either husband or wife (or sometimes both) to find the evidence of adultery needed by the divorce court.

Court reports and the divorce petitions themselves recorded the progress of these divorces, with statements from the petitioner about where and when they had been married, if they had children, the detailed allegations of adultery and other bad behaviour on the part of their spouse. Often, reading these accounts is like delving into the lives of individuals to the extent that you feel rather guilty, prying into details of assignations at hotels, in restaurants, at dances; at men and women being 'shadowed' by their spouse, by friends, or by private detectives as they walk home after an evening out, or as they go to meet friends for a drink or a chat. The newspapers sent their reporters to cover divorce cases, as they often included rather salacious details that readers would love to read and discuss over their morning tea. The information rarely mentioned sex explicitly, but in these tales of men and women meeting people of the opposite sex who they were not married to were details of boundaries being stretched and passions being aroused. A number of key phrases and words were used to imply sexual congress, and these would have been known to, and understood by, newspaper readers.

From the 1870s, the number of petitions for divorce had started to increase from the small numbers seen in the immediate aftermath of the 1857 Matrimonial Causes Act being passed. It was no wonder that divorce suits had formed an increasingly large part of the newspaper diet at the same time, as editors realised just how juicy a good divorce could be. However, on the darker side, the court minutes of divorces contain painful detail of abuse: both of verbal abuse and of physical. Drinking, allegations of adultery even when nothing has occurred, neglect, sexual violence - all these issues are played out both in the divorce court and in writing, preserved for prosperity. Reading between the lines of some of these petitions, you can see women attempting to wrestle control of their lives back from some often quite overbearing men, challenging them and seeking to have some freedom. In one case, a very young woman married to an older man tried to get his permission to have a career on the stage only for him to collude with her father in banning her; in another, a woman was told to see her friends less because others might think she didn't want to spend her time with her husband. Instead, she asked for a divorce.

Although these divorces provided the newspapers with gossip, they were also a microcosm of Victorian and Edwardian life, sometimes showing a power struggle between husband and wife, and man and woman. They also hinted at a problem with the marriages of the middle- and upper-classes, where it was acceptable for a man to sow his oats before marrying, whereas a woman was expected to stay chaste until she wed. After marriage, expectations on both sides might not be met, and either or both parties look for a more compatible partner, or some romance, elsewhere. This might have been less of an issue for working-class partnerships, where sex before marriage more commonly took place without the same approbation, and where divorce was still too expensive an option to consider.

On the surface, the Pollards' case was little different from any other. There were accusations of adultery, of failing to maintain a family, of laziness and of sexual incontinence. They appeared to be just like any other warring couple, driven apart by their different ages, different aspirations, and different personalities. Kate's realisation that her husband was not the driven, ambitious, hardworking individual that she had been led to believe resulted in a distancing from him. She wanted a husband who did not depend on her for income such as Tom did.

Yet one key fact was different. Others might see their divorce make its ways through the court process smoothly, gaining the final decree only a matter of months after the initial filing of the petition. Unusually, it would take Kate Pollard four years to be free of her husband, in a convoluted and well-publicised case. She was initially granted her *decree nisi* in November 1902, only for it to be rescinded eighteen months later; she then tried again two years later, gaining her divorce in 1906. Between filing her first petition in July 1902 and her second in October 1905, several men involved in helping her to divorce her husband would be imprisoned; her solicitor would narrowly avoid the same fate; and one man would see his entire career destroyed. Divorce had made Henry Slater's name; and it would ruin it too.

Chapter 2

The World of the Private Detective

Henry Slater would be just one of many private detectives operating in London at the end of the nineteenth century and early years of the twentieth. Throughout Britain, in fact, numerous individuals had set up shop as 'private inquiry agents', operating, at their lowest level, from their kitchens and living rooms as sole traders, undertaking local work on a small scale. Others signed up as local agents for detective agencies, or for other, more established, sole traders, carrying out ad hoc engagements as needed, and only being paid when they took on a job. When no work was forthcoming, they went unpaid, and many had to retain jobs in other arenas with their detective work being more of a sideline or hobby, or something to put on a business card with pride even when work was pretty much non-existent. Higher up the scale, an individual might be able to find enough regular work to operate full-time as a detective, keeping overheads low, and sleuthing for fees and expenses from clients. In many a provincial town, there was a private detective advertising his - or her - services in the local press, and private detectives operated across the United Kingdom, from Glasgow to Belfast to Cardiff.

But it was in London that the private detective agencies really proliferated, taking advantage of people's natural suspicions about their fellow man in the metropolis to run well-staffed offices and to boast about their successes in the London and national papers. Because of the competition, these detectives advertised certain skills or talents, or areas of expertise, highlighting their central location and their years of experience. Former police detectives vied with those who had worked in many other fields before turning to detective work – actors and actresses with a skill for disguise and accents; commercial travellers and clerks; these private detectives came from a range of backgrounds and social classes. All, however, were drawn to a life of intrigue and variety, where they were being paid to delve into other people's lives.

Henry Slater would prove to have a particular talent both as a private detective and as the man behind an agency that became synonymous with private detection in England during the late nineteenth and early twentieth centuries. He was an innovative operator, utilising both press and technology, and creating novel publicity campaigns to keep his agency in the public eye. Yet he also owed much to an earlier private detective, working thousands of miles away across the Atlantic. That man was Allan Pinkerton. In a published account of his career, Glasgow-born Pinkerton made clear that he – and the other private detectives he employed – represented the law, rather than the police. It was the private detective who prevented crime, and who ensured that those who committed crime were held to account.[27] Pinkerton certainly practised what he preached.

Sometime between 1850 and 1853 – accounts vary – Pinkerton had set up a detective agency in his adopted city of Chicago, utilising his skills at self-promotion to gain high-profile work with the railroad companies and even with protecting Abraham Lincoln.[28] He employed both men and women, such as Kate Warne and the lesser known Hattie Lawton, to act as his detectives.[29] Pinkerton ensured that his successes were publicised, partly by writing a range of memoirs about his famous cases that were duly repeated in the press and became part of the Pinkerton mythology. He was a shrewd businessman who worked for whoever offered him money. Like Slater's Detective Agency, Pinkerton's started with one ambitious man who saw a chance and took it; unlike Slater's, however, Pinkerton's continues to operate to this day.

However, it is a development in British politics a decade before Kate Warne's death that also helped open up opportunities for private detectives from both genders, and all classes, on this side of the Atlantic. The passing of the Matrimonial Causes Act in 1857 created new private detectives, and agencies, in the UK. Although the Act opened up divorce to those of more moderate means than before – an Act of Parliament having previously been required to end a marriage – it required evidence of marital misdeeds. Therefore, individuals were employed to go undercover. They either followed individuals with the goal of finding them meeting with lovers (an act known as 'watching' or 'shadowing'), or infiltrated households, becoming servants within a family, or becoming friends with an individual suspected of having an affair. Women were particularly sought-after as detectives, as it was believed that an errant wife often needed little encouragement to become friends with another woman and to confide in her. Over the next couple of decades, nonetheless, an increasing number of both men and women became private detectives – some for just a short period of time, but others for longer. Some were engaged by the police initially, even with no experience, because their contacts or lifestyles were considered useful. Some male private detectives might in turn employ women to help them on cases where they thought her presence would be less obtrusive than a man's.

One of the early 'private inquiry offices' in London was that run by former Metropolitan police inspector Charles Field.[30] He established himself as a private detective prior to the Matrimonial Causes Act being passed – in the early 1850s – and so his initial work was focused on money-related issues; he described himself as keeping 'an office for the detection of fraud'.[31] For example, he promoted his involvement with the 'Rugeley Poisoner' case, where physician William Palmer was suspected of murdering his friend John Cook, after the latter died in 1855. Palmer was money-oriented, and several others in his circle had died mysteriously prior to Cook, including his mother-in-law, a horse racing friend, four of his children, and his wife. He forged his mother's signature to pay off his creditors, and took out a large life insurance policy on his wife before she died in 1854.[32] Charles Field was asked to investigate possible insurance frauds committed by Palmer, and, working with his assistant Mr Simpson, he established a 'strong suspicion of foul play' on Palmer's part.[33] Palmer would be convicted of murder and executed at Stafford prison on 14 June 1856.[34]

Field recognised that it was his police credentials that gave him authority and respect – he would continue to be described in the press as 'the detective officer' Field for several years after establishing himself as a private detective, and whether or not he described himself as such, he did nothing to dissuade the press from referring to him by his former calling. Although in 1856, he had highlighted his involvement in the high-profile murder case brought against the Rugeley poisoner, and regarded himself as specialising in fraud investigations, he did investigate one couple as part of a long-running matrimonial case. In January 1854, he was engaged to watch Robert Ansley Robinson, a magistrate who was accused of 'adulterous acts' with the wife of Gloucestershire landowner Omwell Lloyd Evans. Robinson was Deputy-Lieutenant of Gloucestershire, while Evans was described as 'a gentleman of some fortune, amounting to about 2000l a year'.[35] Field was employed by Evans at a rate of 15 shillings a day, with additional travel expenses, for a period of three to six months, on the understanding that if Field did not 'succeed' in his task within six months, his services would be discontinued.[36] There was a clear incentive to find the evidence wanted by his employer, and this would be evident in later detectives' work, including Slater's; their success and reputation – both with their client and the wider world – depended on it. In Field's case, he was given an additional payment each day if Field was satisfied with what he had been doing.[37] What can be seen from Field's work is that he recognised the value of publicity, establishing his selling point as a former police detective, and ensuring that he would be recognised as an expert in his field. This talent for self-promotion, and the publicising of particular cases they had achieved success in, would be copied by later private detectives.

One of Field's fellow London private detectives was the Hungarian-born Ignatius Pollaky, a 'busybody' who initiated his career in England by building a relationship with the Metropolitan Police, attempting to make himself indispensable in providing information to them.[38] He had established himself as a private detective in charge of a 'Bureau de Renseignements' (an information office - staffed solely by himself) by 1862. Pollaky used various terms to describe his work - foreign detective, continental agent, private inquiry office superintendent, private detective - but his exploits were recorded in the press, and his language skills and experience of different countries meant that he was in demand to investigate cases both in the UK and in mainland Europe.[39] On his death at the age of 90, and for years afterwards, he was written about as a 'celebrated' private detective known for his perseverance and patience, and also for his 'mysterious' absences from home in order to investigate cases overseas.[40]

A key skill of the Victorian private detective was the ability to make friends - to infiltrate the lives of individuals, and to get them to trust them with their secrets. Another was to be surreptitious - to be able to hide in plain sight, and to shadow individuals effectively. These were skills those from relatively humble backgrounds, and particularly those from the burgeoning lower middle class, could do; many also saw the peripatetic life and work of the private inquiry agent as an attractive career choice that offered variety, excitement, and the freedom of self-employment. From the 1860s onwards, an increasing number of individuals moved into this work; private detection agencies were established, and these advertised in newspapers for new agents, as well as to publicise their own services. One of the attractions of private detective work was the fact that it was an egalitarian profession – almost anyone could set up in business as a private detective or inquiry agent, with minimal outlay. And what of the skills or qualifications needed? Nosiness, determination, an entrepreneurial nature, and the ability to listen, to observe, and to manipulate.

The public was gripped by tales of spying and detection, and had been since Kate Warne's day. The opportunities that emerged for private detectives, and particularly for female ones, following the passing of the Matrimonial Causes Act, were soon followed, in the 1860s, by stories and books focusing on the female private detective – such as Andrew Forrester's *The Female Detective*, which he followed with other books, such as *The Private Detective and Revelations of the Private Detective*. The male private detective was also well catered for, such as with the stories of the fictional 'Monsieur Lecoq', created by French journalist Emile Gaboriau – Lecoq's name being rather similar to that of reformed criminal and later criminologist Eugene Vicocq, who had become head of France's first private detective agency (and perhaps the world's) back in 1833. Therefore, fact and fiction combined from the mid-nineteenth century, publicising and encouraging the work of the private detective, and arguably encouraging the growth of private inquiry agents and offices.

This is not to say that private detectives were universally respected or admired. The fact that this was a profession open to those from differing backgrounds was viewed with suspicion, and the activities of some unscrupulous detectives could darken the industry's reputation as a whole. Back in 1869, the *New York Times* had run an expose of private detectives – picked up in the British press – that noted the existence of some detective agencies that employed young men to shadow other men their age, who worked in 'responsible positions', in order to find something incriminating or immoral that they could then report to their employers. The young men being followed were usually clerks, and they were followed from the moment they left work, to the moment they reached home for the night. The detectives would follow them as they socialised, visiting popular billiard rooms or restaurants, to see how much they spent, or whether they were associating with the 'more disreputable and dangerous associates of either sex'.[41] Today, celebrities are blackmailed after the theft of personal images or videos, but in the 1860s, young clerks were blackmailed for consorting with 'dubious' individuals, or simply for enjoying themselves too much. The unscrupulous private detective was little more than a blackmailer, using the evidence he had gathered to make money, even if he had not been engaged to find evidence in the first place.

This concern about the ethics of the private detective was reflected throughout the 1870s, with British newspapers highlighting cases where detectives had committed fraud, or had used unscrupulous methods to achieve results. In 1876, Manchester private detective Henry Harris was tried for obtaining money by false representation, claiming to be employed by the local police to prosecute shopkeepers selling 'prizes' – a form of lottery. He had visited a druggist in Salford and essentially threatened the man until he paid him money to keep quiet about his lottery.[42] The following year, a piece was published in a newspaper headlined 'The private detective nuisance', which made clear its stance on the industry. It detailed the 'methods of private detection', which it claimed involved plying innocent people with drink and tobacco in order to loosen their tongues and give away important information. The newspaper's disapproval of the private detective appeared to be largely based on the invasion of a British person's privacy, and the detective's need to eavesdrop on others, to 'bore gimlet-holes in doors and panels, to hide... in cupboards and under tables, and to administer small bribes in the right quarter' – as well as the fact that a private detective was perceived to be of a lower class than his police equivalent, and thus he must be 'very inferior' to a police detective, who was in the 'higher walks' of the detecting profession.[43] This attempt at pigeon-holing the private detective as being both duplicitous and sneaky, as well as lower class, and of comparing private and police detectives in terms of social status, would continue throughout the century, and reflected uncertainty as to where private detectives 'fitted in' to society.

This suspicion in some quarters regarding the work of the private detective was both a reflection of their ascendance, and a valid concern about their qualifications and background (financially, morally, and socially). It did little to stem the growth of the profession. The Golden Age of the British private detective was the period circa 1885 to 1910; a reading of the nation's newspapers shows a clear spike in adverts for private detectives in London during this period, and a large number of articles relating to the exploits of these men and women.[44] Likewise, in literature, the private detective became increasingly visible, most notably, of course, with the stories of Sherlock Holmes. Fiction depicted these inquiry agents as more gentlemanly in background than their police equivalents.[45] The stories of their exploits also offered Victorian audiences a chance to vicariously experience a life far different to most of theirs: heart-racing exploits and exotic locations, increasingly combined with science. In reality, of course, the job could be far more mundane, with a lot of time spent watching and waiting, without much happening; or dealing with what could be rather run-of-the-mill marital conflict. Yet even the occasional boredom or frustration was tolerable, as there was always the hope of something exciting ensuing.

There was also the opportunity to become a store detective, either employed by a shop as staff, or working as an independent detective on a piece of work for them. The latter part of the nineteenth century saw a rise in consumerism, and a corresponding rise in thefts from shops, with it being noted that the pressure on women to desire and accumulate nice clothes and accessories had led to a spate of what was seen as 'kleptomania' by middle-class women. The problem of shoplifting led to a further opportunity for women, in particular, who were now also employed as store detectives in the new department stores on both sides of the Atlantic, as Elaine Abelson has explored in her history of shoplifting in the Victorian department store.[46] By the 1890s, the private detective, both male and female, had ample opportunities for work, both within and without the department store.

Private detective agencies by now proliferated both in London and the provinces; in London, many were centred around 'Theatreland' - from Haymarket to the upper reaches of the Strand. This focus on Theatreland was partly, at least, due to a proliferation of thefts targeting theatre audiences as well as actors, and theatre managers' concerns about inside jobs and larger-scale frauds and blackmail schemes taking place that focused on the theatres. One of the highest-profile private detectives of Theatreland was Maurice Moser, a former Metropolitan Police detective who established his detective office at Southampton Street, one of the side streets that leads from Strand up to Covent Garden's Piazza.

The uncertainty about whether private detectives should be applauded or scorned, as seen in some of the attitudes towards the profession, did not mean that private detectives were all chancers, scoundrels, or untrained amateurs, although there were certainly some of these. In fact, by the 1880s, becoming a private detective had become an attractive option for disenchanted or retired policemen.[47] Many of the Metropolitan Police's finest became private detectives, as can be seen in the examples of both Charles Field and Maurice Moser, and these individuals used their existing detective skills in a new role. They were sometimes able to supplement the erratic workload and income by writing and publishing memoirs of their policing career - the genre proving very popular with the book-reading public in the latter nineteenth century, and one that Moser added his own autobiography to. Being a former police detective was a useful claim in press adverts, as some surviving examples show: for example, Uriah Cooke, based at Craig's Court, Charing Cross, was 'late Criminal Investigation Department'; Alfred Knowles at Euston Road was 'late of Detective Department'; and George Trace at the Strand was 'late Inspector, Metropolitan Police'.[48] These former police detectives advertised their prior careers as they felt it gave them some gravitas and reputation in an increasingly popular field. It differentiated them from the inexperienced men or young clerks who simply fancied a more exciting career – as it appeared, anyway – and made explicit the fact that they knew how to investigate a case properly, to find evidence, and to do a good job.

However, this experience and the proudly displayed former job titles of these men did not always work in their favour. These proliferating detective agencies have to be placed in the context of the real-life crimes and investigations that drew the attention of the press and public, most notably the Whitechapel Murders of 1888. Newspaper readers avidly devoured accounts of each murder – five women are considered to be victims of the individual who became known as 'Jack the Ripper', but there were also other murders of women in East London at around this time that were, at the time, ascribed to the same murderer.[49] They learned not only of the dangers facing women walking at night in parts of London, but also of how the perpetrator of these violent, appalling crimes was still walking among them, and debated among themselves how he could be caught.

There was clearly, and understandably, an expectation that the police would do their job, and catch this feared killer. The inability of the police to identify the perpetrator of these horrendous murders drew press criticism, and their late, failed attempt to use dogs – bloodhounds – to gather scents was discussed in some length. Criticism was evident towards the police, and towards male police as well, with one female rights campaigner, Frances Power Cobbe, suggesting that women, and in particular female private detectives, would have had more success catching Jack the Ripper, because of their specific skills, which surpassed those of the Met: the ability to 'pass unnoticed where a man would be instantly noticed; she could extract gossip from other women…she would move through the streets and courts without waking the echoes of the pavement by a sonorous military tread', as well as having 'intuitive quickness and "mother wit"'.[50] One person who would note such comments about women's natural ability as detectives would be Henry Slater, who would use assertions such as Cobbe's to great gain the following decade. Generally, however, press coverage of perceived police failures helped the private detective gain business and reputation: if police detectives could not solve cases, perhaps their private equivalents would be more successful.

This does not mean that private detectives were a singular breed. There was a lot of variety both in terms of their background, and how they operated. As previously mentioned, this was a career open to anyone with a bit of education and nous, and with the increased literacy of the era, many men (and some women) were able to work in the field. Therefore, among the numbers of late Victorian private detectives were the children of agricultural labourers, gardeners, mariners, publicans, and farmers.[51] If not former policemen, then these detectives had often moved into the career from a variety of other jobs, including as omnibus conductors, painters, restaurateurs, and hotel porters.[52]

However, there were many private detectives who had formerly been solicitor's clerks, and also actors. Both these jobs would have given them useful skills in terms of learning about the law, detective work, and adopting different personae. As a private detective, work often involved getting evidence of adultery for divorce cases, and many detectives therefore pretended to be other people, in order to get a married party to become a friend and thus get confidences from them, or, in fraud cases, to encourage an individual to commit a crime in front of them. These were, in effect, acting roles, and so it's clear to see why former actors might find detective work appealing. For those lucky enough to have acted in provincial or London theatres, they knew those who worked there, and could use those relationships to their benefit as private detectives. For the humble solicitor's clerk, they learned both about investigation and the law through their jobs, yet some chafed at having to work for someone else, or having a lack of freedom in their role. They were young, ambitious, and educated, and saw a career as a private detective, working on a variety of cases, either as a sole trader or as the member of a detective agency, to be an attractive option.

Henry Slater was, in this sense, a typical private detective of his era. By 1885, this entrepreneurial Victorian had started work as a private inquiry agent, and after completing a few cases, with mixed success, he started advertising his services, as he would continue to do in larger and more extravagant ways, for the next two decades.

Chapter 3

The Office on Basinghall Street

In the early 1890s, the time when Kate Pollard was finding out that she had made a huge error in marrying her husband, Henry Slater's Detective Agency was at the peak of its success. On Basinghall Street, in the heart of the City of London, there was the bustle of city workers going about their business, and Slater had positioned his agency here, rather than in the popular detective agency hub of the Strand. The private detectives with their offices in Theatreland and the roads between the Strand and Covent Garden competed for business among actors and actresses, and other eager theatregoers, hoping to get their attention before and after shows. Slater, however, ever the renegade, preferred to do his work here, seeing himself as part of the City. The City conveyed legitimacy, and what Slater wanted was for his business to be seen as both acceptable and respected.

It's hard to imagine what life was like here in the late nineteenth century, as much of the street has since been demolished and replaced with identikit modern office buildings; both 1 and 27 Basinghall Street, at various times the hearts of Henry Slater's empire, are now just two of these late-twentieth-century blocks. Yet then, as now, Londoners came into the city each morning on the Metropolitan railway to Moorgate, to work at the Guildhall, one of whose entrances lay on the street, or one of the many offices on the road itself.[53] The church of St Michael Bassishaw still existed on Basinghall Street then, although seven years later, it would be demolished after work to clear the human remains from its crypt exposed weak foundations. It had been closed just a year before, in 1892, and would sit empty until 1900, when Bassishaw House (itself demolished in the 1960s) would be built on its demolished site.

Paintings and photographs of the late Victorian Basinghall Street show a very different road; one shows a remnant of the eighteenth-century city, though, with Georgian shopfronts forming the ground floors of smart, four-storey townhouses. They bring into mind the surviving shops of Gunpowder Alley further east in Spitalfields, their ground-floor frontages an elegant white and green in colour, contrasting with the brick above. They present a somewhat bland, anonymous front to passers-by; there is little sign from outside as to what business those inside are conducting.[54] At 22-26 Basinghall Street was the Wool Exchange, photographed in 1962 as an ornate, late Victorian building with decorative balconies and pillars, a mishmash of styles that conjures up our ancestors' tendency to over-decorate their interiors, cluttering their parlours with an assortment of trinkets and furniture that ends up confusing the onlooker.[55] This Wool Exchange was described in the 1890s as 'Babel let loose' - a loud, busy, frenetic place.[56] It reflects Basinghall Street as it was at the end of the nineteenth century; a place of commerce, of business and of busy-ness. It was here that Henry Slater's Detective Agency held sway.

The agency had been established for nearly eight years now. The first surviving press advertisements for Slater's Private Detective Agency appeared in the British press in the autumn of 1885, and later advertisements also suggest that this was the year the agency was founded.[57,58] Henry Slater's main strategy was to get as much publicity for his agency as possible in the press, and a main part of his strategy was to advertise regularly in the newspapers, making claims that could not be substantiated in the belief that few, if any, would seek to corroborate these claims, but would instead take them on face value.

From his earliest adverts, a couple of themes emerge - themes that would be returned to again and again over the years. The first was that the agency cast its net wide, claiming to trace missing friends, investigate personal and family matters, serving legal documents, and find evidence to use against election candidates. Other adverts would claim that Slater's agency could help stop blackmail, uncover fraud among stockbrokers and dealers, and provide evidence regarding trademark and patent infringements. These adverts suggested that the agency was well staffed, and able to take on a wide variety of cases. However, two aspects of the agency's work highlighted in press adverts were particularly significant: that of shadowing individuals, and finding evidence for divorce cases. These would prove the most regular source of income not only for Slater, but for many other London-based detectives at this time.

Slater's other regular boast was that he was the 'only acknowledged establishment of the description in the City of London' - a boast used regularly in his newspaper advertisements from 1886 until 1899.[59] Although many private detectives in the late nineteenth century were based in London's Theatreland, in Westminster and therefore outside of the boundaries of the Square Mile, it was not made clear in the advert who Slater's had been acknowledged as the only City agency by - because it was most likely Slater himself, and Slater alone. He was careful with his wording, while also omitting any references or sources as to this acknowledgement. He also highlighted his use of female detectives; most agencies, on occasion, needed to employ a female detective, as they were invaluable in divorce cases, able to inveigle their way into other women's lives and to gain their trust and their confidences. But it was Slater who most aggressively promoted their use publicly; even in 1887, he had placed adverts that simply stated: 'Female detectives...a feature of this establishment is the large staff of Female Detectives.'[60] Other adverts highlighted the agency's use of technology - having a telephone line and telegraphic address.[61]

One of Slater's other publicity strategies was to start a 'war' with another private detective, one that would show Slater's to be the better agency. Our only evidence for this directly comes from a newspaper nearly twenty years after the event. In this, the *Dundee Evening Telegraph* stated that Slater's had made its name as a result of an 1887 case involving a 'Mr Moger'.[62] This case, involving a 'diamond-cut diamond', led, according to the newspaper, to a trial that led to extensive newspaper coverage, with each article mentioning Slater's name. It provided a huge amount of free publicity to the agency, and resulted in an equally large increase in its business[63] It's tempting to see this trial as a creation of Slater's, and the press statement quoted above suggests it could have been written by Slater as a form of marketing for his infant agency.[64] It's particularly interesting, because a search of the newspapers from the time specified – 1886 to 1887 – has no reference to Slater in this context in relation to the case. The case was a real one. It was a diamond robbery that was carried out in London in spring 1886, which concluded with the conviction of the five men involved.[65] Slater is not mentioned in the trial reports, nor in other contemporary accounts of the case.[66] However, even if Slater had invented the story of how he became famous, tying his name to the real robbery (presumably claiming credit for the capture of the robbers), the name of 'Moger' is significant. This is a typographic error, 'Moger' being Maurice Moser, Slater's rival private detective. This is the first mention of the two men together, but they would be associated in a professional context for another decade.

Moser was one of Slater's key competitors in the industry. In the 1890s, it was sometimes Maurice Moser who advertised his detective agency's services immediately above an advert for Slater's. Moser was another man adept at self-promotion, and used his memoirs and subsequent interviews to publicise his own agency, which moved locations at least once, but was always based off the Strand.[67] He used similar tactics to Slater, though, stressing that his agency was open twenty-four hours a day, including Sundays, and that he had a staff of detectives from both sexes and all classes.[68]

He had an advantage over Henry Slater in terms of getting publicity and clients. He was, of course, a former Met police detective who could mine his former cases to create an image of himself as an experienced, well-trained individual who people could trust. The publication of his memoirs added to this feel of experience and reliability, but also make people feel that he was an interesting character who had taken part in some exciting work. Henry Slater must have secretly been pleased when Maurice Moser hit the headlines for the wrong reasons, when he was named in a series of divorce cases. He had given the married Antonia Williamson a job at his agency, and she had fallen in love with him, even taking a portrait of him home to hang in her marital bedroom, to her husband's anger. In 1889, unsurprisingly, her husband petitioned for a divorce, naming Moser as co-respondent. The following year, Moser's wife Harriet petitioned for a divorce from him, and he retaliated by petitioning for divorce against her on the (fictional) grounds that she had committed adultery with another man.[69,70] Moser's personal woes benefitted Slater professionally. Antonia's husband – Edward, who was also her first cousin – employed Slater's agency in 1890 to 'watch' Moser and find proof of his adultery with Antonia.[71] Slater commissioned one of his female detectives, Louisa Sangster, to shadow the pair, and at the hearing of Antonia's divorce petition – with her husband's cross-petition – it was Sangster who gave evidence of the 'cohabitation' between the two private detectives.[72] Moser and Slater therefore had beef with each other dating back to their earlier days as private detectives.

Both men were adept at publicising their businesses in the press, but it was arguably Slater who had the upper hand in ensuring that his agency was well-covered in both the advertisements and news sections of the media. One of his popular strategies was to create 'quotes' or references from other parties. Occasionally, he stated where the reference had come from, such as with an advert from 1889, where he quoted the *Financial World*. This publication had apparently spotted a 'compliment' to 'our great English private detective' in the *Financial News*, where Slater had been compared to 'Fouché himself'.[73]

This was not, however, a recent compliment, and it might have actually been intended as an insult. Back in 1887, the theatrical newspaper London and Provincial Entr'acte, in its rather acid-tongued gossip column, noted that Slater's agency should be 'well-pleased' with the Financial News' compliment.[74] Joseph Fouché, to whom Slater was compared, was the Minister of Police under Bonaparte, and was known for his ferocious suppression of the 1793 Lyon insurrection. While Slater may have liked being compared to a minister of police – giving him the gravitas that he was aware those private detectives like Moser, who had formerly been police detectives, had – Fouché's ruthlessness may have been what Slater was really being compared to.

The numerous adverts placed by Slater in the press over the course of two or so decades show that his agency was housed in a large, well-staffed office, close to the Bank of England - he emphasised this location in order to highlight its ability to deal with financial cases. Slater's agency grew over time, employing a number of men on both a short- and long-term basis. Although Slater also promoted his use of female detectives, women formed a minority of the workforce, and, like other successful detective agencies, he also employed them as typists or secretaries.[75] Slater employed ex-police officers as his detectives, as well as those from other walks of life. If he thought someone would make a good private detective, he would employ them. Therefore, among his detectives were former police detectives Joseph McKenna and Charles Fielding (not to be confused with the mid-century detective Charles Field); Francis Stevens, who had previously worked as a baronet's servant; and former clerks Charles Simmonds, Samuel Marrison and Arthur Weeks. Some of his staff started in clerical positions and worked their way up, such as Bristolian Edgar Cartwright. Although many were employed fulltime at the agency, others were engaged on a freelance basis, as work needs dictated.

Throughout the 1890s, Slater's agency was the place to go when you needed someone followed, or a private matter investigated. It was a well-resourced agency, with several full-time detectives on its books, as well as cashiers and secretaries undertaking the routine admin of the office. It also claimed to have detectives on hand elsewhere, to be called on if needed, and unlike other agencies that made claims to have detectives in 'every city of the world', Slater's genuinely did seem to be able to provide other temporary sleuths when the occasion arose. It was a business that made sure it was known about, advertising in the press on an almost daily basis, and never shy to flag up its successes, even when it failed to demonstrate exactly how it had been involved.

One case in point was the Missing Word competition scandal. In December 1892, a competition of this name was published in *Pick-Me-Up* – a weekly periodical – with an impressive prize on offer of £24,000. The competition had been found to be illegal, as it was deemed to be a form of gambling, and the editor, proprietor and printers had been fined a token sum of a shilling. It appeared that although the issue featuring the competition had gone to press, and people had entered the competition in good faith, none of their entry fees had been accepted, and no prizes had been awarded – therefore it was not felt that much damage had been done.[76] However, shortly after the case was settled, Henry Slater placed a series of adverts in the *Evening Standard*, stating that he had been the only detective employed on the case, and that he had been successful. In the same publication, he also claimed another success. Charges had been brought against the Panama Canal Company regarding cheques worth a total of four million francs that had been paid on its behalf to various persons.[77] Henry Slater duly placed an advert stating that he had been the first detective employed to make 'secret investigations' in France in relation to the case.[78] Both the Missing Word and Panama Canal scandals had occupied many column inches in the regional and national press in late 1892, and Henry Slater had picked up on them and implied that his agency had a key role in resolving them both. The phrasing of his adverts was deliberately vague, noting that he had been engaged in some way in both cases, but not whether his involvement had been major or minor. It ultimately didn't matter; what did matter was the newspaper readership associating the resolution of the cases with Slater's Detective Agency, and noting the company name for potential future use.[79]

By this same year, Slater was also advertising in the American newspapers, both to make his company sound a large, international one, but also to take advantage of a different style of work. The early 1890s had seen an intense interest in baccarat – a card game played between a 'player' and a 'banker'. This had led to scandal in 1890, when Sir William Gordon-Cumming was accused of cheating at a game of baccarat during a house party also attended by his friend, the future Edward VII. Following accusations of cheating, Gordon-Cumming launched a slander suit, and the then Prince of Wales appeared in court as a witness. Gordon-Cumming lost the case. Slater stated that he was from 'Slater's Detective Association', the use of 'association' rather than 'agency' suggesting an international network of agents under his name. He stated that he was 'prepared' to help supply baccarat games with Monte Carlo-trained assistants, on condition that the games were honest.[80] The use of Monte Carlo suggested a glamorous organisation with agents used to playing at the top European casinos. There is no suggestion anywhere else that Slater had staff in Monte Carlo, and it is highly likely that, as with much of his advertising, he made claims based on little more than hope and chutzpah. At the most, he is likely to have had a contact in Europe he hoped to find men through if his advertisements were successful.

In February 1893, from his base at 27 Basinghall Street, Henry Slater gave an interview to the *Westminster Gazette*. This had been prompted by rumours that hundreds ('one telegram said 200, another 400') of English private detectives had been invited to head across the Atlantic to work at the Chicago Exhibition.[81] The publication felt that an interview with Henry Slater, the best-known private detective of the time, was needed to shed light on the truth of this rumour. It was clear that when a statement from a private detective was needed, Henry Slater was the man to call.

This was, of course, a position promoted by Slater himself. Slater deemed himself to be at the top of his game during the 1890s, and repeatedly described himself in the newspapers as 'the greatest detective of the age', citing 'vide press' but not naming specific papers that had allegedly called him that; and placing an 'important notice' that he had 'for years been successful in nearly every case entrusted to him', regardless of whether the case was a financial one such as fraud, or a more domestic case such as divorce.[82]

He was clearly as good an actor as the other detectives he employed; when the *Westminster Gazette* reporter visited Slater, he ensured that he was to be found sitting in his 'comfortable office', busy working on what he described as 'the usual pailful of work'.[83] He admitted that he had, six months earlier, paid for a newspaper advert that promoted his decision to send ten detectives out on the transatlantic steamer Teutonic to work at the Chicago Exhibition. This advert had resulted in letters from around the country from readers: some asking for work as detectives themselves, but others wanting to know where Slater's men were, and how they could be recognised. Slater argued that he did not want his men to be recognised - yet he still advertised their existence and approximate location, knowing it would result in good publicity. Slater was confident that financiers and businessmen at the exhibition would want to employ his detectives. They would prefer his British detectives to American ones, because they talked less, and did not exaggerate; they would also prefer those who had not been former 'Scotland Yard men' as the latter always looked like ex-policemen, and could be detected as such by criminals.

The most interesting part of the interview was Slater's description of his staff. 'Men' - by which Slater meant more mature males - tended to be the managers and superintendents of his agency. Most of the detectives on the ground were 'women, boys and girls of 20 to 22 years of age'.[84] He preferred young people because they didn't tend to get drunk on or off the job and 'blab' about their work, but were also good at finding out information about any subject. As with much Slater said to the press, this wasn't necessarily the truth; at the turn of the century, the average age of Slater's detectives (from those identified) appears to have been nearer 30 years old, and predominantly male, although this was substantially younger than those in positions with more responsibility.

In the autumn of 1894, Slater's Detective Agency would move along Basinghall Street, from 27 to number 1, advertising its change of address in the press from the start of October that year.[85] The agency's new base reflected its success by the mid-1890s: it occupied some twelve rooms, spread over two upper floors. On the ground floor was a separate café, which became a marketing point in press adverts.[86] Potential customers might come for a cup of tea and see the signs for Slater's. Others summing up the courage to visit the agency might fortify themselves with a drink first; and those who had already been to commission the agency to watch an errant spouse might afterwards head to the café for a bite to eat.

This was a sign of Slater's supremacy in the detective world, and its success. Its offices were substantial, with separate rooms for both Slater and his manager, George Henry. There were reception rooms for clients and rooms shared by pairs of detectives. Although it isn't possible to know the names of all those employed by Slater, and detectives moved on regularly, he had a core team of detectives based at the office. These were primarily men, but they were from varied backgrounds. In addition, there were detectives employed in the regions, with responsibility for various counties, and others who were taken on ad hoc as work demanded. There is very little known about the women Slater employed, even their names – beyond Louisa Sangster, who was working for him at the start of the decade. It's clear, however, that of his core team, Slater expected loyalty and hard work. In return, he trusted them to differing extents; some he acted as a surrogate father to, some as a friend.

This was Henry Slater at the peak of his powers as a private detective. By 1895, he was in his mid-forties, a well-dressed, successful man with a well-known detective agency that was now in its second decade of existence. He knew the value of publicity: something he would do consistently throughout his career was to use the newspapers to promote himself and his business. Adverts, promotions, interviews: all gave him the opportunity to get his name out there as the manager of an agency that could provide any number of detectives, of both sexes, all ages, with a variety of skills. By the time of the trial that ruined him, he was spending between £3,000 and £4,000 a year to advertise in the press - a substantial sum.[87] He was also good at turning rumours around to benefit him; from being asked about a vague rumour of detectives being sent to the Chicago Exhibition, he managed to make it sound like he was the main supplier of such detectives. Of course, the rumour was likely to have started with Slater himself.

This is what Slater did, and this is why he was so successful. Others had, of course, come before him: from Ignatius 'Paddington' Pollaky, the Hungarian immigrant who had come to London and turned his hand to private detection and in the process become synonymous with the area where he worked, to Maurice Moser, who milked his prior experience for publicity, selling stories to the press, and utilising the telegram name 'Shadows' for his business. Slater, though, was adept at learning from what other detectives did to promote their businesses, and building on it. Moser and Slater were both advertising their use of lady detectives by the start of 1893, but Slater would make them appear as a USP for his business: he was associated with their use, rather than Moser, who did not repeatedly assert his usage to the extent that he would be seen as the innovator.[88] Slater was ultimately a PR man: he knew the power of the Victorian press, and he was keen to give them what they wanted. To do so created publicity for him and for his business, and publicity meant more clients, and more money.

Chapter 4

Changing Direction

Henry Slater later stated that he had stopped taking an active role in his detective agency in 1897, transferring much of the day-to-day work to his manager, George Henry.[89] Certainly, 1897 was a year of change for him. He was so successful financially that he could afford to semi-retire, despite not yet being 50 years old. He was spending at least part of his time at his second home at Clarendon Mansions in Brighton, and this is the address he gave when, on 13 October 1897, he was initiated into the Royal Kent Lodge of the Freemasons.[90] This lodge was, in Slater's time, based at Freemasons' Hall, Great Queen Street, in Covent Garden. Although this was the central hall of the Freemasons, it rented out rooms for various lodges to meet.

The general requirement for those wanting to join the Freemasons was to be of 'good repute'. Usually, a candidate knows other members of that lodge; the candidate will ask to join and will then be invited to proceed. References are taken up so that members can both ask about the candidate's suitability and discuss it. There is then a secret ballot before a candidate is initiated or rejected. The United Grand Lodge of England is the governing masonic lodge for most freemasons in England, and under their rules, any single member can 'blackball' a membership without giving a reason, and this is enough to reject a candidate, and lead to the candidate's proposer and seconder being expected to resign. Yet Slater had applied under a pseudonym, but was still allowed to join, which suggests that methods for investigating suitability were not looked into too much.

This pseudonym was Henry Scott. It was in 1897 that Slater started using this name, asking staff to refer to him as Captain Scott or The Captain. It created the image of a former military man who was in charge of his own army of detectives. Although few records survive of formal name changes at this time, there is no record in *The London Gazette* of such a change. Later, female detective Maud West would use *The Gazette* to disclaim her former identity of Edith Maria Elliott, suggesting that she had changed it by deed poll when, in fact, she continued to use the Elliott name in private.[91] Henry Slater may have taken on changes of name to disassociate himself from his former identity, but all his changes appear to have been done informally.

Using a different name was not uncommon in the private detective world – many detectives used different names when they were working undercover on jobs, and Slater had also used the name of Captain Brown for work. Of his detectives, John Pracy regularly used the pseudonym of John Bray; Henry Iles was Henry Sergeant when on jobs. But in Slater's case, the name change seemed more significant. 'Henry Slater' was the famous private detective, the name of his detective agency, and also the name sometimes used by George Henry. When Slater stepped back from his business, Henry would use the name 'Henry Slater Junior' to make clients believe they were still dealing with the boss. Slater wanted to separate this work identity – the identity that had made him famous – with Henry Scott, gentleman, of London and Brighton. This was a man who, when he applied to join the Freemasons, used a name that was not the one he was widely known by, claiming not to be working, and giving Clarendon Mansions as his address rather than one of his usual London addresses, despite applying to join a London masonic lodge.[92] He had made his name as a private detective – and they could be regarded as rather shifty, untrustworthy individuals. Joining the Freemasons signified acceptance and respectability to Slater.

His actions signalled a change of direction this year, but Slater was the central part of his agency, and it seems that he was unable to leave his business alone completely. Instead, despite what he said, he was still in the office on a regular basis, and being sought by his staff for advice. In fact, he still had his own room at Basinghall Street, and it was expected that he would be there on a frequent basis. Publicity and advertising make no reference to his retirement, and he was such an active, involved individual that it seems dubious whether he would be able to take a back seat and watch the agency operate without him. What is more probable is that he used George Philip Henry as his right-hand man, taking on the persona of Henry Slater Junior and being the agency's manager while its founder sat at the top, overseeing his empire. The original Henry Slater, though, was certainly still hands on, writing to his agents, looking at their daily accounts of their work, criticising and applauding as necessary.

The detectives at Slater's agency were not united about when they thought Slater had semi-retired, or how often he visited the office. Charles Fielding said that since he started at the agency in the mid-1890s, Slater had remained primarily at his Brighton flat, coming to Basinghall Street once a week or once a fortnight. Edgar Cartwright said this was not the case, insisting that Slater had still been 'frequently' in the office at least up to 1901. Others said that Slater had seen no new clients after 1897, only being involved in existing cases, but Cartwright disagreed. In fact, he was able to cite new cases that Slater had personally been involved in, including one where Slater himself had broken into a flat on the instructions of a man seeking a divorce, and found the wife in bed with another man. Slater's second manager, William Hamilton, also pointed out that Slater always supervised the agency's correspondence when he was in the office, although that correspondence was kept in George Philip Henry's room.[93] Slater himself would later admit that he had last seen a client in the agency offices in 1902, not 1897.[94]

Even if Slater had not been in the office every day from 1897, he still kept in close contact with it. Charles Fielding, the police detective turned private eye, said that Slater kept in touch with what was happening with the agency by means of a daily letter written to him by one of the clerks; one of Fielding's duties had been to give the appointed clerk a list of callers they had had that day.[95] It was widely said that the manager of Slater's on a day-to-day basis was George Henry, greeting clients as Henry Slater Junior, as his boss was, allegedly, largely retired. Certainly, by July 1902, adverts were being placed in the press asking potential clients to communicate with 'Henry Slater Junior, assistant manager'.[96] Yet it was Henry Slater who continued to monitor his staff's work, and it seems that although Slater wanted to enjoy the spoils of his career, he was not yet quite ready to let it go completely.

Slater unquestionably had expensive tastes and clearly enjoyed the financial success of his work. He had homes in both London – living at various times at Mount Street in Mayfair and Palace Court Mansions in Bayswater, the road being opposite Kensington Gardens – and Brighton, overlooking the sea. He travelled abroad, and he enjoyed himself. However, he also claimed ill health – perhaps a recurrence of the rheumatism he claimed to have suffered between 1888 and 1891. In January 1902, he travelled to Australia for three months, apparently for health reasons.[97] He could not have been too ill, for while there, he advertised his agency in the *Sydney Morning Herald*.[98] Several Australian adverts survive for this year, but none outside it, suggesting that appealing to potential Australian customers was a short-lived venture for Slater. It raises the possibility that rather than retiring, Henry Slater had gone to Australia in the hope of gaining clients there – or even of opening a detective office down under. Nothing, however, seems to have come of any such attempts.

Henry Slater's success as a private detective had led to both good and adverse press coverage over the years. In April 1900, for example, a case was heard at the Taunton Petty Sessions in Somerset, where a middle-aged man named Henry Kennedy was charged with obtaining £7 by false pretences. The prosecutor was Alfred Collins, who ran the Harmony Restored Inn, a budget accommodation in Ilminster. He argued that seven months earlier, Kennedy had defrauded him after failing to pay for his room at the inn. Kennedy claimed he was actually a private detective, who also used the name of Henry George Slater; there was therefore discussion in court as to whether he was 'the' Henry Slater of Slater's Detective Agency. The local paper duly reported this fact, noting that everybody knew who Henry Slater was. It had a worldwide reputation as the employer of respectable private detectives, and that hearing the name, people would have confidence in its staff.[99] A Slater detective meant a reputable detective working for London's most famous agency; and Henry Slater was therefore, the newspaper implied, the most reputable.

William Hamilton, one of Slater's managers, had worked for the agency for fifteen years, and had never seen Kennedy before; however, in 1895, the firm had used several Lancashire men as temporary detectives on a short-term assignment, and Kennedy was the name used by one of them. He denied that the man was actually Henry Slater, insisting that his boss had never used the middle name of George.[100] He also said that although disguise was 'to some extent the essence of one's business', it was highly unlikely that Slater would let one of his agents use his own name as an alias while on business – and Slater always ensured that his agents had adequate money, so there would be no need to avoid paying for one's lodgings.

Could Kennedy have been Henry Slater himself in disguise? Although Hamilton denied knowing him, Kennedy's own defence argued that Collins could easily have got in touch with him to get his money, as 'he had a well-known London address' – Basinghall Street. The defence believed that an eminent detective such as Henry Slater would have had the money to ensure that he stayed at a higher-class establishment than the prosecutor's address. It seems far more probable that Kennedy took Slater's name and profession to make himself sound a glamorous character, and to try to avoid the charges against him by pretending to be the well-known detective. In this way, Slater can be seen as a success – achieving fame and reputation, even in court.[101]

Although Slater considered himself to be the best-known of the private detectives, he faced considerable competition in London, and this only increased over the course of the 1890s. One of the competing agencies that was advertising immediately next to Slater's own adverts was Attwood's Private Detective Offices, which advertised its 'confidential cases investigated by experienced agents'.[102] Attwood's had been founded by Henry George Attwood in 1882, when he was 37.[103] Like many of the agencies of the time, it was based in Theatreland, moving from Catherine Street to Tavistock Street in the 1890s, and highlighting its location near the Lyceum Theatre. Like Slater's, it claimed to offer free consultations or 'interviews', but rather than stress its affordability, merely claimed to offer 'moderate terms', thus suggesting a respectability in not being 'cheap'.[104]

Henry Slater had promoted his agency as being the City of London's only one. However, this was not true, as much as he may have wanted it to be. Two of Slater's other main rivals by the late 1890s were Barclay's and Burgess's. Barclay's Detectives ('We have never failed in the Divorce Court') were based at various times at Old Jewry and on Moorgate, both in the City, as well as on the Strand. The agency claimed to have been described in the press as the leading London private detectives. Founded by John Barclay, his agency charged 1s 6d per hour for its services, payable by the day, week or month; they were unusual in specifying their charges in their adverts.[105] Burgess's, meanwhile, had two offices – one at 31 Nicholas Lane in the City, and the other in Kennington, south of the river, as well as suggesting (like many others) that it had unspecified 'offices abroad'.[106] Burgess's agency claimed a longevity unheard of elsewhere: in 1901, it advertised its services, claiming to have been established back in 1851, and – in case the point hadn't been made

– stating that it had '50 years' experience' of providing advice on divorce, libel and fraud. This was quite a claim, given that 1851 was six years prior to the Matrimonial Causes Act opening up divorce to the masses, and that in its earlier years, divorce was still something that relatively few couples sought or gained. William Burgess, the founder, had formerly been an estate agent, and so his agency had likely developed from being a house and estate agency since being established. However, Burgess's agency challenged the veracity of Slater's claim to be the only City of London agency, and showed how hyperbole could be involved in agency adverts.

These were just a couple of London's agencies, employing a variety of individuals as their detectives or private inquiry agents, as well as office staff. Outside of London, there were fewer agencies, but cities across Great Britain and Ireland certainly had their own private detectives. There were detectives in Belfast, Cardiff, Edinburgh, Sheffield, and numerous other places, for divorce cases, missing persons and fraud took place everywhere, and detectives would therefore be needed. For detectives based in the provinces, the London agencies could provide them with additional work, for if they were commissioned to 'watch' individuals outside of the capital, it could be cheaper to commission an agent in the provinces to work on the case rather than send one of their own detectives out.

The competition between the more successful, larger detective agencies was reflected in the press, where readers could scroll through columns of adverts for rival detectives and agencies. Slater's use of multiple adverts, forming a column of their own, was clearly designed to focus the reader on his agency, and believe that his was the primary detective agency in London. He was clearly aware that he had to keep ahead of his rivals, and that there was much at stake. Slater had advertised his employment of female detectives, but other agencies were doing the same, and he had to find new ways to highlight his female employees' qualities. What could they do that other agencies couldn't? His answer was to create the bicycling detective. This was a two-fold publicity tactic: he had something other agencies did not – not just a lady detective, but a mobile one; and he was creating the impression of a technologically advanced agency using relatively new forms of transport rather than going out on foot. It was novel, but subject to hyperbole, as Slater referred to an 'army' of cycling lady detectives in his adverts, which is unlikely. These cycling advertisements ran for a relatively short duration, from May 1895 to March 1899, with their peak being the autumn of 1896, and no adverts relating to this 'phenomenon' being placed in either 1897 or 1898. Adverts were placed only in the London and Brighton newspapers, despite Slater's insistence that his agency 'have an army of lady cyclist detectives throughout the Kingdom for confidential services of all descriptions'.[107]

In one series of adverts in 1902, Henry Slater used three different marketing angles to publicise his agency. In the first, he headed the advert 'Young Lady Detectives', highlighting that he had a 'staff of female detectives'. In the second, he noted that he employed 'quick change' male and female detectives of all ages. In the third, he highlighted his agency's use of wireless telegraphy.[108] It was vital that Slater's did advertise, and grab the attention of newspaper readers, as there was significant competition from newer, or younger, detectives and their agencies. That he was seen at the top of the list of London detectives, his name synonymous with the profession, was clear from one divorce case, where the cuckolded husband only realised that his wife was committing adultery with one of his army colleagues when he was sent an anonymous letter. The letter-writer enclosed a press cutting advertising Slater's agency, 'pointing out the necessity of having wives watched if a divorce was required'. Other agencies advertised their skills in watching wives, but it was an advert for Slater's that was used by this letter-writer, knowing that using such a famous agency's advert would be understood by the recipient.[109]

Alongside this pressure to remain at the top of the informal league of London detective agencies was the need to make money, and to ensure that clients paid up. Court cases show that Slater's Detective Agency had to instigate action against clients for not paying it what the agency thought was due; for example, back in 1895, William Hamilton brought a case against Annetta O'Brien Clifford of Bushy Park, claiming that she owed nearly £70 for work she had commissioned the agency to do. Five years earlier, the court heard, Mrs Clifford had wanted to prove that her first husband John Schofield had misbehaved, in order to obtain a divorce from him. She had engaged Slater's, and the agency had assigned two detectives to watch her spouse for some six weeks, at a cost of a guinea a day for each man, plus additional expenses. Slater's found evidence of adultery, and this was duly included in Mrs Clifford's divorce petition, which she filed on 4 February 1891. The agency charged Mrs Clifford its specified amount, but she decided to pay just £30, arguing that this was 'fair renumeration for the services they had rendered to her'. The court found otherwise, and made Mrs Clifford, who had since remarried, pay an additional £50 - more than Slater's had originally charged.[110]

Divorce cases such as this were Slater's bread and butter, as they were for the majority of detective agencies. Although they might highlight their ability to work on other types of case - such as missing persons, fraud, and so on - watching husbands and wives for evidence of adultery is what most agencies relied on for their income. Throughout the 1890s and early 1900s, Slater's took on a steady stream of cases brought by husbands and wives, such as the case brought by Catherine Eleanor Smith in 1899, who had been in a largely long-distance marriage since 1883, her husband working largely in South Africa. She had become suspicious that he was secretly returning to England without telling her, and his letters from abroad did nothing to assuage her suspicions. She therefore employed Slater's agency to make enquiries, and it turned out that he was not living in South Africa at all - but at Teddington Hall, a rather grand mid-Victorian property, with another woman, posing as a Mr and Mrs Darrell. The agency's evidence helped Mrs Smith gain a judicial separation, and custody of her children.[111]

Most agencies and detectives would have been satisfied with this steady stream of divorce work, but the main problem was the sheer number of detectives competing for the same, finite, number of cases. Hence Slater's various publicity tactics, such as the twenty-four-hour office and the cycling detectives, and the constant advertising. He wanted to make sure his was the first name people thought of when they were thinking of employing a private detective, and that is perfectly understandable.

Luckily for Slater, he had developed a close working relationship and friendship with a solicitor. This was Albert Osborn, of the London law firm Osborn and Osborn, which he ran with his brother Oscar. The firm was based at 56 Copthall Avenue, just a five-minute walk away from the agency, and Osborn was a frequent visitor to Basinghall Street, with a direct phone line to Henry Slater's room. Osborn and Slater passed work each other's way; Osborn was Slater's solicitor, but he would commission Slater's agency on divorce cases, Slater sending his detectives out to find evidence of adultery to use in cases Osborn was working on. In return, Slater would encourage potential clients to use Osborn and Osborn if they decided to petition for a divorce after using the detectives' services.[112] When Hugh Knowles sought to help Kate Pollard to gain a divorce from her husband, he went to Henry Slater; but it was no coincidence that Kate's divorce lawyer was none other than Albert Osborn. The Pollard divorce case stood to make both men a substantial amount of money.

Chapter 5

Finding Evidence

Slater's involvement in the highest-profile, and ultimately disastrous, divorce case of his career had started on 20 September 1901, when Hugh Knowles called at the agency's offices on Basinghall Street and asked for the agency's help in obtaining a divorce for Kate Pollard. Henry Slater's respected agency established a strategy for this commission: a select group of detectives would be chosen to shadow Thomas Pollard to find evidence of him committing adultery. Slater's agency accepted Knowles' commission, and what followed was an often chaotic series of events involving several detectives, a lot of money, and a naive Thomas Pollard, over the next year, involving different locations and strategies, and various individuals all with an eye on the money.

Thomas Pollard was on hard times, living back with his parents in Plymouth, and only supported by an allowance of 10 shillings a week from his wife. He was described as a 'poor, broken-down, semi-drunken man', but this was not a reason accepted by the divorce court for a wife to divorce her husband.[113] Adultery, however, was.[114] The hope was that he was as much of a bounder as Kate had suggested - that he was an alcoholic, and had paid for sex with prostitutes. Knowles had plenty of money to throw at the case, but initially, it was thought that it wouldn't be necessary to pay too much. Surely Tom Pollard would quickly be caught sleeping with another woman? But on sending detectives down to Plymouth for some initial shadowing, it became clear that nothing incriminating could be found against Pollard. He was not visiting the city's pubs;

and neither was he having a relationship with any local women that they could ascertain.

After a month, George Henry, Slater's manager, suggested a new, more risky strategy. He proposed that a detective should be sent down to instigate a friendship with Pollard, and from that position of trust, persuade him to 'misconduct himself' so that they could get evidence. Initially, George Henry and Albert Osborn sent instructions to detective Henry James Iles, who used the alias Henry James Sergeant.[115] Iles had been working on cases for Slater's across Devon and Cornwall, and so could get to Plymouth quickly.[116] On 3 October, he made the acquaintance of Thomas Pollard. He made several trips to the town – not yet the city it would later become – to watch Pollard over the next few months; on 18 December, he had drinks with Pollard followed by dinner.[117] Pollard was a lonely man, and Slater's detectives, starting with Iles, found it easy to befriend him.

Plymouth was a shipping port that during the Industrial Revolution had grown in size due to its import and export trade. It had formerly been three separate towns, with Devonport – home to a centuries-old naval dockyard and thus previously known as Plymouth Dock – and East Stonehouse. These three places would not be merged until 1914. Part of the towns were associated, in the mid-nineteenth century, with prostitution; there was a perception, not entirely unjustified, that prostitutes – deemed to be 'utterly degraded and outcast' – lived and worked across such southern dock towns.[118] In the Victorian era, there was a group of East Stonehouse streets that formed a red light district, and Damnation Alley – the former name of Castle Street – was home to several brothels at this time.[119] It was also known as 'the rag' due to the behaviour of residents there, which involved drinking at unlicensed beer houses as well as prostitution.[120] Plymouth was also home to the Theatre Royal, built on George Street in the 1810s as what was believed to be the country's only fireproof theatre. It was, ironically, subject to a severe fire in 1878, and had to be repaired.[121] There were often actresses and chorus girls residing in the town, and there was a suspicion about these often young women, with lingering doubts about their morality. With such women being present in the town, it was believed that a still young, idle man whose marriage had ended must inevitably be living a somewhat dissolute life among them.

Cyril Broughton Smith was one of the Slater's detectives working on the case. At the time, he was 33 years old, but was one of Slater's junior agents. Smith, a muscular man with a slight moustache, was sent down to Plymouth in early November 1901 to make Pollard's acquaintance. It was felt that Henry Iles needed support, as he had been unable to find any evidence of Tom Pollard having affairs with any women.

Within two weeks, Smith had made Pollard's acquaintance, and had sent a report back to the office. This report contained a proposal – he had conceived of an idea as to how to procure successful divorce evidence. He intended to arrange a meeting between Pollard and two local chorus girls, in order that Tom would 'compromise' himself with them.[122] His proposal apparently shocked the office so much that someone – presumably either Slater or George Henry – felt the need to send an urgent telegram back to Smith, stating: 'under no circumstances carry out your proposition, and return immediately.'[123] Smith had only recently been employed by the agency – he was seen as a 'new man'. Henry Slater himself was said to be displeased with George Henry for having sent relatively inexperienced detectives down to Plymouth in the first place. Yet Cyril Broughton Smith's proposal did not result in his employment being terminated; nor did it stop the detectives from working on the case. In fact, they worked on it using very similar tactics to those proposed by the junior detective.

By early 1902, with Smith in purgatory in London, another detective was ordered down to Plymouth. This was Frederick Stanley Davies, a 30-year-old, heavy-set, impressively moustachioed man, the son of Welsh parents, but who had been born and bred in London. On 26 February, he departed for Plymouth on a three-week assignment.[124] He initially introduced himself to Tom as 'an old friend from London', and they soon established a friendship, wandering around the city together, buying clothes, and stopping at various places for drinks - all funded by £240 given to Davies by Hugh Knowles.

On 10 March 1902, more drinks were had in a local pub, in which Fred Davies told his new friend that Plymouth was rather dull - in fact, he was getting sick of it. Why didn't the two of them take a trip to the Channel Islands, for a change? Their conversation was overheard by a Great Western Railway clerk, Frank Mead. He noticed that Pollard was dressed in a manner that made it clear he was not well off, and that he confessed as much to Davies. Davies duly took Pollard to a bootmaker in the town, where he bought a pair of boots for the man from shop manager William Lee, and then a new hat.[125] After having all this money spent on him, Pollard agreed to head to Jersey with Davies.[126]

Whilst on Jersey, Davies and Pollard stayed in St Helier. The town was home to the 2-year-old Jersey Opera House, and thus home, like Plymouth, to female performers as well as prostitutes who catered for the large number of visitors to the island.[127] It was seen as a suitable place to try to persuade Pollard to have a sexual encounter; if Plymouth had failed, St Helier might succeed. The two men stayed at the Star Hotel in St Helier, where Davies posed as Pollard's valet to those they met, and, having already paid for both men's travel, he also paid for all their hotel expenses.[128]

One night, just after 11pm, Davies walked Pollard to a boarding house at 7 Hilary Street. They knocked on the door, and it was opened by the owner, a middle-aged woman named Alexandra Macnamara.[129] She had two Frenchwomen staying with her at this time: 27-year-old Marie Travert, and Marie Leroi, who occupied neighbouring rooms in the house. Neither woman could speak English, although Travert understood it; both women were willing to sleep with men for money. Davies gave Travert ten shillings, and asked her to go and buy some 'refreshments'. She returned with three bottles of wine, and the men started to drink – Davies's goal was to get Thomas Pollard inebriated. Davies then took Marie Travert aside and suggested that she should try to seduce Pollard, and then gave Pollard half a sovereign to pay for Marie Travert's services. She started flirting with Tom, and was soon able to persuade him to accompany her to her room. Davies then spoke to Mrs Macnamara, and commissioned her to 'witness' Thomas Pollard *in flagrante delicto* with Marie Travert. Despite this, Davies still insisted on going upstairs shortly afterwards and forcing open Pollard's door, in order to catch him with Marie. When the two men left Hilary Street, Davies gave Marie Travert and Marie Leroi ten shillings each, claiming that he was looking after the money as Pollard, his 'master', was 'a little bit wrong in the head'.[130]

The next morning, the two men left the island and headed back to Plymouth, where they arrived on 18 March. They had been gone a week. Slater's usually made its detectives submit daily reports of their activities, but in this case, none were made by Davies on his return. However, one of the letters Davies had sent to the agency just before they left Plymouth claimed that Pollard had promised, if he was well enough, to accompany Davies to Jersey, and that Davies 'thought he would be successful over there'.[131] Davies would later argue that he simply meant that he was more likely to get Pollard to talk about his past career in an unfamiliar environment, but then said that he went to Jersey because Pollard was so 'notorious' a figure locally that he didn't want to be seen with him in Plymouth. Clearly, Davies had wanted to get Pollard drunk, and then in a compromising position, and felt it would be easier to do this away from people who knew Pollard; but he was willing not only to lie but to make false allegations about Pollard when asked to explain himself. Meanwhile, back in London, it was made clear in Basinghall Street that '[the agency's] instructions to their detectives were not to see the light of day'.[132] From this point on, John Pracy was ordered to keep watching

Pollard; Davies had managed to spend £34 in Plymouth and Jersey, without the case being closed.[133]

Although Davies had been successful in getting Pollard to sleep with a woman who wasn't his wife, his mission, and its result, was seen as 'dangerous' by the agency. Certainly, George Henry was aware that it looked - correctly - as though they had made Pollard engage in misconduct, and decided that a further attempt needed to be made to ensure they had sufficient evidence against him. Accordingly, in May 1902, Henry Iles was sent back to Plymouth with a photograph of Pollard. Iles' aim was to get statements from local women who may have had sexual relations with Kate's husband. The photograph was originally one of Tom and Kate Pollard together, taken just after their marriage; she had presumably given it to Hugh Knowles to pass on to Slater and Osborn, and they had cut her off it to enable their detectives to show just the man's face on its own to local women.[134]

Iles claimed to have seen Pollard at 11pm one night, talking to a woman named Maud Goodman in the street.[135] Maud was to become a key part of the Pollard divorce case. Although subsequent reports failed to provide any reliable background for Maud - not even her age is specified - there were only two women of this name in the local area at the time, one being a mother-of-four who lived a quiet life in Devonport. The other, likely to have been the Maud in question, was a 22-year-old woman who was born and bred in the town. Maud had lost her mother before her second birthday, and had lived variously with her father and two brothers, and with her maternal grandmother and uncle, during her childhood. By 1901, she was working as a servant, but by the following year, she was boarding at the house of Minnie Wilson at Summerland Place. Maud admitted to entertaining men in her lodgings for money.[136]

One of Maud's fellow lodgers with Mrs Wilson at 8 Summerland Place was a woman who became a firm friend of hers - Louisa Ford. Louisa, known as Louie, was older and more experienced in life than Maud. She was one of six children, brought up by her widowed mother – who worked as a charwoman – in Devonport.[137] At around the age of 16, in 1886, she had married a seaman named Charles Ford, who spent most of his time at sea, leaving his young wife at home bringing up their daughter. Her married life was spent in a house shared by at least six other households. Louisa had her daughter Mary in the winter of 1887, and a son, Frank, in early 1901. The 1901 census records her as a widow, and so it is possible that young Frank was not Charles Ford's son.[138] By 1902, Louisa was boarding at 8 Summerland Place with her children, and she would be a long-term resident.[139] Despite the 12 year age gap between her and Maud, they were friends who spent time together walking the streets of Plymouth, socialising.

Albert Osborn approached Minnie Wilson, and ascertained that Maud Goodman was a woman who might be willing to falsely identify Pollard as someone she 'knew', in the carnal sense. He then spoke to Maud herself to set a chain of events in place that would, he confidently believed, enable Kate Pollard to get her divorce, and Slater's agency (and himself as Kate's solicitor) to get a hefty fee.[140] Thomas Pollard was certainly a visitor to Summerland Place. In fact, a physician friend of his, Dr Albert Eccles, knew how often Pollard went there, and had asked him on one occasion to check on one of his own patients who lived in the road.[141] The insinuation later was that Summerland Place was the location of various houses of ill-repute, and that Pollard visiting there regularly meant he was probably a client of one of the prostitutes there. This rumour may have been picked up on by the detectives and given them an idea to 'match' him with one of Summerland Place's female residents.

In July 1902, another Slater detective, Francis Stevens, ventured to Plymouth. Stevens had started work for Slater's three years earlier, being made a manager after a year, on a salary of £15 a week. The two men were close friends, and when Slater took his three month sabbatical to Australia, he wrote Stevens regular, chatty letters. On Slater's return to England in April 1902, however, Stevens noted that his employer's demeanour towards him had changed, and that he had become cool towards him.

However, Stevens would remain working for the agency until later that summer, and so he duly travelled down to Plymouth on another job, during which he stayed at the Grand Hotel on the Promenade - an impressive, Italianate-style building barely 30 years old. It was an impressive place for a private detective to stay, but it appears to have been a regular haunt of Slater's staff. While on his assignment, Stevens submitted regular reports to Slater, as was the agency's style, and usual for detectives - but he was apparently blissfully unaware that he had colleagues also working in the city, employed on another secretive task.

As Davies had been cultivating Pollard's friendship, another of Slater's men, Charles Fielding, had remained in London, and noticed how often solicitor Albert Osborn was in contact with George Henry, the manager, via telephone. Fielding was asked to make copies of the other detectives' reports into Pollard, and noticed that he had not had any reports from their activities in Jersey. George Henry smiled at this, and said, 'Oh, they must not see daylight.' At one point, Fielding also overheard Henry speaking to Osborn on the office landing. Henry said, 'We're not getting on very well with the Pollard case at Plymouth.' Osborn slapped the manager on the back and said, 'I will go down and see what I can do for you.' 'I wish you would, Albert,' a relieved Henry responded.[142] Osborn promptly followed the line of detectives catching the train to the south-west.

On 10 July, Stevens was therefore surprised to find Osborn walking into the Grand Hotel at Plymouth. The two men greeted each other, and went for lunch. Over their sandwiches, Osborn told Stevens that he had travelled down to meet a Mr Pollard. As they relaxed, replete, a man came through the restaurant door, grabbing Stevens' attention because he was 'very tall'. Osborn saw him too, and muttered to Stevens, 'That fellow Pollard is altogether too straight... What I cannot do one way, I must do in another.'[143]

Stevens was now drawn into a different investigation to the one he claimed to have been sent to Plymouth for. By the time he had arrived, both John Pracy and Osborn were well and truly frustrated with following Pollard around, watching him in the forlorn hope that he might willingly commit adultery with one of Devon's many prostitutes or other young women. Pracy had soon returned to London, but on the evening of his departure, Stevens went to dinner with Osborn, where the two men were soon engaged in a conversation about this difficult case, Osborn commenting that he was 'sucking the Pollard people dry'.[144]

Certainly, the detective agency and the solicitors were making a lot of money from the case. Between the autumn of 1901 and the end of March the following year, Hugh Knowles had paid Slater's Detective Agency £1,170, in sums ranging from £15 to £250.[145] Fees, hotel costs, food and drink – all were paid for by Knowles, who was hoping that this expenditure would result in Kate Pollard gaining a divorce. There was therefore a strong desire to find evidence, or to fabricate it, not only to satisfy Knowles, but also to achieve a further 'success' for the agency, further cementing its reputation as the best detective agency not just in London, but across the nation.

Chapter 6

The Honey Trap

The scene was set for a honey trap; the location was 3 Summerland Place, where Maud was staying in a lodging house with Louie Smith.[146] Summerland Place was in the centre of Plymouth, an easy walk from Plymouth Hoe. Today, it's hard to imagine how the area looked; the Plymouth Blitz of 1941 destroyed much of the town, including Summerland Place and the infant school situated at the bottom of the road. The modern city therefore obscures what the town was like during Edwardian times, when lodging houses nuzzled up next to each other along the road, punctuated by family homes and also by businesses, such as the antiques shop further up Summerland Place. These lodging houses were run by women, and although some men stayed there, they were largely home to other women - milliners, dressmakers, singers, and servants.[147] The extent to which prostitution was carried out among its inhabitants cannot be ascertained, but some - including Maud Goodman - admitted that they were paid for sex. They lived among those who did not judge them for their behaviour, and felt secure in their lodgings as a result, surrounded by a network of women with precarious financial positions who knew that their community had to do what they could to earn money.

In 1902, Maud and Louisa were staying at number three, together with their friend Nellie Bell; 60-year-old Emma Smith lived at number four.[148] These women moved around, often within the local area and sometimes even the street - Maria Congdon, for example, was running number four as a lodging house in 1901, before moving to number eight. A look at the 1901 census shows that of numbers one to nine Summerland Place, seven houses were run as lodging houses by women, of whom all but one were widows. Only Minnie Wilson, operating a lodging house at number nine, was not - she was considerably younger than her neighbouring lodging house keepers, being only in her mid-twenties.[149] The women staying in these lodging houses were often friends with each other, and so there was a lot of running between the various houses, with girls visiting neighbours in order to see their friends.

When Maud Goodman met a man in June 1902, she was able to bring him back to Summerland Place and entertain him overnight without disapproval from her landlady or other friends. Maud and her circle admitted seeing men for money, but although she was seen as a loose woman by some of the detectives, within her community, there was greater tolerance and comradeship. However, it was Maud's sexual encounter that June that brought her into the Pollard divorce case.

On 9 July 1902, the day before he met with Stevens at the hotel, Albert Osborn had sent a message to Maud Goodman, asking her to meet him at Minnie Wilson's lodging house on Summerland Place. When she duly arrived, he took a photo of Thomas Pollard out of his pocket - the same one being hawked by Iles the previous month - asking her if she knew him. Whether Osborn thought he might genuinely be the man Maud had slept with is not clear. It seems doubtful, given the detectives' earlier reports that it was hard to get Pollard to misbehave, however drunk he was. What seems more likely is that Osborn knew that Maud had a past, and that she was a young woman of uncertain financial status, who might be persuaded to lie about her lovers if she was offered a bit of cash. He had also, unknown to her, already approached two of her friends, and learned that she had had a man over at her place the month before. He now presented her with the photo of dark-haired, middle-aged Thomas Pollard, and Maud responded that she thought she knew him, but was not sure. She knew what Osborn wanted her to say.

Osborn said that if she signed a piece of paper confirming that she knew him, it 'wouldn't do any harm', giving her a half-sovereign.

Maud at first refused to sign, because she did not want to 'give away' one of her gentlemen visitors – it might get him into trouble; she then seems to have paused the conversation to go with Louisa Ford to the Victoria Hotel – presumably to talk things over with her friend and decide what to do.[150] She later claimed to have told Minnie Wilson that she 'thought' she knew Pollard, but that she would not give him away. What she does not appear to have previously known is that Minnie Wilson had been shown the photograph some two weeks earlier; on seeing it again, Minnie realised why Maud had been asked to look at it, and warned her, 'the photograph has been shown before. It is in connection with a divorce case, so be careful what you say.'[151] Maud ignored the warning, and on her return to the lodging house, she asked Osborn if they could go to a nearby hotel, the Swan, where she would sign the paper in its private bar; she wanted to be away from Minnie when she signed, claiming that this was because Minnie would not approve of her giving the man away.[152] Osborn agreed, and when Maud duly signed the paper, he gave her a further sovereign.[153]

When Stevens became involved, he rapidly suspected they were investigating something dodgy – a piece of 'dirty work' that he did not want to be drawn into. When he learned about the two women being offered a sovereign to identify Thomas Pollard from his photograph, he told Osborn that this was a dangerous thing to do if the women were subsequently called on to be witnesses: 'It might cost you very dear, and these women could give you away.' Osborn, however, refused to believe that any court would trust the testimony of two Devon women before that of a well-known solicitor, and responded, 'Any judge or jury would believe me before these women, and we can do all right on this.'[154] Osborn, who could charge nearly £700 for his work in a divorce action, was open about his attitude; he regarded himself as having 'a perfect right to pay for evidence' if he could not get it any other way.[155] The other option open to Slater's detectives – a recognition and acknowledgement that there was no case against

Thomas Pollard, and that they should communicate that to his wife – was, seemingly, never considered.

Kate Pollard filed a petition for divorce on 14 July 1902, the documents drawn up by Osborn's office. As grounds for divorce, she accused Thomas of committing adultery with Maud Goodman.[156] However, there were still concerns in London about whether enough had been done to identify Tom Pollard as an adulterer, and Pracy and Osborn continued to visit Plymouth to ensure that everything was in order. On the evening of 2 August, Pracy found Maud and asked her to identify Tom Pollard in person. He took her, dressed in a distinctive red outfit, and her friend Louisa, to the environs of the Clock Tower, where they saw a man with his back to them, having just come out of the pub opposite.[157] Pracy pointed him out, saying 'There's our man.' Maud told him she would not be able to identify him unless she saw him face to face. They then shadowed the man to the Hoe, where Maud now saw his face, and said, 'I think I know the gentleman. Anyhow, he is like a gentleman I stayed with.' She laughed, and Louisa noticed Pollard turn to look at her.[158] What Maud did not know at the time was that Thomas Pollard was there because he had received an anonymous letter asking him to be at the Clock Tower to meet the letter-writer. He had duly gone there, but, unsurprisingly, nobody had turned up. The letter writer was from Slater's agency.[159]

There was pressure on all those involved in the Pollard case to tie up loose ends and organise the paperwork required to get Kate Pollard her divorce. Maud Goodman had told Osborn that she had 'frequently committed herself' with Thomas Pollard, or so he claimed, but it's clear that although Maud had had relations with men, she was vague as to whether one was Pollard at all.[160] He looked like a gentleman, and she had been with a gentleman, but that is as specific as she got.

Immediately after shadowing Pollard at Plymouth Hoe, Pracy had taken Maud back to her lodgings, and presented her with a statement to sign. This stated that she had identified a photograph of Pollard as being the man she had slept with, and that she had subsequently identified him in person.[161] Maud argued that she could not sign – she was not as certain about Pollard's identity as the statement made out. Osborn told her if she didn't sign the statement, which also said that she had had relations with Thomas Pollard in March, April, May, and June 1902 'at various places', someone else would.[162] At 11pm, Maud persuaded Osborn to finally leave her alone – but early the next morning, he called for her, again pressing her to sign the statement, and sending for pen and ink. Eventually, and under pressure, she wrote her signature on the paper. She received £1 from Messrs Osborn and Osborn in return. Her friend Louisa 'Louie' Ford got another pound.[163]

Maud was astute, and realised that the men from London had money to spend, and that she was in a position of relative power. On 7 August, she wrote to Osborn demanding more money – or, as she put it in her letter, 'a present for her trouble'. Osborn sent her a letter containing £2, to be shared between herself and Louisa Ford.[164] Pracy then came down to Plymouth, accompanied by Kate Pollard's sister Jane, in order to positively identify Thomas Pollard as Kate's husband.[165] While there, he also visited Maud Goodman to ask her to attend the divorce case in London, but Maud refused: 'I don't want to go.' Panic ensued in Basinghall Street and at Osborn's office, and Osborn then went down to Devon himself in order to persuade Maud. She eventually agreed, but only if Louisa, Nellie Bell, and Maria Congdon could come with her. Osborn duly arranged to put the girls up at Matcham's Hotel on Aldwych, with detectives Pracy and McKenna 'looking after' them – presumably, at least in part, to ensure that Maud kept to her side of the bargain and did not run back to Plymouth until after she had given evidence.[166]

That November, the women ran riot at Matcham's, and demanded to be entertained while in the capital. They were working-class Devonians with little opportunity for travel, and they

– understandably – saw this as an opportunity. There was little sense that they realised what they had got into, and the seriousness of the situation at that point. Joseph McKenna, one of the detectives tasked with looking after the three women, despaired of them, regarding Maud in particular as 'troublesome'. The women were noisy both at the hotel, and outside it. The day after they arrived, a Sunday, they were taken out in hansom cabs, and to a Sunday League concert.[167]

Thomas failed to appear at the divorce hearing, allegedly because he was penniless due to poor health, and could not afford to attend. Maud Goodman, however, was there, and stated that she had committed adultery with him. Maud's allegations were backed up by the evidence given by Slater's agency, and Albert Osborn was present as Kate Pollard's solicitor.[168] After Maud's evidence, her friends assumed their role was over, and made their way back to Paddington. They were accompanied to the station by Joseph McKenna, who, before they boarded the Plymouth train, was persuaded to give Maud another £4.[169]

A *decree nisi* was issued to Kate Pollard on 24 November 1902. Everything seemed as usual; it was another successful divorce case for the detective agency, ensuring that its boast of a 100 per cent success rate in such work remained intact. Or so it initially appeared.

Chapter 7

The Agency Burns

While the Pollard divorce case was progressing in the summer of 1902, there had been trouble brewing at home. Henry Slater's cavalier approach to his friendships would cost him one friendship in particular, and because of this, ultimately his career. If Slater had kept this friend, Francis Stevens, on board, it is probable that nobody would have exposed the antics of Slater's detectives in Plymouth, and the Pollard divorce might have gone through without comment, leaving the agency claiming another success.

Henry Slater had initially met Stevens as a client, when he turned up at Basinghall Street in 1899 to consult the detective about how to obtain a divorce from his wife, Emily.[170] Stevens was in his thirties, and had spent the 1880s and early 1890s working for Sir John Greville Smyth, as a footman, coachman and valet.[171] By the time of the visit to Slater, he had become a sanitary engineer and builder, working with his brother – although he didn't boast about these jobs as much as he had his former one.[172]

At around this time, Stevens also consulted a phrenologist about his future. He was apparently told that 'nature intends you for a Sherlock Holmes'.[173] He soon met with Slater, and felt that his meeting was a good omen. He and Slater had soon forgotten the purpose of Stevens' visit, instead discussing fortune telling, with Stevens telling Slater about his trip to the phrenologist. Slater apparently suggested that Stevens also consult a palmist, and Stevens duly did so. He reported back that the palmist's predictions were 'very nice'.[174] Slater offered Stevens a job at the agency, and the two men duly became close friends, discussing their personal beliefs. Although Slater tried to keep his personal life very much separate to his home life, Stevens was one of the men he trusted, and so he opened up to him in a way that was unusual for him. He also helped Stevens to divorce his wife, enabling him to remarry a month after the final decree was issued.[175]

Stevens had discovered the detective agency's dubious tactics in Plymouth in July 1902, when he bumped into Osborn. Osborn and Slater had wanted as few people as possible to know about the Pollard investigation, and subsequently gave Stevens some work to do on the case as a way of keeping him quiet. Slater, though, regretted this decision, and appears to have started distancing himself from his friend. He sensed that Stevens knew too much both about him and the Pollard case, and began to criticise Stevens' methods of working.

On Stevens' return to London, Slater really started to make life unpleasant for him, hoping it would cause him to leave the agency. As noted previously, Francis Stevens had noticed Slater's coldness towards him after the latter had returned from Australia. He had, nevertheless, filed regular reports to his boss from Plymouth. On 12 August 1902, Slater rebuked him for failing to include a woman's name and address on one report, adding, 'You are not a baby or a child!'[176] This rebuke took place back in the Basinghall Street office, in front of other employees. Slater followed it by claiming to have been down to Plymouth himself, to make enquiries about Stevens; as a result of these, he claimed to have found out that Stevens had been buying items for his own home and claiming them back on expenses. Slater was furious, accusing Stevens of 'obtaining goods by fraud, misappropriating my money, robbing me right and left for some time.'[177] A stung Stevens swore, calling Slater a '___ liar' and adding, 'Captain, this won't do. Unless you apologise to me before 12 o'clock tomorrow, I shall put it in other hands.' Slater, however, shouted back, saying, 'Oh, oh, you are a thief. I have proved it.'[178]

On 29 August 1902, Stevens left Slater's agency - some reports state that he was sacked, others that he left voluntarily. Given that two days earlier, he had served a writ for slander on his employer, it seems more likely that Slater told him to go. The day after Stevens left, by no coincidence, Simmonds' Detective Association was established. This was funded with £100 of Stevens' money, and £400 from another former Slater's detective, Charles Henry Simmonds, whose name was used for the agency. Stevens had carried on communicating with Edgar Cartwright at Slater's, and when Slater found out, Cartwright had to leave. He did so in September, and promptly moved to Simmonds'. Within a month, Stevens had taken a step back from the new business, or so he claimed, with it now being formally operated by Simmonds and Cartwright.[179] Operating from King Street, Cheapside, they were in direct competition with Slater, deliberately setting up in the City of London near to Slater's headquarters, rather than elsewhere, such as Westminster.

The members of the association had kept in touch with former colleagues at Slater's. Thomas Craig had left Slater's in July 1902, and was soon persuaded to join the rival agency.[180] Simmonds' agency wanted to do more than compete with Slater – it was its owners' intention to ruin him. The agency started placing newspaper advertisements for its services, but it was a matter of grievance to its owners that Slater's regular advert in the main newspapers was often at the top of the column, where it would be read first by potential clients, and this new firm wanted to do something to stop his pre-eminence. Simmonds, Stevens, and Cartwright founders admitted to Craig that they were 'trying to do all the injury they could to the business of Messrs Slater's'.[181]

Stevens knew what had been going on in the Pollard case, and wanted to expose it as part of his plan to ruin Slater. Therefore, as soon as he had established the association with Simmonds, Stevens persuaded Edgar Cartwright to steal papers relating to the Pollards from Basinghall Street. These included an incriminating memorandum written by Slater's detective Cyril Broughton Smith, which clearly implicated the agency in paying Maud Goodman and

Louisa Smith to seduce Pollard. Smith wrote that it had occurred to him that 'a look in at the theatre after supper' would, in his view, be a means of persuading Pollard to sleep with one of the chorus girls afterwards. He noted, however, that he would need to pay the girls – this was an admittance that the agency would be procuring girls in order to create evidence.[182] Smith had also noted that he doubted that 'an ordinary loose woman of Plymouth would serve the purpose' but that Maud and Louisa were more 'classy' and so more likely to tempt the formerly well-to-do Thomas Pollard.[183] Cartwright stole this note, among other documents, before suddenly leaving Slater's and joining the revengeful Stevens in the new business.

Between 1901 and March 1904, the agency – bankrolled by Hugh Knowles – would spend over £2,000 on the Pollard case.[184] Initially, the expenditure – listed in their accounts as 'watching Pollard' – appeared worth it; Kate Pollard petitioned for divorce, and she had, of course, obtained her *decree nisi* from the Divorce Division of the High Court.[185] However, the King's Proctor then intervened, asking the court to rescind the decree. He alleged that the detectives, acting on the part of Kate Pollard, had arranged that Thomas Pollard should be 'induced to commit adultery' in order to gain her divorce. Kate denied the allegation, but now both she and Slater's detectives were under investigation. The agency was now being run by George Philip Henry; although Henry Slater may not have been as hands-off as he claimed, instructions to the detectives in this case came from his manager, consulting with solicitor Osborn – one of Slater's old colleagues and friends. It was, though, his name on the business – he was inextricably linked to a rather grubby case involving lies, sex, and money, and his world was about to implode in two inter-linked court cases.

Members of staff, either concerned about the tactics used by the agency in the case, or sensing which way the wind was blowing, started to leave. The presence of many competing detective agencies in the capital meant that there were plenty of employers who would welcome an experienced Slater's detective with open arms. Some went to Simmonds' Detective Association, or at the least, kept in touch with Simmonds and Cartwright; Charles Fielding, a long-standing member of staff, was sacked by Slater in the summer of 1903, as the detective chief suspected – correctly – that Fielding had kept in touch with both Stevens and Cartwright after they had left Slater's agency.[186]

It was always worth keeping enemies on side. Slater failed to realise this, and his attitude towards his staff caused him issues. Although he was good friends with both Albert Osborn and George Henry, and appears to have been loyal to them, in other cases, he could play hot and cold with individuals. In terms of his former friendship with Francis Stevens, though, when he decided he no longer wanted his friendship, Stevens refused to take it lying down. Even his aim in setting up a rival agency was explicitly, as he told Charles Fielding, to 'take away Slater's business'.[187] He and Cartwright chose to set their agency up in the City of London – many more agencies established themselves further west, and so in choosing the Square Mile, Simmonds' was directly encroaching on Slater territory. The City of London was home to few agencies, with Slater's by far the largest and most successful. But now, 'Simmonds' Detective Association' would compete with it from offices at 29-30 King Street, Cheapside.

The first advert for Simmonds' Detective Association appeared in the press in October 1902. The agency employed similar tactics to Slater's and other detective agencies of the time, bombarding newspaper readers with adverts for its services, placing multiple adverts in a single edition, and using quotes from previous satisfied customers (whether real or fictional). Simmonds' was before Slater's alphabetically, and had the advantage in where its adverts appeared in the press. Like Slater's, Simmonds' highlighted their use of female detectives; and the agency also highlighted how it owed its existence to Slater, without giving him publicity through mentioning his name, boasting that its founder was 'Henry Simmonds, manager (many years with leading London private detective)'.[188]

Simmonds emphasised its use of 'tact and skill', and suggested that, unlike Slater's, it could guarantee secrecy ('our system is unique and the only one, from past experience, by which secrecy can be assured.').[189] Faced with a sometimes bewildering number of claims and boasts from a multiplicity of detective agencies that proliferated across the capital, potential customers looked for evidence of professionalism, longevity and secrecy; but the frequent use of outlandish claims by different agencies also suggests that customers wanted to use 'big' agencies, flamboyant ones with recognisable figureheads. Both Simmonds' and Slater's agencies claimed to have agents and branches across the world, but in reality were firmly grounded in their respective London offices, from where their founders battled each other through newsprint. What Simmonds' staff had learned from their experience working for Slater's was that creativity, verging on fakery, was a fundamental part of the detective's work.

Henry Slater had, at the start of July 1902, placed an advert in the *Daily Telegraph* stating that he specialised in giving 'his personal attention to all cases of slander and libel'.[190] He certainly would be giving his personal attention to such a matter by early 1903. For helping establish an agency that would rival his former employer's was not sufficient for Stevens in his desire for revenge. He had made good on his threat to sue his former employer, and finally, in March 1903, Henry Slater appeared in court for the first ever time, accused of slander by his former friend and fellow detective.

In court, Stevens detailed the change in attitude from Slater after their previous friendship, and accused the latter of doing 'everything' to annoy Stevens. The personal items Slater had accused him of charging to the company amounted to little more than a pot of Devonshire cream – and Stevens insisted this was paid for with his own money. Slater's public denouncement of him had resulted in his colleagues referring to him as a 'cream pincher' and thus had a huge effect on his reputation within the agency.[191] Stevens ensured that he mentioned the Plymouth trip in his evidence, and this seems a deliberate ploy to make sure Slater knew that Stevens knew the secrets of the Pollard case. Slater should have taken heed of Stevens' warnings; this was a man who would do anything to get revenge on the man who had spurned his friendship.

In response, Slater argued that his words had not been slanderous – they were simply 'vulgar abuse'. He seemed surprised that Stevens would bring action against him, especially after months had gone past. The jury, however, made their minds up on the matter remarkably quickly, not even needing to leave the jury's box to confer. Instead, they found that Henry Slater – who was advertising himself as 'the greatest detective of the age', even placing an advert to this effect on the day the verdict was given – had slandered his former detective.[192]

On Thursday, 5 March, Stevens was awarded £500 damages.[193] These were described as 'heavy damages', and in addition, Slater had to pay Stevens' costs.[194] There was an even heavier price to pay in terms of Slater's reputation. Coverage of the case did not refer to him as famous, or as the owner of the most well-known detective agency in London, let alone Britain. He was simply 'the private inquiry agent'. It was instead Stevens who emerged triumphant from the case, not only the winner, but described in more salubrious terms as the former employee of a baronet.

The competition between Simmonds' agency and Slater's agency continued after the slander suit was settled; the *Daily Telegraph* of 23 April 1903, for example, contained a column of adverts from detective agencies, including four from Slater's, and four from Simmonds'. Simmonds' offered lady detectives, a 'secret system' of working, and boasted that Simmonds himself had been described in the press as 'Sherlock Holmes in real life' – a boast that Simmonds' agency had employed in its adverts since it was founded.[195] It was, of course, a quote that had originally come from Henry Slater. Slater responded by stating that his agency was higher class, offering 'secret society agents in the highest circles in every town throughout the world', and that he could offer clients 'young lady detectives' who could impersonate any character – 'from a crossing sweeper to a princess'.[196] There was a slight sign of desperation on the part of Slater here, making big claims in order to respond to the upstart agency.

But was it Slater who placed the adverts, or his manager, George Henry? Despite, as shown, Slater claiming to have virtually retired by this point, the evidence of Slater's presence in the agency is a sign that he was not as hands-off as he wanted others to believe. It was Henry Slater who told Stevens off in person, in front of his colleagues, not George Henry. However, this could have been done on one of what Slater regarded as an infrequent visit to the office, and the language used in some of these later adverts is more florid than earlier ones that were certainly placed by Slater himself. The likelihood is that there was a co-working arrangement between the two men; George Henry taking on the management role when his boss was not around, placing adverts, seeking to gain an advantage over competitors. However, when serious events took place, such as the need to put Stevens in his place, it was Henry Slater who came into Basinghall Street to take charge.

As if a grubby slander suit making Slater out to be a vindictive employer wasn't bad enough, it must have been a portend of things to come. Stevens, no longer with Slater's agency but bankrolling Simmonds' one, had secrets – he knew why detectives had been sent to Plymouth, and how they had created evidence in the Pollard case. He knew that Slater would not want him to tell anyone this, but instead of directly blackmailing him, he did something else. He set up his own detective agency that would directly compete with Slater's – a newer, younger, trendier agency, staffed by those who had trained under the older Henry Slater. It was no coincidence that the agency was named for Simmonds. Charles Henry Simmonds dropped his first name for their publicity materials. He now shared Slater's first name and initials – H.S. – drawing a direct parallel between the two agencies. It also ensured that the younger agency came first in any alphabetical list of detective agencies as well as perhaps causing some confusion among potential clients, who might pick Simmonds thinking it was actually Henry Slater's agency. Private detection was a competitive industry, where agencies had to think creatively to win business; Simmonds' took it further, by trying actively to destroy their detectives' former employer. Some of those involved in Simmonds' agency would soon become key witnesses for the prosecution of Henry Slater.

Stevens was clever, as he knew he was not allowed to directly compete with Slater as a result of leaving his employ. Instead, he had paid to help Cartwright and Simmonds establish the rival agency, and only worked on one case for them - and that only because they had been short staffed.[197] He kept his distance from anything that might implicate him in trying to ruin Slater; but he certainly gave other people directions on what to do. The agency had used the Lothbury branch of the London and Westminster Bank for its business banking, and had a very healthy income.[198] One week before Edgar Cartwright had left Slater's, Stevens persuaded him to steal Slater's bank passbook, and to write to the Inland Revenue stating that the king of private detectives was paying less income tax than he should have done. He did so knowing that Slater would be examined in the slander case, and he hoped that a tax investigation might be the subject of some cross-examination in court.[199] He wanted to ensure that he won the case, by whatever means. He also paid for Simmonds' agency to send out circulars to 2,000 of Slater's current and former customers - having arranged for the customer list to be stolen from Basinghall Street. The circulars stressed that this new agency would carry on work 'at a more moderate cost' than Slater's. Although Cartwright believed - or so he said - that the circulars were merely designed to show people that they wouldn't charge so much because they would be running up smaller bills undertaking the work, it was clear that the new agency, under Stevens' directions, was trying to undersell Henry Slater's organisation.[200]

As Slater was dealing with the slander suit, and as yet, unaware of the sheer level of machinations being undertaken by Simmonds' staff, there were also rumblings that the Pollard case was not done and dusted. First of all, Thomas Pollard had no idea that his wife had been granted a divorce; he claimed to have only realised when he read a press report about it on 25 November 1902. He then started receiving mysterious letters from another detective agency – a familiar one, as this was Longley's, based at 3 Featherstone Buildings in Holborn. Longley's may have been a quite short-lived agency, as there are only surviving press adverts for it between 1901 and 1903, but it was run by a former Slater's detective. It was also where both Thomas Craig and Cyril Broughton Smith would work for a time, with the latter having a close connection to the agency. It was so close that it would later emerge that Longley's letters were actually written by Smith. Slater's detective and manager William Hamilton had also now moved and was now based at 5 Featherstone Buildings. There were clearly strong links between this location and aggrieved former detectives at Slater's agency.[201]

However, Stevens had even more to do with Longley's involvement than most people realised. Just prior to his slander suit against Slater being heard, and furious with the older detective for having turned his back on him, he had written letters to Cartwright, threatening to 'ruin him [Slater] body and soul', knowing that he had information both about Slater personally, and his agency professionally, that could finish him. The stealing of financial information and client lists, the notifying the Inland Revenue of possible tax fraud, and the circulars promising to undercut Slater's rates were all the signs of a vengeful man – but Stevens had not finished yet.

Stevens now started to tip his friends off about how the Slater's men had obtained evidence of adultery in the Pollard case. These friends were presumably at Longley's agency, for on 1, 3 and 5 January 1903, Thomas Pollard was sent three letters by Mr Longley. The first asked him to come to Longley's London office, where the agency could give him information that would help him, and ultimately the King's Proctor. Another asked him to 'keep his own counsel' about what had happened at Plymouth, and not to try to trace Maud Goodman himself. He was told to bring the divorce citation, any letters or telegrams he had received from his wife while he had been at Plymouth, a photograph of her, and copies of press reports in the Devon papers to London for the private detectives to look at. Thomas went along with these requests, and on 6 January, the agency wrote to him to tell him that Mr Longley himself had called on the Treasury solicitors and had submitted a preliminary statement for the King's Proctor's attention.[202] In April 1903, having won his slander damages from Slater, Francis Stevens wrote to Edgar Cartwright, laughing, 'The King's Proctor has had all my papers... and will suck all he can from them.'[203]

As a result of Stevens' interventions, the King's Proctor decided to investigate. He believed that Slater's detectives – allegedly with the knowledge and support of Slater himself and his solicitor, Osborn – had engaged Maud Goodman specifically to lie in court and state that she had committed adultery with Thomas Pollard, in order for Kate to successfully gain her divorce. They had faked evidence in a divorce case, and he was about to expose them.

As the strands of the Pollard divorce suit were unravelling, so too was Slater's Detective Agency. Over the course of the second half of 1902, and throughout 1903, Slater faced the slander suit, but also other problems at work. His agency had now lost several key members of staff – experienced detectives who did the bulk of the donkey work at Basinghall Street. They had gained valuable knowledge and contacts while at Basinghall Street, and were now utilising them elsewhere, in direct competition to Slater's agency. Stevens, Simmonds, Cartwright: they had all left Slater's, and so too had Thomas Craig and Samuel Marrison.[204] Of those left at the office, some knew too much about how the evidence had been procured in the Pollard case, and others had been directly responsible for arranging it. George Henry and Albert Osborn had been deeply involved, and for the latter, in particular, being found out would have severe repercussions for his career and his reputation. He was aware of the possibility of being found out, as was George Henry.

The office, in 1903, was abuzz with rumours that the Pollard case was being investigated by the King's Proctor. Henry Slater appeared unflappable, commenting, 'That's all right. If Osborn has been fool enough to go down to Plymouth and get women to make false statements, we must put up with the consequences.'[205] Yet he admitted that the evidence obtained in Jersey - where Marie Travert had been paid to sleep with the drunken Thomas Pollard - was 'too dangerous' to be used in the case.[206] Osborn was the man who appeared more concerned. After Pracy mentioned Osborn's payments to Maud Goodman, to persuade her to give evidence in the divorce case, Osborn tapped his pocket and muttered, 'That is what has done it.'[207]

Under the surface, Slater himself was equally perturbed. He had demanded that all files and reports on the case should be given to him. He had asked George Henry to visit him in his private office, to burn some of the incriminating reports in his hearth. These were from the detectives who had worked in Plymouth, and the aim was to ensure that no incriminating evidence survived. Slater hoped that nobody had seen him burn the records.

Yet in other ways, on the surface at least, for much of 1903, business at Slater's Detective Agency continued as usual. The agency continued to take on other cases, under George Henry's management. Henry Iles remained working for Slater's, and was commissioned to work on a divorce case in 1903. The commission came from a railway contractor named Richard Walter Wright, who lived in South Africa. He believed his wife, Dora Mary, was having an affair with an Italian medical student named Pico. It was a tantalising case referred to in the press as having 'an air of adventure...an air that recalled the hot Southern blood feuds' but actually relied on evidence of misconduct in a Lugano hotel; so more of a cold Swiss feud than a hot Southern one. Slater sent Iles off to Switzerland to find evidence of the wife's affair, and, later, he had to serve the divorce papers on Mrs Wright in Lugano.[208]

Closer to home, the agency was commissioned to try to track down John Wilcox, who had disappeared from home in January 1901. He had only been married a year, but told his wife, Edith, he had 'got tired of her' and promptly vanished. Nothing more had been heard from him until Slater's detectives were able to track him down two years later, finding him walking with another woman in the Strand. The lovers were shadowed to Waterloo Road, where they went into a house together. 37-year-old Mrs Wilcox obtained her divorce on the basis of Slater's evidence, and it was another divorce success for the agency.[209]

In April 1903, Slater's detectives were commissioned to watch Major Charles Montgomerie Ryan of the Devonshire Regiment, whose wife Ethel wanted a divorce on the grounds of adultery and cruelty. Ethel picked the country's best-known agency, Slater's, to investigate her husband and find evidence of his adultery. Ethel gave either Slater or George Henry a photograph of her husband in uniform so that detectives could identify him. The agency also referred her to Messrs Osborn and Osborn, suggesting she use them as her divorce lawyers. The two firms' reciprocal arrangement, referring clients to each other, was clearly still in place.[210] Slater's duly provided evidence of Major Ryan committing adultery with Edith Smith at the Wilton Hotel in Pimlico on 12 April 1903, at the Royal Academy café in Piccadilly the following month, and at both the Royal Café in Pimlico and the Midland Grand Hotel at St Pancras in July. Mrs Ryan filed for divorce the following month, and obtained her *decree nisi* in June 1904.[211] However, despite the evidence accumulated by Slater's agency over the course of four months, Slater could not add this to his list of successful divorces that his agency had worked on. The Ryans never finalised their divorce, agreeing instead to a maintenance agreement and continuance of their existing separation.[212]

Henry Slater spent this early part of 1903 preoccupied with the slander case. Cases such as the Ryan divorce case, and the Wilcox case too, would have been dealt with by George Henry and the staff of detectives. However, Slater was also something of a control freak, and continued to receive updates about cases, while also visiting the office regularly to ensure that it continued to run smoothly. Had he really retired, and stayed away from the business, he might not have insulted Francis Stevens nor faced court for what he had said; more fundamentally, perhaps he could have avoided getting drawn into the Plymouth case. But he was unable to stay away. It was his name on the adverts and the letterheads and the bank account. It was his agency, and he could not resist keeping his toe in the detective world, always wanting to know what was going on.

When the calm in Plymouth was disturbed this year, Slater might soon have regretted his decision to stay involved. Frederick Murray, managing clerk of Devon law firm Messrs Watts, Ward and Anthony, was contacted by the Treasury solicitors in London and asked to act as the King's Proctor's representative in Plymouth.[213] He agreed, and it was made clear to him that he needed to get in touch with Maud Goodman. He went to Summerland Place to talk to her about the Pollard case, and, panicked, she wrote to Osborn immediately afterwards. He replied, stating his doubts about Murray's credentials, and commenting that if the King's Proctor had to get involved in the Pollard case, 'there would be no harm done if you truthfully told the facts as you have told them to me.'

Maud then went to Murray's office at 4 Princess Square, accompanied by Nellie Bell, and found Thomas Pollard in the office with him. Maud was asked to identify him, and taken by surprise, she exclaimed, 'I do not know the gentleman!' She was right; she had never 'misconducted' herself with Pollard. She then clarified the situation: Pollard was certainly the man she had seen on the Hoe, but he had not been the man she had slept with at Summerland Place.[214] On leaving Murray's office, Maud then bumped into Joseph McKenna, the Slater's detective, on the street. He was out working on a different case, he said, and meeting Maud was apparently a coincidence, although this seemed highly unlikely. The pair had a brief conversation. McKenna told Maud to simply tell the truth and nothing but the truth, but then asked her if she would 'look over some statements'. 'It is no good you getting the papers,' a flustered Maud told him, 'as I have some doubt about the matter.' McKenna replied, 'If you have any doubt about the matter, you ought not to say anything you are not sure of.'[215] Maud then decided not to look at the statements, and McKenna agreed not to press her any further about it.[216]

It was all starting to get a bit serious. Mr Murray now came to Maud and told her that the King's Proctor was definitely intervening in the Pollard case. She now wrote again to Albert Osborn, who told her to 'tell the truth' – but this truth was anything but, as Albert then told her that she must give 'the same information as you gave to us in the matter'. Frederick Murray wanted Maud to see Pollard again to check that this really was the man she had slept with, but Osborn warned her against doing so – 'there was no reason' she should.[217]

By December 1903, Slater knew that his friends and colleagues had made a massive error in their conducting of the Pollard investigation. At the same time, his advertising tactics changed. Although he, or Henry, continued to place multiple adverts in a single column of a newspaper, the wording of these had altered. Many asked for personal friends to trust him with their problems – he even asked for schoolfriends to get in touch, those who had 'experienced reverses' in their personal or business lives that he could help with. Henry Slater was now in his early fifties, and facing such a reverse himself.[218]

Some of the adverts of this time were placed in the name of the manager of Slater's agency, suggesting they had been drafted by George Henry. However, they undoubtedly had Slater's approval. Perhaps he was dredging his past to find new clients - suggesting that the agency had had a tailing off of customers. Henry Slater always separated his work and home life, and had only mentioned his real identity to Francis Stevens. To the rest of the agency, who Henry Slater was remained unknown. For such a compartmentalised personality, it strikes a discordant note that Slater's Detective Association now wanted to make contact with individuals from the owner's past.

Slater's was trying to get business whichever way it could. Henry Slater had always boasted about his firm's success in divorce cases, and this continued: his adverts from late 1903 still stressed that he had been successful in every one of his divorce court cases since 1885. However, he now placed adverts for his other services, saying he could obtain evidence for 'merchants, manufacturers and traders, who consider that their patents and trademarks are being infringed, or that their employees are tampering or being tampered with'.[219] In the light of what was going on behind the scenes, these adverts are significant: they show a concern that Slater's might be exposed for underhand activities as part of its divorce work, and a desire to therefore emphasise and concentrate on other types of work, in case the divorce shadowings had to end. There was also, though, a bit of bravado in the number of adverts still being placed, the money being spent on taking up most of a column in multiple adverts, and the number of newspapers being advertised in - including the *Standard, Truth, Morning Post* and *Daily Telegraph*. Slater and his team still wanted to be seen as the number one agency, one that could not be brought down. It is for that reason that another advert was placed, stating that he had, for many years, been almost 100 per cent successful, and that his 'reputation for ability and secrecy is, therefore, always at stake.'[220]

Slater knew that the success of his business was based on his reputation – yes, his professional reputation, but also his personal one. He had created an image of himself as the greatest detective of the age, and therefore he knew the importance of shaking off competitors. But by the end of 1903, newer, fresher competitors were right behind him, and his reputation was at stake like never before.

Chapter 8

At the Divorce Court

While Slater's detectives were working on other cases, behind the scenes, the King's Proctor was studying the evidence that had previously been submitted by Kate Pollard's divorce solicitors. His plea was filed before the divorce court on 11 June 1903, with further particulars being added in July and August.[221] On 2 October 1903, the Earl of Desart, the King's Proctor, set down a cause to revoke Kate Pollard's decree nisi. The King's Proctor, who was just a year older than Henry Slater, stated that 'diverse material facts' had not been known to the court, namely that Kate Pollard had arranged for people to induce her husband into committing adultery, with the aim of obtaining a divorce. He had several points to make. Firstly, he believed that Thomas Pollard had initially been the subject of such a plan in Jersey in March 1902. He also believed that Pollard had not committed adultery with Maud Goodman despite the divorce petition saying otherwise. Finally, he was confident that Maud had given false evidence at the divorce hearing.[222]

The facts laid out by the King's Proctor were stark. Albert Osborn and Slater's Detective Agency - the parties' names underlined in red - were stated to have made a series of attempts to induce Pollard to commit adultery in Plymouth between November 1901 and 15 July 1902. Osborn (Kate's solicitor), Slater (as the owner of the agency) and George Henry (as its manager) were deemed responsible for having instructed three of the agency's detectives to go to Plymouth, make Pollard's acquaintance, 'make him intoxicated' and 'introduce him into the company of women of loose character'.[223] On 14 September

1903, Kate Pollard made her reply to the King's Proctor's case. She simply denied every allegation made by him, and asked that his case be rejected. Unfortunately for her, and for Slater's agency, it was her own request that was rejected.[224]

In the new year, speculation started mounting in the press. In January 1904, a story appeared in a couple of newspapers regarding a 'private detective scandal', although the agency concerned was not named. Readers were warned that 'before long' there would be some 'remarkable disclosures' relating to misconduct by detectives, and that a 'certain London private detective' had been working in conjunction with 'a London solicitor' to concoct divorce evidence.[225] These rumours, which were undoubtedly about Slater's Detective Agency and Albert Osborn, were used as a means to disparage the entire private detective profession. Although some private detectives – notably those who were former police officers, the articles stressed – conducted their work honourably, there were others who depended 'on creating evidence, or intimidating persons who dare not face the publicity of the courts.'[226] The Pollard divorce case was, and would continue to be, a means by which private detectives were disparaged. It was not just small fry who might be tempted into fabricating evidence – it was those working for the top agency in the country doing the same. Nobody was exempt.

Only a couple of newspapers were discussing the impending scandal, and only in vague terms, but it was a sign of what was to come. Two months after the initial speculation, on Wednesday, 16 March 1904, the case returned to the divorce court to decide whether the Pollard divorce decree should be rescinded. The case was conducted by Sir Edward Carson, the solicitor-general, on behalf of the King's Proctor, with Sir Edward Clarke heading the defence.

Maud Goodman had been reluctant to appear at the divorce court again, and her presence there was the direct result of pressure by Osborn and Pracy. She, Louisa Ford and Nellie Bell had returned to London accompanied by Slater's detectives, as there was concern that without their presence, the girls would simply have stayed home in Devon. Albert Osborn ordered a two-wheeler and a four-in-hand cab to take the group from Paddington station to their hotel; Louisa Ford was cross that she was only given a bottle of beer and a sip of Scotch whisky during the long journey, and resented being taken in a waggonette rather than a hansom cab or 'electric brougham'.[227]

When Maud and Louisa gave evidence at the divorce court, their truthfulness was brought into question. Under cross-examination by Sir Edward Carson, Louisa admitted having telegrammed Osborn before coming to London, it being insinuated that she wanted him to give her instructions about what he wanted her to say. She denied having told Murray, who was working on behalf of the King's Proctor, that she intended to leave his side (she was supposed to be a witness for the King's Proctor), and 'go on Osborn's side'. She admitted to Carson that 'when I came up for Osborn's side, I was better treated than when I was in Mr Murray's party'.[228] Given her prior complaints about Osborn's parsimoniousness when it came to transport and drink, it's clear that it didn't take much to change her mind as to whose side she was on. Maud, in turn, denied telling Osborn that she had frequently slept with Pollard – she had simply told Pracy that Pollard was similar to a man she had slept with, not that he *was* that man. She also added that after she had first met with Frederick Murray, John Pracy had caught her and told her to 'stand by us'.[229]

Within the confines of the divorce court, the allegations against the Slater's men were detailed, and several of the agency's detectives were called on to tell the court what they knew of the case. John Pracy was one of these men. He stated that he had worked for Slater's agency for fourteen years, thus making him one of the company's most experienced detectives. Pracy talked about his actions in Plymouth, insisting that when Maud had seen Tom Pollard on the Hoe, she had laughed, and said, 'That's the old rat.' Pracy asked her to be quite sure, and she said she was. Furthermore, Pracy said, Maud had looked at the expression on Pollard's face and said that he was probably thinking to himself, 'That's the little devil that has caused all the mischief.'[230] There was a reason Pracy had worked for Slater's for so long: he was loyal to his employers and would not admit to anything being remiss in how evidence had been gained in the Pollard case. He was also adamant that no pressure had been put on Maud Goodman to say particular things.

On 23 March, another Slater detective, Charles Fielding, gave evidence. He started by setting out his police credentials, for it was these that would establish him as a trustworthy witness rather than his subsequent stint at Slater's agency. However, it was this latter job that was of interest to the divorce court. Fielding described his varied duties at Basinghall Street, which included keeping reports on their 'chief clients', one of whom was Kate Pollard. Fielding had been ordered to make copies of the original reports in the case, and to forward them to Albert Osborn at his firm. Fielding was privy to much operational information: he knew that Davies had been at Jersey, but he hadn't seen any reports from him while he was there. This was unusual in itself; Fielding would have expected to have received these reports in order to copy them and send them to Osborn – but he hadn't. He had noticed this omission and went to George Henry to tell him that he had not seen any Jersey reports. Henry's response was to laugh, saying, 'Oh, they must not see daylight!'

On another occasion, Fielding said he had heard George Henry and Albert Osborn discussing the case while standing together on the landing outside Fielding's office door. The manager had told Osborn that the agency was 'not getting on very well at Plymouth with the Pollard case'. Osborn slapped Henry on the back, and asked, 'Shall I go down and see what I can do for you?' George Henry responded, 'I wish you would, Albert.' Shortly afterwards, Osborn travelled down to Devon. Fielding's evidence not only suggested that

Osborn had been complicit in faking evidence in Plymouth, but also demonstrated a closeness between the agency and the solicitor.[231]

Yet the agency itself was beset by suspicions and competition between detectives; Fielding had been 'let go', or sacked, by Slater's on 25 July 1903, following what Fielding felt was months of being shadowed by his distrustful colleagues. Although nobody directly told him their concerns, he knew they were perturbed at his friendships with the likes of Edgar Cartwright and Charles Simmonds. They thought he had been giving these two men information about what was happening at Basinghall Street, sending them telegrams; but it was clear that Slater and his manager were paranoid about their detectives either defecting to other agencies, or establishing their own rival companies. This was not groundless, as the example of Stevens *et al* showed that this was indeed a risk, but it resulted in an unpleasant work atmosphere. There were, at this time, around thirty detectives employed by Slater's, and if they weren't under suspicion by the boss, they were instead being put under pressure to be successful in the cases they were given, and to be better than the others they worked with. It resulted in a pressure cooker environment.[232]

The third detective to give evidence that March was Thomas Craig, who had been employed by Slater's until July 1902. Like Fielding, he had clear memories of what had happened, remembering in particular Davies's involvement. Before the latter had gone to Jersey, he had told Craig that 'he had tried to get Mr Pollard with a woman, but he was not a man of that sort.' Equally damning was the fact that George Henry had told Craig that if he could somehow get Pollard with a woman, he would pay him £2. Craig's evidence implied that certain of Slater's staff - from George Henry to Cyril Broughton Smith - were clearly corrupt, openly admitting getting Tom Pollard drunk and enticing him to commit adultery. In August 1903, Craig said, he had been asked by William Hamilton to sign a statement claiming that until he had left the agency, he had never heard any suggestions of enticement. He had signed it because he had been asked to, despite knowing that it was a lie. He now justified this saying he was so used to lying in his official reports at Slater's that it had become second habit. When Craig was asked for particular examples of when he had given false statements while at Slater's, he was able to do so immediately, citing 'the Whiteside case and Colonel Hill's one'.[233]

These men's evidence was added to by Edgar Cartwright's. Cartwright, the Slater's detective who had helped set up Simmonds' rival association, admitted making threats to 'smash up' Slater's business. It was strongly suggested that he had a grudge against his former boss and had been willing to perjure himself in court in order to get revenge. This parade of private detectives had the effect of showing the court that it was a cut-throat industry, where detectives were encouraged to fake evidence and lie in order to get results and beat the competition. What remained unclear was the extent to which Henry Slater himself had been involved.

Sir Edward Clarke, himself a former solicitor-general, believed that the case was remarkable, but that the divorce was based on valid evidence.[234] It was his job to persuade Sir Edward Carson, representing the King's Proctor, of this. Clarke found it particularly remarkable that the King's Proctor had intervened not on the basis that Tom had never committed adultery. The intervention had instead been made because Tom had allegedly committed a further act of adultery that had never been mentioned in the divorce petition, one that neither Kate Pollard nor Albert Osborn had been aware of when the case had originally come to court.[235]

Clarke argued that Osborn had known nothing of the subterfuge, and that it had been entirely the part of Slater's Detective Agency. He called the solicitor forward to explain his role. Osborn admitted having worked with Slater's for several years, but claimed he had not heard of the Pollard case until July 1902, when George Henry mentioned it to him during a meeting the two men had with Hugh Knowles. 'Henry said he had suggested to Mr Knowles that a solicitor should go down to Plymouth,' said Osborn, 'as possibly he might be able to get information from the women there which they would not give to one of the agency's men.' Osborn's detailing of how he had gone to Plymouth and talked to Maud made clear that he and Slater's men had been motivated by a clear desire to find evidence for their wealthy client.[236]

On Wednesday, 30 March 1904, the President of the Divorce Division of the High Court resumed the hearing of Pollard v Pollard (King's Proctor intervening) before its special jury. George Henry was asked about the payments made in the case, and said that these were done by Edgar Cartwright, as the agency's cashier. He also denied that Davies had been dismissed from the agency because he had been found to be in communication with the men who had established Simmonds' Detective Association.

William Hamilton, another Slater's manager, although not as senior as George Henry, was also then examined. He denied knowledge of any reports from detectives admitting misconduct in the case, or of any arrangements to get Thomas Pollard drunk. Hamilton claimed that Slater's attendance had been 'tapering off' since 1895 – earlier than other accounts claimed, but, perhaps coincidentally, also the year that another of Slater's detectives, Longley, was said to have left the company to set up his own agency – and that it was largely George Henry who was in charge, seeing clients and giving instructions.[237] Hamilton also distanced himself from the agency's core staff, insisting that he was a freelance private detective and picked and chose what work he wanted to, across different employers – he was not 'entirely dependent on Slater's', and he had 'no reason to grumble' about the salary he was paid.[238]

Hamilton, like George Henry, was asked about Davies's role in the agency. He saw Davies as a good all-rounder, who had initially been an office boy at Slater's. George Henry had never mentioned to Hamilton that Davies had gone to Jersey, and he didn't think there had been any reports from Davies about it. He knew that Thomas

Craig had made a statement to the King's Proctor, but otherwise insisted he knew nothing about what had gone on in the Pollard case. His examination then ended, and it was now time to call Henry Slater.

It was Henry Slater's evidence that exposed not only the machinations of his agency, but also his own, fiercely guarded, true identity. The exposure arguably ruined his agency as much as the actions of his detectives, for it made him look like both a fantasist and a liar. One of the first things his evidence exposed - and which would be relentlessly highlighted for months after - was the fact that Henry Slater was not, called that at all, let alone Henry Scott.

The initial questions he was asked were more of a barrage: who was he? When did he last take an active part in the business? What did he know of the Pollard case? Did he know who Hugh Knowles was? Slater denied having taken any active role in his own business since 1897, and therefore he knew nothing about the Pollard case at all. He had not known who Knowles was until he was pointed out to him today in court. He did know, however, that Knowles was a client of his agency. He was asked whether it was true that in October 1901, he, George Henry and Albert Osborn had met to discuss making Pollard drunk and getting him to sleep with another woman. Slater denied ever sanctioning it, authorising it, or knowing that it was going to be done by others. His answers were short, terse, and negative. Yes, he had gone to Australia in 1902 for his health. Yes, he had received some business communications from London, but they did not contain details. Yes, some papers had gone missing, but he thought they had been taken earlier, not once the agency realised a court case was likely.

That was the business side of things, where Slater could simply deny everything and not go into detail. He could cope with that. But this case was also about more than how trustworthy the agency was - it was about him as an individual. Private detectives often had a bad rap in the press and in court; they were sometimes seen as shifty individuals, faking identities in order to get results. They posed as policemen; they posed as lonely souls in search of friendships with the people they had actually been paid to spy on. Even the notion of watching individuals and exposing their secrets was the antithesis of what it meant to be British: people deserved their privacy, but private detectives' success was built on pulling the curtain aside and revealing individuals' peccadilloes and sexual misdeeds. Therefore, to expose the founder of the most successful detective agency was to prove that detectives could not be trusted, that they were no better than the people they snooped on.

The first question that had been put to Henry Slater on 30 March was therefore the most damaging. What was his name – no, not the name he went by, but his original name? Was it true that he had had many different names, and a large number of occupations before he became a private detective? The questions had initially come from his own counsel, who wanted confirmation of his real name; but then, under cross-examination from the intimidating Sir Edward Carson, they became a maelstrom of questions designed to expose Henry Slater's real identity, and his own, long career of fooling people.

Chapter 9

Will the Real Henry Slater Please Stand Up?

His real identity was something Henry Slater had tried to discard once and for all in the 1890s. He had become a successful private detective as Slater; he had realised the value of a pseudonym in creating a persona, even a mystique, to an ordinary individual. He used various identities according to his mood and what he wanted to achieve, including the names of Captain Scott and even Henry Slater.

For 'Henry Slater' was just another pseudonym, taken on for the purposes of his job. As noted earlier, it was not unknown for detectives to take on a second identity, and most of Slater's detectives had an alter ego. These identities helped obfuscate individuals' origins, and provide cover for their work. Both male and female detectives created these new identities for themselves, sometimes for a specific job, or, conversely, using a distinct name to separate their work and home identities. Therefore, the female private detective Maud West – who set up her long-standing business in 1905 – was, as mentioned earlier, known by a different name when at home with her family. Conversely, her daughter Evelyn later became known as Maud West Jr at work, in part to suggest continuity at her mother's business.[239]

In Slater's case, he had a lifelong desire to disguise himself, to conceal his identity, and in the process, he would frustrate future researchers into finding out too much about him. Yet his original name was easily found out, partly because Slater had made the mistake of entrusting his friend and colleague Francis Stevens with it. It was first mentioned in the divorce court, and mentioned by the *Daily Mirror* in its coverage of the case on 17 March 1904. At the time of this first mention, it was one of the least noteworthy parts of the case; the *Mirror* headlined its story 'Divorce Suit's Secret Mystery' with its subhead detailing the 'sensational story of detectives' endeavour to prove a husband's guilt'. The mention of Slater's name came after a full column on the basics of the case, when the solicitor-general stated that there was some doubt about who he was: 'There was a Mr Henry Slater, who also passed under the names of Captain Brown, Captain Scott, and Mr George Tinsley.'[240] Slater's identity would be focused on as a means of discrediting him. By painting him as an untrustworthy individual who used a series of fake names, both his detective agency and the profession of private detective itself were discredited.

As was uncovered at the divorce court, Britain's greatest detective was not really Henry Slater – he was born, and lived a significant part of his life, as George Tinsley, and for the first few years of Slater's agency maintained one name at work and another at home. But where and when he was born was clouded in vagueness. He was born around 1849, but his birth was not registered. This was not unique; the registration of births was not made compulsory until 1875. If George had been consistent about where he was born, though, that would make him easier to track across the decades, but he was not. In 1861, the first census in which he can definitely be found, his place of birth was given as Marylebone. In 1871, George himself stated that he had been born in Brompton, but in 1881, he had decided that he had been born in Paddington. Given that these areas were not far away from each other, it seems probable that he was born somewhere within the triangle made from these three areas, but it is frustrating that the area cannot be narrowed down further.

There may also have been some social politics at play. Brompton was a 'good' area, sandwiched between Kensington and Knightsbridge, and home to many affluent families. George may have decided to list this as his birthplace to denote that he was from a good family, part of the machinations of a young, ambitious man. In 1881, he was thinking of becoming a private detective, and Paddington was associated with several private detectives. 'Paddington' Pollaky, as his name suggested, was based in the area. Wendel Scherer, a German native, was one of the other private detectives who lived and worked in Paddington. Stating his birthplace as Paddington may have been a subconscious or conscious decision by George, but like much of what is assumed about George Tinsley's life, not much is verifiable.[241]

Not even his parentage can be determined. At the age of 27, Tinsley claimed to be the son of a farmer, also named George Tinsley. This man cannot be found in any census. Given Henry Slater's later tendency to obfuscate his humble origins, it seems possible that he lied about his father's identity at this point. One of the few things that actually appears to be true is that George Tinsley spent part of his childhood living with his maternal grandfather. At the age of 12, in the first census in which he can be found, George was living with his grandfather, Richard Elliott, at his coffee-house at 1 Albion Place.[242] Although George lived in London for decades, his grandfather was not from the capital, but a rural migrant to the city. Richard Elliott was from the Berkshire village of Lambourn - then a pretty place, with a high street that consisted of simple Georgian houses; barrows in the local landscape reminders of the area's long history of settlement. Richard Elliott's birthplace was renowned for its horse-racing, with race meetings taking place on the nearby downs during the eighteenth century, but it was still a rural idyll of a kind, with limited job prospects.

Nothing is known of Richard's first wife, who would have been George's grandmother, not even when she married his grandfather. She was dead by 1847, as in this year, Richard married his second wife, widow Elizabeth Fromont.[243] Elizabeth died in 1858, and three years later, Richard married for a third time.[244] The birth, marriage and even identity of George's mother are unknown.[245] All that can be known for sure is that Richard Elliott continued to run a

Chelsea coffee shop until his death early in 1872.[246] George Tinsley's background was, from the start, somewhat anonymous.

To return to the first mention of George Tinsley: his residence with his grandfather in 1861. This was not as salubrious nor genteel a setting for the 12-year-old boy as you might think. Whereas today, Chelsea is synonymous with wealth and privilege, in the mid-nineteenth century, it was a more mixed area. There was, as there had always been, pockets of salubriousness and moneyed lives: but this was not the whole story. Chelsea was a mix of rich and poor, of old and new, as London expanded outwards to create suburbs out of former rural idylls. The coffee house was part of Chelsea life; the most famous one in the earlier part of the nineteenth century was Don Saltero's Coffee House in Cheyne Walk, which had existed since the late seventeenth century, and had become a well-known attraction, featuring an eccentric assortment of 'exhibits', until it was demolished in 1866.[247]

Richard Elliott's coffee house was not near Don Saltero's; it was further away from the river, up towards South Kensington, in the area known as Little Chelsea, and less well placed for river trade. Other residents of Albion Place at the time included the 83-year-old Ann Hodkinson, whose occupation was rather sadly given as 'depending on friends' - this is what was stopping her from poverty and an application to the workhouse. Neighbours included a tailor, greengrocer, confectioner, hosier in this retail-dominant road; but there was also a whip-maker, dressmaker, hatter, railway worker and carpenter among the more salubrious residents. Richard Elliott's coffee house was at number one, at the top of the road nearest to the busy Fulham Road (Albion Place would soon be demolished, replaced by the Odell's Place ropewalk, which has also since been replaced).[248] By the time of George's visit or stay, he had been widowed, and it was just him and this boy at the premises. Many of George's age would be working by the age of 12, but he had no occupation - not even as an errand boy - recorded against his name. He was in that in-between world between education and work, watching his grandfather ply his trade. His life revolved around his grandfather's coffee shop, and the local Sunday school at Chelsea's Park Lane chapel.

The Victorian coffee house was not a unified entity – as an 1863 account put it, the individual establishment adapted to the 'circumstances of the neighbourhood'. This could mean, in some of the more well-to-do areas of London, a well-furnished room where the coffee was served in china cups, and where customers 'smoke cigars and play critically at chess', paying a shilling for the privilege. Meanwhile, in rougher areas, a cup of burning hot coffee cost just a penny, with customers, predominantly drawn from the labouring classes, using the place as a home-from-home – somewhere to eat, drink, or even sleep. Here, food was restricted to the basics loved by workmen: bread and butter, bacon, eggs and a variety of other meats, such as kidneys or cold beef and ham. Newspapers – dailies, local papers and foreign publications – as well as periodicals such as *Punch* could be found, and were popular sources of both news and entertainment to the coffee-shop customers.[249]

By the mid-1860s, there were estimated to be around 1,000 coffee shops in London, with the average cup of coffee costing between a penny and threepence.[250] Richard Elliott certainly provided both food and drink, for he described himself at various points as having an eating house and coffee house. He did not have a live-in servant, although he may have had help during the day; primarily, though, this was a family concern. In 1851, it was Richard and his second wife Elizabeth working there; in 1861 Richard was perhaps joined informally at work by young George Tinsley; and in 1871, third wife Sarah was working with her elderly husband. This was a changing era in terms of drink preferences, and the ubiquitous coffee was increasingly being joined by tea, as imports of the latter had passed those of coffee by 1853.[251]

By the time of his grandfather's death, George had moved on from the coffee shop. Richard didn't leave a will, and his wife, Sarah, inherited whatever goods he had owned. However, George had been left with an education: he was literate and numerate, and would be able to work in a wider variety of settings than his grandfather as a result. He was schooled in the days before compulsory education – it was only in 1870 that new schools were built through the local rates to provide education to an area's children up to the age of 10, and it would be a further ten years before children got a compulsory education that continued until they were 13.[252] George still benefited from the expansion of education for middle-class males that took place from the 1840s onwards, though. The fact that he was both literate and numerate (to an advanced level, according to his later trial record) suggests that his family believed in education, and ensured he was taught well.[253]

His education but lack of wealth also left him in something of a limbo: what class did he belong to? Whereas further back in England's history, the classes were strictly defined and ordered, change was underway, and the classes were in flux. George's father, he had said, was a farmer, and if this was the truth (which is by no means to be assumed) a yeoman would traditionally have been part of England's middle-ranking society, although a tenant farmer would have been lower down the scale. His grandfather, the coffee-shop keeper, was of a more indeterminate class: serving a mix of people, not a labourer but more akin to the labouring class than those further up the social ladder. George, though, was able to aspire to more – to be part of the lower middle-class, where young men received an education that enabled them to take on clerking jobs, white-collar positions where they could, feasibly, work their way up the employment ladder.

At the time when George was looking for work, employment in England was changing. An industrial society involved increasing amounts of bureaucracy and administration, more sophisticated banking methods and efficient correspondence. Staff were needed for these increased administrative functions: young, educated clerks were the answer. In 1851, there were around 44,000 clerks, accountants, and bankers – by 1871, the figure would be nearly three times that amount.[254] The pay was respectable and there would be raises; a job was relatively safe for those who were reliable. However, the expansion in education in the middle of the nineteenth century – with public schools increasing their numbers, and many new schools being established – saw a 'formidable increase' in educated young men emerging from their schools from the mid-century onwards.[255] The number of jobs deemed to be suitably middle-class for these young men, though, did not keep up, and so there was substantial competition for these, as the middle-class expanded.[256]

George was working by the middle of the 1860s, but he was an easily bored individual who took a series of jobs with little idea of what to choose as a longer-term career. Initially he worked as a pawnbroker's assistant, helping customers who wished to pledge their goods – even their clothing – or to redeem them later. Many people from the working classes would have pawned regularly in order to get some money short-term; their Sunday clothing might be pledged on a Monday, then claimed back at the end of the week, when the individual had been paid, and in order for the clothing to be worn again to church that weekend.[257] All types of goods could be pledged – not just clothing, but accessories, shoes, tools of the job – pretty much everything had a value.

The pawnbroker served an important function within his community, but this community was likely to be a poorer one, with the shop up a side street in a working-class area of London. The pawnbroker's shop was open long hours, especially on a Saturday night; one contemporary account noted that attempts were made to close such establishments by 10pm on a Saturday because of fears that 'pawnbrokers kept their shops open on Saturday night in order to enable the lower classes to get money and spend it in drink'.[258] The reality was that they opened late to give locals the opportunity to redeem the Sunday-best clothing they had pawned earlier in the week ready to wear again the next day – Sunday.[259]

It was not a place where an ambitious, educated young man such as George would have wished to stay too long, although it served as a useful training ground for his future career – the pawnbrokers were described in the nineteenth century as 'the best unpaid detectives in London' because of their ability to spot stolen goods being brought into pawn, and to identify 'fences'.[260] He would have learned the importance of good communication, the ability to talk to a wide range of people, the importance of making (and keeping) money, and also have made friendships; the more successful pawnbrokers employed a number of youths to act as their assistants, and in some cases, these young men shared accommodation either above the shop or nearby. It was, therefore, a good introduction to the world of work, but unsurprisingly, it was not somewhere for an ambitious and upwardly mobile man such as George Tinsley to stay too long. Unsurprisingly, then, he soon moved on, becoming a jeweller's assistant. This had similarities to his former job, involving long stints standing up, serving customers, in a shop – but it would also have spurred George on further to improve himself.[261] Seeing customers buying sometimes expensive items, having the cash to buy items that were decorative rather than simply functional, would have made him want what they had, for he was constantly wanting to do better, to be better, and by that, he meant both socially and economically.

From the jeweller's shop, George moved on to become a solicitor's clerk. Initially, he was working for Messrs Pritchard, a firm based on Great Knightrider Street in the City of London. He did not live in the City, but instead commuted in from his home in Battersea. After a short spell at Pritchard's, and now aged 21, George Tinsley moved on to the firm of Freshfields. This firm had been names after solicitor James William Freshfield at the end of the eighteenth century, and in the early nineteenth century had several wealthy clients with slave-owning plantations in the Caribbean. It was a successful and well-thought-of firm, and Freshfield became an MP and magistrate before retiring in 1857. By the time George joined the firm, James

Freshfield's middle-aged sons James William, Henry and Charles all had key roles at the company.[262]

At Freshfields, George was very much a junior, working in an administrative role at the company's office at 5 Bank Buildings, Lothbury.[263] He dealt with the solicitors' post – both sending it and collecting it – and was something of a messenger, taking documents and delivering them, as well as collecting other items and bringing them back to Freshfields. He may also have been talking or writing to clients and other solicitors, sending requests for fee payments, managing the solicitors' diaries, and ensuring that the Freshfields team had adequate stationery for their needs. Mundane, yes, but he was in contact with solicitors and their varied clientele and cases, seeing the type of cases that were heard at court, and learning about the evidence that was needed for cases to proceed. The firm was dealing, at this time, with high-profile worldwide clients such as the East Indian Railway Company, the National Bank of New Zealand, and a Chilean mine company, Copiapó – but there would also be lower-key cases to be dealt with.[264]

The job was a good one for someone of George's status – he was a man who could read and write, and who was, as he later showed, an intelligent and quick-witted individual. He felt he was on an upward trajectory, and that for a young man with prospects, it was time he also found a wife. Luckily for him, in Battersea, he had met Emma Elizabeth Cartwright. Emma was the same age as George; she was the daughter of a house painter and decorator, and born and bred in south London. They married at St John's in Battersea on 16 April 1870, with Emma's sister Eliza as one of their witnesses, and Eliza's fiancé as the other.[265] Both George and Emma signed their names as literate individuals: Emma's more of a rapid scrawl, but George's a rather stylish script, with a sharp, pointed 'g' and 'y', and a flourish over the T of his surname – a script that would help identify him years later.

Unlike George, Emma's family are well documented in the archives. Her grandfathers had been labourers, and her mother, Eliza, had been a servant prior to her marriage. Emma's father William was, certainly up until his marriage in 1850, illiterate, although her mother was able to at least write her name.[266] Dates also show that Eliza and William had their first child, Emma, out of wedlock, as she was born nearly two years before their marriage.[267] William had steady work as a house painter and decorator, but the Cartwrights were not 'posh', and their status was upper working-class rather than lower middle-class, if such a distinction can be drawn – but to George, they represented a solid, stable family unit, well established in south London, where Emma had been born and brought up. He and Emma settled near the Cartwrights, and George continued to work as a solicitor's clerk, leaving home each day to make the journey from Battersea to the City.

George maintained his job at Freshfields throughout 1870 and early 1871. In January 1871, he became a father, when his first daughter, Edith Elliott Tinsley, was born.[268] Her middle name was George's mother's maiden name, but she was named equally in memory of his coffee-shop-operating grandfather, Richard. George was now a respectable husband and father, responsible for maintaining his young family. However, this domestic bliss could only last so long for a young man with ambition and an apparent dislike of monotony, and a family tragedy may have been the impetus for George's life to change once more.

In July 1871, baby Edith died. Only 5 months old, she was by no means the only baby to die in Victorian England, and George and Emma were not the only parents to have such a loss. Yet every infant death was a sad event for its parents, and Edith's untimely death made George re-evaluate his career. For reasons unknown, Freshfields soon dismissed their clerk, leaving him unemployed – and by early 1872, Emma was pregnant again. What would George do to make a living again, and look after his wife and the imminent arrival? The answer was to become a shorthand writer. George later claimed to have been established as such back in 1868, but although he may have been teaching himself shorthand at this date, he certainly wasn't engaged in using it full-time; he would, however, have found it a useful skill in taking notes at Freshfields. He used Pitman shorthand, simpler than another popular shorthand system of the nineteenth century, that of J.G. Cross, and the teaching of it was also offered as a correspondence course. George could therefore learn this new skill while holding down his full-time clerking job.

In learning a new skill in the late 1860s and early 1870s as a reaction to an entry-level clerking job that was failing to satisfy him mentally, George was following in the footsteps of Charles Dickens nearly half a century before. Dickens, too, had been a solicitor's clerk who found his work rather dull. In his spare time, he, too, had learned shorthand - in his case, Thomas Gurney's system, known as Brachygraphy. It had taken him over a year to learn it sufficiently well to start work at Doctors' Commons as a shorthand writer, eventually working as a parliamentary reporter.[269] George Tinsley denied, in later life, having been dismissed from Freshfields, claiming instead that 'I left to take a situation as shorthand clerk'. He had indeed got a job as a shorthand clerk or writer by late 1872. Having been dismissed by Freshfields, he now started working as such for the bill discounter and mortgage agent Henry Salter. Salter was based at 11 Pancras Lane at the time, a few minutes' walk east from George's former workplace. The keen-eyed George Tinsley, writing shorthand reports for Salter, made sure he tracked what Salter did at work, and how he carried out his clients' wishes.

Work was only a part of George's life, however. Outside work, he enjoyed amateur dramatics - a common activity among London's middle classes. He took part in plays, but particularly liked to perform in what were known, offensively, as 'nigger minstrels'. As an actor, albeit strictly amateur, George chose his first pseudonym, and his first use of the name Henry. His stage name was Henry Seymour. Acting highlighted a key part of his personality and identity: a man who could shift-shape, almost, taking on different roles and names, hiding his origins and becoming whatever character he wanted to play.[270]

This shapeshifting, this boredom and desire to change jobs, to change identities, was not what a Victorian wife wanted to see in her husband, the father of her children. While Henry was playing with these different roles, acting in his spare time, perhaps desiring a full-time career on stage while working a menial clerking job in the City, Emma Tinsley was continuing to keep her house in order in Battersea, deal with her grief over the death of little Edith, and also now look after a new baby, as daughter Lilian May had been born on 30 August 1872. By the time of her baptism, in November that year, her father, George, was working for Henry Salter full-time and had moved his family to a new home in Buckhold Road, Wandsworth.

George's work identity shifted over the next three years, until he was working full-time as a self-employed shorthand teacher. Another house move followed: this time to Middleton Road in Battersea, where another daughter, Amy Eva Daisy, was born in June 1875. 25 Middleton Road, where the Tinsleys moved to, was part of a row of modern houses, completed only four years earlier. From this new, modern, respectable base, George continued to place his adverts in the local papers, always aware of the power of the press and of publicity. He thanked the local community for their support to date, and made a 'written guarantee' to be able to teach anyone, male or female, Pitman's shorthand to a rate of 120 words per minute. He charged a guinea for each lesson, and was happy to both visit his students' homes for lessons, or for them to be taught at his house.[271]

George Tinsley advertised in the *South London Times* regularly: sometimes weekly, but more commonly fortnightly. The sudden start of a publicity campaign in 1875 raises doubts about Tinsley's claims to have been servicing his local community for seven years. The advertisements suggest a fairly new business, seeking more customers, with George keenly aware of the need to make his neighbours alert to his existence. His adverts show an awareness of the importance of newspaper publicity, and a desire to make his own name known. His brand was, from day one, himself. He also took on additional duties as clerk to the Battersea Burial Board, a job which he found occasionally tedious and that only lasted around a year. The job offered respectability within his community, but was not exciting.

What was exciting for George was his participation in the arts. No longer taking part in minstrels, he joined a choral society, the Wandsworth Choral Glee Union. This had been established in late 1874, with the patronage of Sir Henry Peek, spice importer and Conservative MP for the Mid-division of Surrey, and Daniel Watney, a local distiller.[272] Its first concert was put on at the Wandsworth Assembly Rooms on 22 March 1875, a Monday evening, and it was seen as a great success. It had a varied programme, including the 1863 song 'Maggie's Secret' and 'The Timid Little Maid', which was written in 1859. There were solos and duets, with a piano accompaniment.[273] As a keen amateur performer, George Tinsley was keen to feature in the union's concerts, but there is no mention of him by name in the review of this initial concert.[274]

However, while he was a member, there was dissent in the ranks. The Union's committee consisted largely of Wandsworth tradesmen, and other members did not always approve of how they conducted the society's business. Despite the success of the Union's initial concert, within a fortnight, a rather noisy protest erupted, following the committee's decision as to which members would have the largest roles in their next concert. Four of the society's singers, offended at being omitted or sidelined, duly gathered very early on the morning of Good Friday to make their way to the houses of the committee members. At each house, they woke the offending men (as well as their families and neighbours) by 'coarse singing, yelling and howling', as well as throwing stones and dirt up at the windows. At one house, the men nearly pulled the garden gate off its hinges and broke some glass, the owner appearing to threaten them with court unless they paid to rectify the breakages. The case was deemed so serious that the *South London Chronicle* duly called for them to be forced to apologise to the society, or to be kicked out.[275] George was unlikely to have been part of this fracas, for he had been seen as having had a crucial role in their earlier concert success - which had made them a good amount of money. George, with his gift for publicity, was an asset to them. Therefore, three weeks after the Good Friday protests, George Tinsley was unanimously elected chairman of the Wandsworth Choral Glee Union.[276]

George was soon bored of life in south London. By 1881, and now aged 32, he returned to clerking work and he relocated his family north of the Thames, to Chiswick. The new family home was on Dale Terrace, part of a short road that ran just south of Chiswick High Road and Chiswick Common, down towards Hogarth's House - and beyond it was the river. The terrace formed the lower part of Dale Street as far as the Duke of York pub, on the corner of Devonshire Road - part of an area of Chiswick that had formerly been market gardens but was, by the time the Tinsleys moved there, known as Chiswick New Town. The houses were small, terraced Victorian homes, but they had a large bay window downstairs at the front to let the light in, and neat little front gardens to separate them from the road. The houses' construction was part of a late-nineteenth-century development of suburbs spreading out from Hammersmith, and the creation of a large residential area, with shops and pubs catering for this new, larger population.[277] This part of west London was well-connected - the tube station at nearby Turnham Green had opened in 1869, making a commute to the City take just half an hour, and Acton Green station (later to be renamed Chiswick Park and Acton Green) followed in 1879.[278]

Chiswick represented suburban family life: safe in these small, terraced houses, where neighbours looked out for each other, and where privacy was an unlikely possibility. For Emma, George's long-suffering wife, the change - even though it was within the same city

– was huge. She was away from her family and friends, people she had grown up with, and away from her support network. She had young children to look after, but was increasingly aware that she had an additional child in some ways – her easily bored husband, who appeared unable to stay in the same house, or the same job, for very long before his urge for change kicked in again. And for George, this was not the life he desired either. There was little excitement in a clerking job; little excitement in Dale Terrace, sandwiched between identical homes and identical families. He was supposed to be a dutiful husband and father. He was expected to maintain a solid, but boring, job, to pay the rent and the bills, to ensure his family had what they needed, and to stamp down on his dreams of theatrical stardom or excitement. For all that George was the Victorian patriarch, with a lot more independence and choice than his wife, he was still expected to conform to Victorian ideals of masculinity and domesticity. He was not, however, prepared to conform.

In relatively confined surroundings in Dale Terrace, George and Emma would have got to know their new neighbours, whether they wanted to or not. Next door to the Tinsleys, at number 15, were the Moon family. Alfred Moon was in his fifties and an annuitant – a pensioner – and so to make a bit of money, they took in boarders, as was common. In 1881, one of their lodgers was John Henry Polmear, a 22-year-old from Devon, who had joined the Metropolitan Police as an officer. He was different to the other neighbours, who were painters and coachmen, grooms, and dairymen. Did he get to know George Tinsley, and tell him tales of his professional life, the cases he dealt with? Or perhaps he even told George about the opportunities that others could get working with the Met or the courts, as private detectives. It was certainly while he was living in Chiswick that George decided that he had had enough of clerking and of teaching – and instead, he decided he wanted to become a private detective.

Chapter 10

Dubious Tactics

When he initially started work as a private detective, in 1885, it was under his birth name of George Tinsley. Although he found work, he did not find immediate success – in fact, he seems to have struggled to behave professionally, and in the earliest case he was involved in that we know about, there were stories that he had been drunk while working, and that his evidence could not be trusted as a result. Partly in a bid to distance himself from this negative coverage, George Tinsley now decided to change his name. However, there was another, darker reason: he wanted to ruin a competitor.

The competitor was his former employer, Henry Salter. Salter was from East London, being born in Stepney in 1822. He had originally gone into business as a mortgage broker in 1868, having previously described himself as a bookseller, a stockholder, and agent.[279] His company was formally Henry Salter & Sons, as his eldest sons, Henry and Edward, worked for him, initially, like Slater, as clerks. It was not unheard of for brokers to also undertake detective work: brokers dealt with money, and private detectives also worked on financial cases as well as divorce suits. They might track down fraudsters, or missing money, for example. Salter did this, and successfully managed his business for fourteen years. As a new operative in the field, Tinsley wanted to get rid of the competition, and he had a plan to do so.[280]

He decided that the name he was now going to use professionally was Henry Slater – Henry Salter's name with two of the letters transposed. When questioned at the High Court on 30 March 1904, Sir Edward Carson queried this; he had gone into the same work that

Salter had done, hadn't he? Was that in order to try to get some of his clients? Although Slater admitted he had followed Salter's line of work, in terms of stealing his clients, he was uncharacteristically coy. At first he answered, 'You can put it that way if you like', and then, when asked again, said nothing. Only when the solicitor-general forced him to answer did he admit that yes, he had wanted to take Salter's business away by confusing potential customers about who he was, and that the intention was to 'do' him. His plan initially failed, in that the emphasis of his business was, like Salter's, on the mortgage broking, and Slater was not good enough at that. But he discovered that he was good at the private inquiry work – as long as he stayed away from alcohol – and so he soon restricted himself to that work. But he liked the sound of the name Henry Slater and so he stuck to that until 1897.

It's clear that Slater here used similar tactics to Francis Stevens and his associates, when they left to establish Simmonds' Detective Association. This was something of a cut-throat world, but even so, Slater was getting his just desserts when Simmonds' agency used the same strategy as Slater had used when he tried to ruin Henry Salter. Stevens had learned from the master as to how to get business, and how to get ahead of competitors; Slater must have regretted trusting him so much. Slater's agency was so well-known that the identity of Henry Slater was indelibly linked to it. When Slater, in 1895, decided to start distancing himself from the agency, he realised that he now needed to change his identity again, so that people would not just associate himself with private detective work. He therefore became Captain Brown. He liked the idea of a new identity, and the following year, he decided he wanted to be known as Captain Scott. This name was apparently suggested at Basinghall Street, where the other members of staff variously referred to Slater as the guv'nor, the captain, or the boss. Slater preferred the captain, and chose Scott as it reminded him of 'Great Scott'.[281]

This is what he initially claimed, at any rate, but as with much of what Henry Slater said, it was not the whole truth. He certainly never drew attention to one aspect of his life: his tendency to make enemies. He had been accumulating these since his time at Freshfields, and some had long memories. In October 1890, a man named Harry H. Sheppard wrote to the comic magazine *Ally Sloper's Half Holiday*. He was a long-term subscriber to the 6-year-old publication, and had read with interest an earlier article regarding the fictional Ally Sloper's daughter, who had been offered a job at Slater's Detective Agency. Harry Sheppard wanted to point out to the magazine's readers that 'there is no such person as Mr Henry Slater…this gentleman's real name is Tinsley, and Messrs Freshfield, the well-known solicitors, could furnish you with certain facts not to his credit…'.[282]

Why was Harry Sheppard so keen to enlighten the publication about George Tinsley's spell at Freshfields, which, he implied, had been less than satisfactory to his employers? A bit of research shows that the letter-writer had been a neighbour of George's in Battersea. Harry, who was nearly twenty years George Tinsley's junior, had lived with his family not far from the Tinsleys' home. Significantly, Harry's family also worked in law. His father, Liverpudlian Hobart Sheppard, was a solicitor's articled clerk manager in the 1871 census, and Harry's cousin, William, was also a solicitor's clerk. Although Harry was only in his teens when George left Freshfields, his family still remembered his time there two decades later, by which time, Harry himself had become a solicitor.[283] It feels likely that a member of the Sheppard family worked with George at Freshfields, and remembered his work there in a negative way.

Sheppard's attack on Slater impacted him more than he wanted to admit, because it was not the only exposé he had been subject to. Sheppard had revealed to the press that the private detective was not born Slater but Tinsley, and that he was a darker character than the public persona he had as boss of a famous private detective agency. In the divorce court, Sir Edward Carson had queried Slater's explanation of why he had adopted the name of Scott. It emerged that another man named Perryman had also attacked Slater in the press, accusing him of previously being 'Tinsley, the exposed thief', and describing him as 'Tinsley, the thief who is still parading about as Slater's bogus detective agency'.[284] At this point, to distance himself from the allegations, Slater had become Captain Scott. To Carson, Slater maintained that Perryman had a grudge against him purely because Slater had 'reported some inquiries about him to Mr Marks of the Financial News'.[285] Slater had been giving information to the press to blacken the names of other people.

If, though, Slater had reported someone for misdeeds, would that individual respond by calling him a thief, and in addition, referring to him by his birth name, a name that Slater was keen to keep quiet? It is likely that the man angry with Slater was Charles Wilbraham Perryman, who in the 1890s published a newspaper called the *Financial Observer and Mining Herald*, aimed at investors. The Cheshire-born Perryman was in and out of the courts throughout the 1890s and into the Edwardian era, appearing both as the plaintiff and defendant in numerous libel cases.[286] If this was the same Perryman who had made accusations against Slater, it was more understandable if it had been due to Slater discussing him with a rival publication. Perryman was both litigious and fond of insulting those he took against, seemingly adept at finding the aspects of individuals' personal lives that he could use against them. Although many of those who Perryman took against were willing and able to take him to court, it seems that Slater was not.

Slater's reaction was extreme, as he claimed that at this point he had changed his name again, and that he had changed it by deed poll. As with the change from Tinsley to Slater, there is no evidence that he ever legally changed his name. He was, though, very keen to put distance between him and the allegations made by both Perryman and Sheppard. There is no evidence that he had been guilty of theft, or other misdeeds while at Freshfields, but this is clearly what was being imputed. Given his willingness to try to ruin Henry Salter, another of his previous employers, it is also clear that Henry Slater was a more complex man, with a darker history, than he wanted to present to the public.

This complexity is evident from the home life of Henry Slater. Just before Harry Sheppard's attack on Slater, in 1889, George Tinsley had taken a three-year lease on a five-bedroomed villa in Park Road, Tottenham.[287] The house was named Chirgwin Villa after its owner, a performer named George Henry Chirgwin, known as 'The White Eyed Kaffir'. It was a large house with a conservatory, stable and coach-house, and only minutes from both Harringay and West Green stations - but it was a world away from George Tinsley's former homes of Battersea and Chelsea.[288]

It was in Tottenham that the Tinsleys' fourth and final daughter, Winifred Maud, was born in May 1890. Emma registered her daughter's birth, and gave her husband's occupation as newspaper reporter. It was not unusual for private detectives to give other occupations when asked to record themselves: they might be embarrassed about it, or they might simply want to preserve some secrecy. George Tinsley, the former shorthand reporter and clerk, was certainly doing some reporting for the newspapers, even if it mainly consisted of tipping them off about people he didn't like. But given that the one thing Tinsley had always been fairly honest about was his occupation, it feels strange that at this one juncture, Emma recorded him as a reporter and not as the established private detective that he actually was.

Their new home in Tottenham proved to give the Tinsleys anything but a peaceful life. Within months of moving in, Emma was involved in an accident which left her in shock and needing to recover.[289] Then, in August 1892, the family was away from home. In their absence, their landlord, George Chirgwin, turned up at the house with his coachman. The latter climbed over a wall and unbolted the gate to let Chirgwin in. They made their way into the stable and from there, entered the house through its back door. At

10.00 pm that night, Emma Tinsley saw the coachman outside the house and reported the matter to her husband. George Tinsley - using his real name - duly took Chirgwin to court for trespass. The case was heard in December that year at the London Under-Sheriff's Court in Red Lion Square, before Under-Sheriff James Burchell and a jury. Slater was listed as George Tinsley, private detective, and appeared in court dressed in a 'dark blue Melton overcoat lavishly trimmed with fur'.[290] The court heard that Slater's tenancy with Chirgwin permitted the owner or his agent to view the premises twice a year 'or oftener' [sic] in order to check that the house was in a good state of repair. This could be done during any reasonable hours - which 10.00 pm was clearly not.

Chirgwin claimed that he had only wanted to ask his tenant, Tinsley, if he wanted to extend the lease on the villa, and insisted that the Tinsleys had been at home and had even invited him in for some refreshments. Chirgwin, in fact, denied everything put to him: he didn't enter the house forcibly: 'We never climbed over no gates. The gate was open.'[291] What he did admit to doing was going through all the bedrooms and taking a lot of items away. He couldn't give an inventory, but insisted the things had all been his.[292] In fact, he had visited the house twice, the first time to take things, and then returning later in the evening with his coachman, the coachman's wife, and Chirgwin's two daughters. They had only been 'driving about' and decided on spec to go to Chirgwin Villa and see if the lease needed renewing. Chirgwin, who was defending himself in the case, said he had always got on with Tinsley, regarding him as a 'very nice man'.[293]

George Tinsley, however, did not agree with Chirgwin's explanations, and believed he had waited until he knew the house was empty before sending his coachman clambering over the garden wall. Tinsley won the case, but the jury only awarded him damages of one farthing; on hearing this, Chirgwin asked, to laughter in court, 'Shall I pay it now?'[294] The jury evidently regarded the case as somewhat trivial, and George Tinsley's solicitor pointed out that Chirgwin had 'seemed to look upon the thing as of little consequence', and instead had been intent on amusing the court instead.[295] For Tinsley, the thought of someone being allowed to enter the house without his permission was an invasion of his highly valued privacy and worthy of a court case. Luckily for him, the press didn't pick up on the connection between George Tinsley and Henry Slater, or the unlikely fact that Tinsley, an apparently unknown private detective, was wealthy enough to be able to have a very smart fur-trimmed overcoat to wear in court; the emphasis was more on the involvement of the well-known Chirgwin.[296]

What wasn't reported in the press coverage of this case was that by this point, George and Emma Tinsley had separated.[297] When Chirgwin visited the Tottenham house, it was Emma and her children who were out for the evening; she had to get in touch with George about the matter as the tenancy was in his name. The couple would remain separated for the rest of their lives, although they never divorced. George paid her a regular allowance, never spoke negatively of her, and maintained a relationship, of sorts, with both her and his daughters. Emma continued living in Tottenham until at least 1903, before moving out of London.

Following the break-up of his marriage, 'George Tinsley' would only exist for his wife and children, and in other people's long memories. Otherwise, in his personal life, he was Henry Slater, and would soon become Captain Henry Scott. Slater now wanted the accoutrements of bachelor life for a while. He established two homes for himself – a flat overlooking the sea at Brighton, and another flat in a mansion block across the Bayswater Road from Kensington Gardens. At this point in his life, by now approaching 50 years old, he had reached the pinnacle of professional success; he had his seaside home and his city pad, as well as wealth and status. Then it all started to go wrong.

Chapter 11

Before the Chief Magistrate

The King's Proctor's case at the Divorce Division of the High Court concluded on 21 April 1904, when the jury found that a false case was presented on behalf of Kate Pollard, and that Thomas Pollard had not committed adultery. Kate's divorce decree was rescinded, and although she was granted a judicial separation, she had to pay the court's costs.[298]

This was not the end of the matter, by any means, although many of those involved had assumed it. In fact, it was just the start of what would be seven months of court appearances for Henry Slater, and a wealth of negative publicity for him and his beloved detective agency. At the High Court, Sir Edward Carson had made clear that three individuals in particular - Slater, his manager George Henry, and solicitor Albert Osborn - had been involved in what, he said, was 'one of the most disgraceful incidents that could be brought before a court of justice'.[299] It was clear that such alleged behaviour could not go unpunished, and that the case would not end with Kate's divorce being, in effect, cancelled.

It was now a criminal case, and the police moved quickly. On Friday, 22 April, just a day after the conclusion of the King's Proctor's case, several men were arrested. Slater, George Henry, and Albert Osborn were, naturally, arrested, but so too were two of Slater's key detectives: John Pracy and Frederick Davies.[300] The first attempt to arrest Henry Slater was unsuccessful; despite him having stated in court that he rarely attended the office, police had still gone first to Basinghall Street to arrest him. He was - unsurprisingly - not there, although the staff who were there believed he was due to come in on Saturday morning. However, although it was 6.00 pm on a Friday evening, police did find John Pracy still at his workplace. As Chief Inspector Frank Froëst read the warrant out to him, Pracy muttered, 'I did not think they would pull me in.'[301] He clearly believed that those in charge of the agency – Slater and Henry – together with Osborn, would face the music as they were responsible for the duties of the detectives. It came as a rude surprise that the three detectives from further down the ranks were also being arrested. This was his only comment, however; on being brought before the magistrate at Bow Street, the charge was read to him, but he made no reply.[302]

After failing to find Slater at work, the police needed to track him down at one of his homes. At 8.00 pm, Detective Sergeant Francis Carlin of Scotland Yard located the boss at his London home – Palace Court Mansions.[303] On the surface, Henry Slater remained confident and sure of himself when arrested, telling the detective he was innocent, and had not been at the office 'for thirteen months prior to last March'. He was not active in the business, and shifted the blame onto George Henry as manager (while also acknowledging that it was he, Slater, who took the money). He said he knew nothing of the case, although at the same time, he admitted that someone had shown him a letter about the case. He concluded: 'I am as innocent as a child. I was away at the time.'[304]

Detective Sergeant Walter Bex was the man charged with arresting Frederick Davies. He found him at 8.15 pm on Friday evening, at home in Wood Green, north London. Davies was surprised by the speed with which the police had acted: 'You soon got the warrant! I thought there was going to be a new trial. How many more are there in it?' Bex said he couldn't answer that question, and took Davies straight to Bow Street.[305] Albert Osborn was more concise when he was arrested at home in South Kensington by Francis Carlin, initially just muttering that it was very annoying.[306] This was likely to be a reference to the fact that he had been arrested at 12.45 am;

and in fact, he was remarkably polite given the time of night, adding, 'I suppose I must go with you. I am quite ready to accompany you.'[307]

Slater, Osborn, Pracy and Davies all appeared at Bow Street Police Court, or magistrates' court, on Saturday, 23 April 1904, charged with conspiracy to obstruct and pervert the due course of law and justice. They filed into the upper court of the building one by one: Osborn at the front, followed by Slater, then Davies. John Pracy brought up the rear. They sat down, the first two men's appearance contrasting sharply with the more junior detectives. Osborn leaned against the back of the dock, using his knee to balance his expensive silk hat. Henry Slater, who was tall, struggled to position himself comfortably, eventually copying Osborn's stance. Dressed in a smart tweed suit, he sat with his hands in his trouser pockets, affecting a nonchalant attitude. Fred Davies, conversely, turned up in an old overcoat and carrying his cloth cap in his hand.[308]

The men were now sat facing before Sir Albert de Rutzen, the chief magistrate. Guy Stephenson led the prosecution team. For the defence, Charles Gill and John Valetta appeared for Osborn; Richard Muir for Slater; and Solomon Myers for both Pracy and Davies. The main point of the men's appearance on this day was to hear the formal evidence of how and when the detectives and Osborn had been arrested, and then to ask for their remand. After the arrests had been detailed, Guy Stephenson stopped, and said that the case could not be continued, for he had just heard that George Henry had been arrested. Unlike his colleagues, George Henry did not live in London, but in Southend, near Slater's estranged family, and so he was not arrested until the day after his colleagues. In order to arrest him, the Metropolitan Police had to wire - send a telegraph - to the Southend police. They duly arrested Henry at his home in Great Eastern Avenue, with the manager exclaiming, 'I did not expect this!', and on the Saturday afternoon, Detective Sergeant Carlin of Scotland Yard received Henry into custody from his Essex colleagues.

Slater's Detective Agency was based on Basinghall Street for many years; originally at number twenty-seven, in the 1890s, the company took over three floors of number one. (© Nell Darby)

Slater's rival - and nemesis - Simmonds' Detective Association had its base at 29-30 King Street, Cheapside. (© Nell Darby)

A view of Plymouth before World War 2 destroyed much of the city centre. This is the environment Slater's men would have come to know well. (Author's collection)

Francis Stephens had been staying at Plymouth's Grand Hotel whilst on a detective assignment in July 1902 – and was surprised to find Albert Osborn there, working on the Pollard case. (© Nell Darby)

Maud Goodman and Louisa Ford were asked to identify Thomas Pollard on 2 August 1904, initially at the Clock Tower. Pollard had been summonsed there by an anonymous letter-writer (in reality, either Osborn or Pracy). (© Nell Darby)

Plymouth Hoe was where people went to watch and be watched. Pracy shadowed Thomas Pollard here, and again tried to get the Plymouth girls to identify him as he walked along the Hoe. (© Nell Darby)

The initial stages of the Pollard case took place here, in the Divorce Division of the High Court of Justice on London's Strand. (© Nell Darby)

Sir Francis Jeune was President of the Probate, Divorce and Admiralty Division of the High Court of Justice from 1892 to 1905. He dismissed Kate Pollard's divorce petition after the King's Proctor's intervention. (public domain)

Henry Slater lived at homes in London and Brighton in 1904. He was arrested here, at his London home in Palace Court, off the Bayswater Road. (© Nell Darby)

The investigation into the Pollard case moved from the Divorce Court to here, Bow Street Police Court, in the spring of 1904. (© Nell Darby)

The interior of Bow Street Police Court, where the initial criminal proceedings against Slater, Osborn and Slater's employees took place. (public domain)

The trial of Henry Slater, Albert Osborn, and the five private detectives, took place here at the Central Criminal Court, better known as the Old Bailey, in the autumn of 1904. (© Nell Darby)

Sir Edward Carson was the Solicitor-General at the time of the Slater trial, and as such, was in charge of the prosecution of the six individuals in 1904. (public domain)

Sir Rufus Isaacs QC, defence counsel for Henry Slater. In 1901, he was living at Palace Court Mansions - which was Henry Slater's address in 1904 as well. Isaacs became Solicitor-General in 1910. (public domain)

George Tinsley spent the formative part of his childhood in Little Chelsea, where his grandfather's coffee shop was located. (© Nell Darby)

George Tinsley seems to have attended Park Walk Chapel in Chelsea as a boy; it was demolished within his lifetime, and replaced by St Andrew's Church (pictured on the right) – something that caused issues in terms of his bequest to it. (© Nell Darby)

114 Fleet Street – the site on the left of this image – was where pawnbroker Joseph Avant was based. He employed George Tinsley as an assistant here in the late 1860s. (© Nell Darby)

Another of George Tinsley's jobs was as a jeweller's assistant; he worked for a jeweller here on Cornhill. (© Nell Darby)

31 Old Jewry was the headquarters of Freshfields Solicitors in the 1880s; George Tinsley was said to have been fired by the firm when he worked there as a solicitor's clerk. (© Nell Darby)

Henry Salter & Sons, mortgage brokers, was a firm based largely at 11 Pancras Lane in the City of London. Salter employed George Tinsley as a shorthand clerk; in return, Tinsley took Salter's name (turning it to Slater) and tried to steal his business. (© Nell Darby)

On moving to Battersea, the Tinsleys first lived at 4 Falcon Grove this is where, in 1871, their eldest daughter Edith was born and died. (© Nell Darby)

From Falcon Grove, George Tinsley moved his family to the other side of Battersea Hill; they were living at Auckland Road in 1872. (© Nell Darby)

Formerly known as Middleton Road, Buckmaster Road is just one road away from Tinsley's former home at Auckland Road. In 1875, he was working as a shorthand tutor at this address. (© Nell Darby)

Basinghall Street, as with much of the City of London, has changed dramatically since Slater's time. During much of the agency's existence, the parish church of St Michael Bassishaw was located on the street; Slater and his staff would have witnessed its demolition in 1900. (public domain)

The Bank of England, pictured from Lothbury. This is an area Henry Slater would have known well, having worked in the City of London for decades. His agency's bank account was also with the Lothbury branch of the Westminster Bank. (public domain)

By 1897, Henry Slater was taking a step back from his agency and enjoying the spoils of his career. He claimed these included trips to Australia for his health – and a flat overlooking the sea in Brighton. (public domain)

After moving away from Tottenham, Emma Tinsley lived in Southend with her children, including here, at Chelsea Avenue. (© Nell Darby)

In 1905, Thomas Pollard fled England on board the SS *Victorian*. With him were his lover, Emma Toll, and their baby, bound for Canada. It was while on board that he was, for the second time, served divorce papers. (public domain; credit: Internet Archive Book Images)

The 1921 census records George Henry Gordon living here at 3 Haslemere Road, Crouch End, with Elizabeth Akers (© Nell Darby)

The town of Hyères in the Côte d'Azur, where the man once known as Henry Slater died in 1926. (Author's collection)

The tombstone of George Henry Gordon, who was buried at the Marylebone Cemetery in East Finchley; nearly 30 years after his death, Elizabeth Akers was buried with him. (© Nell Darby)

Henry Slater, Albert Osborn, Thomas and Kate Pollard, and John Pracy, as pictured in the *St Helens Examiner* of 30 April 1904 (public domain)

Slater's counsel now asked for bail for his client. Muir felt that Slater was truthful when he said he hadn't been to his office in months, and took no active part in the agency any longer; therefore, there was no need to remand Slater into custody. Sir Albert disagreed. It was an important case, and he wanted to remand all the accused for a week. Both Slater and Osborn would need to find two sureties of £3,000 each, and the other men would be bailed if they could find two sureties of £500 each. Charles Gill queried this; the charges were not so serious, and didn't warrant such a large amount. Significantly, he said that there was currently an 'immense' amount of prejudice against the men, and 'the case against Mr Osborn had been presented in the worst possible aspect'.[309] This shows that the case had both generated a lot of publicity already, and that it presented not only Osborn but also Slater in a very negative light. They were both men of standing, wealth, with impressive careers in their field. Even if private detectives were sometimes viewed with suspicion, seen as interfering in people's marriages, there was still a respect for Slater as a successful business owner. For Osborn, the stakes were equally high. He was a solicitor - he was expected to abide by the laws which he worked with on a daily basis. These two men, with their homes in affluent west London (as opposed to Davies and Pracy, in the north and east of the metropolis) and their comfortable lives, had the most to lose not only in court but in the pages of the press and the minds of potential clients.

One advantage Osborn had over the Slater detectives was that he had contacts and money. While he was still in court, four of his friends volunteered to provide sureties for him, and late that afternoon, they visited Sir Albert de Rutzen in his private room to do so. At 5.00 pm, Albert Osborn was released on bail. Nobody immediately came forward to do the same for Slater or the other two men, and they were taken to spend the rest of the weekend in the confines of Brixton Prison.[310] Brixton was where London prisoners were usually held on remand, and although conditions there had improved since its days of chronic overcrowding in the early nineteenth century, spending nights inside its walls would have been a shock for the detectives. The impact would have been heaviest on Henry Slater, who despite his humble origins at the Chelsea coffee shop, had become used to a wealthy lifestyle. Did it give him a fear of what might happen to him at trial, or was he confident about his chances? He tended to be a self-possessed individual, and although prison life was undoubtedly unpleasant for him, it is likely that he saw it as something brief to be endured and not repeated.

On Monday, 25 April, George Henry appeared at Bow Street Police Court charged with conspiring to obstruct and prevent the course of justice.[311] He was remanded into custody by Sir Albert de Rutzen, and ordered to be brought up to the court with his colleagues on Saturday, 30 April. Now, the question of bail had to be decided. Although his defence solicitor, Rollo Graham Campbell, argued that any conviction against Henry would not result in a heavy punishment, and that he had not tried to evade justice (in fact, when he had seen two police officers at Southend, he had immediately asked if they were looking for him - suggesting that his statement of surprise on being arrested was not entirely truthful). Henry was merely a 'paid servant' of Slater's, Graham Campbell argued, did not take any profits from the agency, and so was unable to find a large amount of money for his bail.[312] Sir Albert was swayed by these pleas for a low amount of bail, reflecting George Henry's financial situation, and said he should pay the same as Pracy and Davies: either two sureties of £500 each, or four of £250 each. Henry was still unable to provide these immediately, and so he was taken into custody. The magistrate had demanded a far higher amount from both Slater and Osborn. Slater was more fortunate than George Henry; on the same day that his manager was taken into custody, two of Slater's friends - not named in the press - visited Sir Albert in his private room to pay his sureties. These were accepted, and the two men - together with several other friends of Slater's - left in cabs, heading for Brixton Prison to release their friend.[313]

One man was still absent from Bow Street, but not for long. On the following day, Tuesday, 26 April, Cyril Broughton Smith was remanded at Bow Street, being the sixth and final man to be arrested.[314] At 11.30 that morning, he had been arrested by Detective Sergeant Brown at Bedford Row, Bloomsbury.[315] He was asked for his home address, and told Brown it was 3 Featherstone Buildings in Holborn – the office where Longley's Detective Agency was based.[316] Brown knew Smith didn't live there, but still recorded the details. Smith had been unsurprised to see a police detective at his door, saying that he expected it would happen. But alone among the detectives, as soon as he was arrested, he admitted that he had falsified evidence. He tried to explain it away to Brown, saying he had been talked into making false reports, and he had been keen to make a good impression at the agency: 'I was anxious to send in a good report of my work.'[317]

Smith was remanded on bail. His confession did not bode well for the subsequent court cases, but in court, he asked for the information Detective Sergeant Brown had recorded to be read out. It stated that he was among the people who had made observations on Thomas Pollard at Plymouth, it was he who had initially made the acquaintance of Pollard, and it was he who had thought of getting him to commit adultery with chorus girls.[318] Smith then asked to change his account, saying that he had given an incorrect impression of being talked into writing the reports. He needed to correct the record as 'such a statement as that would get the other man, who worked with me, into trouble.'[319]

Was Smith reflecting the loyalty of his network of private detectives, or was he trying to implicate one of them? He said that he didn't want to get a colleague into trouble, but then denigrated him, describing him as 'only a watcher' (unlike himself).[320] He made clear that this other detective had already compiled a written report about Pollard – with the clear insinuation that it was this watcher who had written that Pollard had committed adultery. Whereas the others denied all knowledge of anything untoward happening, Cyril initially admitted it, but rapidly tried to blame someone else once he appeared in court. As previously suggested, the detective arena could be a cut-throat one, and it looks as though Cyril Broughton Smith, despite knowing many other detectives at Slater's, Simmonds', and Longley's agencies, was willing to throw them under a bus if it meant avoiding court, or a conviction.

On the morning of Saturday, 30 April, the six men appeared at Bow Street Police Court - Albert Osborn; John Pracy (charged under his detective pseudonym of John Bray); Frederick Davies; Cyril Broughton Smith; George Philip Henry; and finally, Henry Slater himself, described as being 55 and of no occupation.[321] All six were charged with conspiring to prevent and obstruct the due course of justice in the Pollard case, and Albert Osborn was additionally charged with procuring and inciting Maud Goodman to give false evidence.[322] Henry Slater was charged under the name of Henry Scott, one of the identities he had adopted to give himself a military air, but the press alternated between the names of Slater and Scott in their coverage, knowing that this was Henry Slater of Slater's Detective Agency who was in court, but trying to remember the name he had been charged under.[323]

The case was of intense interest. It appealed to the Edwardian public for a variety of reasons; not only because it was unusual for the King's Proctor to intervene in a divorce case, and for his action to result in a criminal case, but also because of the people involved: namely the head of Britain's most famous detective agency, and a wealthy London solicitor. In addition, the case involved a sex scandal: the men charged were accused of procuring a woman to say she had had sex with Thomas Pollard, a married man. Although nothing of Kate and Hugh Knowles' relationship was explicitly referred to in court or the press, there must surely have been keen-eyed members of the public who read the papers and wondered who this man was who bankrolled the detectives - why would a man pay so much money and be so invested in getting a woman a divorce from her husband, unless they too were romantically involved? Given these factors, it is no wonder that on 30 April, Bow Street Police Court was crowded; and the spectators included the King's Proctor himself.[324]

Charles Matthews, for the prosecution, set out the case, pointing out that although Hugh Knowles had spent a lot of money with Slater's agency to make enquiries, the detectives were 'practically useless' until Osborn had taken charge, securing the services of Maud Goodman and thus obtaining 'instantaneous success'. Although Matthews noted that Slater had been out of England from January until April 1902, he intended to prove that on one occasion, Slater had told one of his staff to put Cyril Broughton Smith's report into the case 'in the drawer, and don't let anyone see it.' It was therefore hard to disprove the fact that Slater had still been a party to the conspiracy of his detectives and Osborn.[325] After detailing the alleged involvement of each of the accused, the case was adjourned for a week.[326]

The following Saturday, 7 May, saw, again, crowds of people attend the police court. The six men took up not only the whole dock but a seat in front of it as well, and it was noted in the press that they listened to the case presented with as much interest as the public gathered within its four walls.[327] During this session, Charles Fielding was called to give evidence about Slater's agency and how it operated. Slater's reputation meant that Fielding's evidence was exaggerated in some parts of the press; although his comment that the Basinghall Street building was on three floors was reported accurately, his guess that the agency employed thirty detectives – itself a good number – was inflated by one newspaper to 300 detectives, including Smith, Davies and Pracy.[328]

This may have seemed believable to readers, for Slater's was the pre-eminent detective agency in London, and had, thanks to its advertising, achieved almost mythic status. Even though the result of the Pollard divorce case was now making Slater news for all the wrong reasons, it also reinforced the image of the agency as being a powerful, influential one, full of detectives dashing about the country on various commissions. Whether it had thirty or 300 members of staff, it was still large and famous – and now, many of those aware of it had ensured that they got seats in the police court to see just some of those members of staff, as well as its famous owner, listen to the evidence from the dock.[329]

Chapter 12

Cartwright's Revenge

Two years earlier, Slater's former employee Edgar Cartwright had proved an enemy to match Francis Stevens. Edgar had started work at the agency as a clerk on fifteen shillings a week. In 1898, he was promoted to cashier, with a pay rise that took him to fifty shillings a week.[330] Although he had never had a quarrel with his boss, he didn't feel very grateful towards him; he felt that Slater was 'fake', and so was his professed friendship. He felt disgruntled, and gave his notice. His last day in the office was going to be 2 November 1901 - shortly after Cyril Broughton Smith had been sent down to Plymouth. However, Slater was nothing if not persuasive, and he convinced Edgar to stay on. He would end up staying at the agency for another ten months. Throughout this period, he would often try to give his notice, as he felt that the agency was taking part in 'dirty business' - the Pollard case.[331] Each time, Henry Slater would persuade him to stay on, assuring his cashier that he was going to check more rigorously on his other employees' behaviour. Despite Slater's later insistence that he had taken a back seat at the office since around 1895 or 1897, Cartwright saw him attending to cases himself for the duration of him working there. On one occasion, he noted that Slater had been so actively involved in a case that he had broken into a flat and found a couple there: 'and as a result, the lady's husband obtained a divorce.'[332]

It had been rumoured that the Treasury - the King's Proctor - was going to act against Slater's Detective Agency back in July 1902; Edgar Cartwright remembered the rumours flying round the agency at around the same time that one of its detectives, Thomas

Craig, had left its employment. In response to the rumours, Edgar had asked George Henry about them, and remembered the manager being 'upset', but keen to deflect the blame onto Albert Osborn - the manager had told Cartwright, 'If anything happens, if Osborn is fool enough to go to Plymouth to get false statements - we must put it all onto him.'[333] The lack of solidarity in Basinghall Street also applied to the relationship between the solicitor and the detectives.

Edgar Cartwright was an ambitious young man, who wanted to progress - and this undoubtedly played a part both in his initial desire to leave Slater's and the promises Slater in turn made him to get him to stay. He claimed that Henry Slater had promised him that George Henry would be sacked as manager, and that the new managers would be Francis Stevens, Henry Iles, one of the firm's lady detectives (who didn't merit a name in subsequent press reports), and Cartwright himself.[334] Of course, this change in personnel did not happen, and although Cartwright said he felt no animosity towards Slater, it is clear that he felt he had been let down. As a result, he felt no loyalty towards the man who had employed him for several years, and given him a good living.

In September 1902, Edgar again decided to leave Slater's, and gave a week's notice. However, on 22 September, Slater accused his employee of meeting a friend outside the office, which he deemed to be a serious offence. He ordered Edgar to leave immediately. Slater rightly feared that Edgar Cartwright was in communication with Charles Simmonds and Francis Stevens, and knew that if his former employees joined forces in a new agency, it would be a serious competitor to his own firm. As soon as Stevens had left the company, Slater had worried, to the extent of arranging for Charles Fielding to be shadowed in case he was in communication with him. When he realised that Fielding was still in touch with Stevens, Slater dismissed him without explanation.[335] Slater was both absent from the office, yet, in his former detectives' accounts, he was present - still taking enough of a day-to-day interest in his business to monitor his staff and to deal quickly with anyone he suspected of communicating with competitors.

Samuel Marrison had left Slater's employ two months after Cartwright. On the day Edgar had been told to leave, Slater himself had told Samuel to give all the Pollard papers to George Henry – together with papers related to two other cases. Samuel did as he was told, and saw them being examined in one of the agency's rooms by George Henry, Henry Slater, and Frederick Davies. In the afternoon, Samuel had to go into George Henry's office, and saw papers burning on the hearth; he recognised one burning corner as being part of a report Davies had compiled into the Pollard case. On another day, John Pracy told him that Osborn had to give £10 to Maud Goodman for a statement. Pracy added that as Osborn had left Maud's lodgings, he had tapped his pocket, and said, 'That's what did it.'[336] Samuel Marrison believed that Osborn had bribed Maud Goodman to give a false statement, in order for Slater to keep his 100 per cent success rate in divorce cases.

Shortly before he had left the agency, Edgar Cartwright had overheard a conversation between Albert Osborn and George Henry. George Henry had commented that some of the Plymouth witnesses – Maud and her friends – were becoming 'troublesome'.[337] Osborn replied that he could 'communicate with a man named Thompson, and see that everything was all right'. Who Thompson was is not recorded; he is only briefly mentioned.[338] He is not described as a detective, but was presumably a local man who could serve as a conduit between the agency and their reluctant witnesses. Whether Thompson duly tried to ensure the girls' loyalty or not is not recorded.[339]

The ordinary detectives employed by Slater's did not earn a fortune in their jobs, nor did they have wealthy friends. Cyril Broughton Smith was employed on the 'daily system' between January and June 1902, where he would go to the office each day on the off-chance that Slater's could offer him work. If there was no work, there was no pay. He therefore had to undertake work for others, akin to being a freelance detective. In mid-June 1902, for example, he had left London to undertake a commission for someone else, and was away from the city for several months. In the winter of 1902, he got work at Longley's agency in Holborn, doing 'chance inquiries'.[340] Both Fred Davies and Cyril Broughton Smith were described in court as having a bearing that showed their lack of status, and they also struggled to find the sureties required to make bail; the struggle the two men had to provide these contrasted sharply with the relative ease with which both Slater and Osborn were able to find their far higher sureties. Henry Slater must have felt protected by his wealth and success; his former detectives, however, had a very different experience.

The men who had become dissatisfied with Henry Slater were men he had trained, and so they knew all his tactics. They also had the additional benefit of youth; for he was now a middle-aged man, perhaps past his prime, and more motivated by money and the thought of a comfortable life than the thrill of shadowing individuals. What he should have feared more than competition, though, was the thought of his secrets being exposed. His detectives knew about the lies that agencies sometimes came up with in order to get their commissions, and it was only loyalty to their employer that stopped them revealing those lies. When they left that employer, however, that loyalty stopped. When Cartwright left Basinghall Street on 22 September, he took with him not only his own papers, but the reports written by Cyril Broughton Smith and Frederick Davies about the Pollard case.[341] This was more damaging even than Cartwright's subsequent appearance as a witness in Francis Stevens' slander suit, where he spoke against his former boss.

Edgar Cartwright appeared twice at Bow Street in May and June 1904, detailing how the agency's office worked, and what he understood the staff's involvement in the Pollard case to be. It was clear that Slater's former detectives might have motive to paint him, and his organisation, in as bad a light as possible in court. These were aggrieved individuals, and they were trying to establish themselves as competing detectives away from Slater's agency. This was recognised by the barristers during cross-examination, but unfortunately for Slater, his ex-employees' negative comments were gleefully reported on in the national press as well as in local newspapers up and down the country, which would inevitably influence readers' views of him.

Henry Slater came across as a man who would say anything to people to keep them happy, but who was not a man of his word. He was laid back in terms of how he managed his agency, leaving it largely in the hands of others, yet expected undivided loyalty, spying on those he suspected of having contacts with other agencies. He showed no ability to compromise or negotiate; if someone fell out of his favour, they could expect to be shown the door with no niceties along the way. This two-sided aspect to his personality was also evident with how he approached the agency's finances. He spent large on advertising and on ensuring that he had a comfortable life out of the takings, yet he could be angry at what he saw to be over-expenditure by his staff. The slander case, Cartwright argued, was down to Slater's attitude towards the accounts; he had ordered Cartwright not to question Stevens' compiling of accounts, yet then questioned them himself. He was quick to accuse Stevens of misappropriating money at Plymouth, yet his staff trusted Stevens and believed Slater to be in the wrong.[342] He also made regular promises to change the management structure of the company in order to increase trust - with several members of staff allegedly being concerned about the decisions being made in the Pollard case - but never did so.

Under cross-examination at Bow Street, Edgar Cartwright had to admit that Simmonds' agency wanted to ruin Slater's, and how it had tried to do so. He also talked about his own involvement in informing the King's Proctor about what the agency had done to obtain evidence for the Pollard divorce case. He had taken away documents when he left Slater's - documents he knew would be damaging to the agency – and had told Simmonds and Stevens about them, as well as the elusive Mr Longley – all of them former Slater's detectives turned competitors. It was Longley who received a letter from the King's Proctor asking them to call his office, and it was Edgar who gave the King's Proctor information, asking for his name to be kept out of it. It was also Edgar who tipped off the Board of Inland Revenue with allegations about Henry Slater's income tax returns. He explained that he had wanted to 'do everything I could to ensure Stevens' success [in the slander suit]. He had been most scandalously treated.'[343]

Edgar Cartwright, along with Charles Simmonds and Francis Stevens, was resentful of Slater, and the three men had joined forces to ruin him, choosing loyalty to each other above any lingering loyalty to a man who had given them jobs and trained them well. This was picked up by Slater's solicitor Richard Muir in cross-examination, who said it was equally scandalous for Edgar to 'betray his master upon a matter which comes to his knowledge as a servant'.[344] There was a clear class angle here. Slater and Osborn represented the wealthy, educated elite, whereas the others were from further down the social ladder and should have known their place. As the case played out, however, Slater's pretensions to elite status were exposed, and it became clear that his origins put him on the same social level as the employees he looked down on. His staff knew that he used fake names; Stevens knew what his real name and background was. Slater had made the mistake of not keeping quiet about his origins when he sought to be friends with Stevens, and when their friendship ended, Stevens told others. They all knew that Slater was no better than them, and the loyalty that he might have expected – as Muir expected – based on the perceived class difference between them, was no longer valid.[345] Therefore, Slater should have been worried about Edgar Cartwright's evidence, for he was a man who resented Slater and who wanted to ruin him. During an incredible thirteen hours of cross-examination, Cartwright was even accused of telling

Stevens that his 'wildest dream was to get Slater convicted, so that there would be no competition against my business'.[346] Detective work was a vicious arena, and during his years in business, Slater had made several enemies. Unfortunately for him, they were mainly the men he had employed.

Francis Stevens had followed Edgar Cartwright onto the stand at Bow Street, and his cross-examination not only showed his plans to ruin Henry Slater, but that he also knew Slater's real identity, and was planning to use it against him. One of the letters he had written to Cartwright while the latter was still working at Basinghall Street stated, 'If we can knock George Tinsley, I may'. Stevens mimicked Slater and his sayings, referring to Edgar as 'my boy' because it was one of Slater's favourite expressions.[347] The man who had earned the respect of his detectives because of his reputation had, by late 1902, earned their derision. It seemed appropriate. George Tinsley had earned the dislike of others in south London in his earlier life - Harry Sheppard being a prime example - and had taken the name of his boss Henry Salter (albeit with a letter transposed), as well as experience learned from Salter, in order to create a rival company to his. In 1902 and 1903, his own employees took revenge and established their own rival company to him, using the experience that he had given them. One wonders what Henry Salter, reading the accounts of the case in the newspapers, thought of Slater's comeuppance.

Chapter 13

Off to the Old Bailey

On the afternoon of Tuesday, 12 July 1904, it was clear that something significant was about to happen. Bow Street Police Court was crowded, eager spectators cramming into the Upper Court to see the accused men in the dock, and to listen to the decision of chief magistrate Sir Albert de Rutzen.[348] It was the final day of the Bow Street case, and the six men were waiting to hear what their fate would be. Would the case be dismissed, and the men discharged, or was this only one stage in a drawn-out legal process to decide whether they had reputations and jobs anymore?

The prosecution wanted all six men to be tried on a charge of conspiring to pervert the course of law in connection with the original Pollard divorce suit, on 24 November 1902. In addition, prosecutors wanted Slater, Osborn, George Henry, Pracy, and Davies to also be tried for conspiracy in connection with the hearing of the King's Proctor's suit at the divorce court on 16 March 1904. Cyril Broughton Smith would not face trial on this count, as he had not given evidence at the divorce court on that day.

The defence barristers for both Slater and Osborn had previously made their statements at a hearing the previous Saturday, where Richard Muir, for Slater, argued that no case had been made against his client. He stressed that as soon as Cyril Broughton Smith had suggested encouraging Pollard to commit adultery, Slater had repudiated the idea. His client was therefore innocent.[349] Charles Gill, for Albert Osborn, made clear that the case was a vindictive one that originated in a conspiracy between Francis Stevens and Edgar Cartwright to bring about the downfall of Slater's Detective

Agency and in so doing, benefit their own rival agency. In addition, Thomas Pollard was clearly a 'public-house loafer, willing to accept a drink from anyone'.[350] Ultimately, the case should not go any further simply because Kate Pollard had only got a judicial separation, rather than the divorce she had sought – therefore, the law had not been perverted.[351]

De Rutzen started by saying he had carefully considered the evidence; but it was not good news for the men. All six were going to be sent for trial at the Old Bailey. They were ordered to stand up, and were cautioned. All the men denied the charges, but only Slater and Osborn gave longer statements to the court. Osborn insisted that he believed Maud's evidence had been true, and stressed his own honesty in having given the court all the documents in his possession.[352]

Henry Slater, meanwhile, insisted again that he had been in ill-health and took little part in his business. He had never met Hugh Knowles until he saw him at the divorce court. He wasn't party to the burning of documents at Basinghall Street, and he had no knowledge of what Osborn had been up to – he had only learned of it when the King's Proctor had intervened.[353] Slater, and his counsel, insisted that no case had been made out against him during the previous three months' hearings at Bow Street. It's not difficult to understand why they would say this. All the evidence was against Osborn, Henry and the three detectives in terms of deciding what to do, visiting Plymouth and Jersey, and trying in different ways to persuade Thomas Pollard to commit adultery. Slater had not been to either place; he had not even been in the office, according to his statement. His defence against the accusations was that he knew nothing – he was ill, he had retired, he had been in Australia – and that all the actions taken by his friend, his staff and his manager had been done without his knowledge.

And yet. Slater and his staff differed in their memories of when he had started to take a step back from day-to-day work in

Basinghall Street. There were distinct memories of his involvement in destroying reports; he was also in regular communication with the office, whether or not he was personally there at all times. Osborn was a friend; Henry had worked with him for a substantial amount of time, was his trusted second-in-command, and Slater had even trusted him enough to use his professional name. It was hard to avoid the conclusion that he was heading the organisation that encouraged its staff to perjure themselves and to fake evidence in order to maintain Slater's professional reputation and success rate in divorce cases - he took ultimate responsibility for what happened in his agency. As he had said, as well, even his relationship with George Henry was not an equal partnership in terms of the law - it was always Slater who was in charge, right up to the point where he was arrested.

The case so far had been both about professional jealousy and competitiveness, and about personal reputation. Charles Gill was undoubtedly right in ascribing blame to Stevens. He had been so outraged by the abrupt end of the friendship between Slater and himself that he launched a slander suit, and then tried to do everything to ruin Slater's agency, establishing his own rival and using Slater's own tactics to steal his clients. Cartwright, loyal to Stevens, was also willing to blacken Slater's name, eagerly giving evidence against his former employer and joining Stevens in competing with his old agency. Reputationally, both Slater's agency and Slater himself had already taken a substantial hit. Albert Osborn was at risk of ruining his company's reputation, and his own as a lawyer, because he was accused of paying a young woman to lie about sleeping with another man. Maud Goodman's reputation, however shaky it may already have been, was further dragged through the descriptions of her as tiresome, keen to get money, willing to lie. Finally, Thomas Pollard was presented as a mess - he had been tempted into bed with Marie Travert (although not with other women on other occasions), and he was an unemployed, layabout drunk.

This, then, was the result of the proceedings at the divorce court, and at Bow Street Police Court. What would be the impact of the individuals after yet another court case, especially when it was a trial at the internationally famous Old Bailey, or Central Criminal Court? The waiting was interminable; the endless legal meetings and revisiting of events equally so. The Pollard affair had been rumbling on since late 1901; it was now the summer of 1904, and there was no end to it. Slater's Detective Agency had effectively been on trial now at two different courts, but still had a third to go. In the meantime, from being charged at the end of the Bow Street case, to their first appearance at the Old Bailey, there were over three months of waiting for Slater, Osborn, Henry and the three detectives.

It was now clear that Slater and Osborn, as well as the detectives, were in some danger of being found guilty and imprisoned. At Bow Street, Slater's and Osborn's defence team had argued that there was no case against their clients, and the two men surely felt that they were somewhat above the law - it was the underlings, Slater's staff, who had undertaken the bulk of the work in the Pollard investigation, and who should be held responsible for any underhand dealings in the case. Despite this argument, Slater and Osborn had been charged along with Slater's detectives, and would appear with them at the Old Bailey. The case against the agency boss and his solicitor friend had not, as they had confidently predicted, been dismissed.

Although the Old Bailey trial would be the conclusion of the case, it was also the culmination of a long drawn-out process that had already led to huge changes for Slater and his staff, for Slater's agency was a mere shadow of its old self by the time the trial started on 17 October 1904. The agency continued to advertise in the press, but these last adverts were different from those that had gone before. Ones in the provincial press in June 1903 comprised a stark black box within which was the basic text: 'Slaters Detectives. [sic] 1 Basinghall St. EC'.[354] There were no boasts of success rates, or bicycling detectives, or female detectives, anymore. There were no glowing references from unnamed newspapers or mentions of longevity. There would be a few more adverts: the agency advertised in *Truth* every week in March 1904, and once more in April. The name of the newspaper was a deliberate choice, Slater (or perhaps George Henry) trying to tell its potential clients to ignore what it was reading elsewhere and believe that the agency was honest and truthful in its dealings with the public. The adverts seemed a last, desperate roll of the dice – and last, they were. In a way, it didn't matter what the result of the long drawn-out Pollard investigation would be. The gossip, the press coverage to date, and the linking of Slater's name with a trial would be enough to cause the cessation of the agency after more than a decade.

Of course, Henry Slater had already been taking a back seat from the business, but several of his detectives had left. He, his manager and three more of his detectives were busy with their solicitors. Even if the agency had thirty detectives, some would have been paid, like Cyril Broughton Smith, on a daily rate, and were not trained to manage the office. There was nobody left to undertake publicity beyond the few adverts that were placed to show the public the agency was still alive. Henry Slater was busy trying to cover his own back – and thus realised that he had no time, or inclination, to ensure the agency's survival. It was also clear that with the owner and the manager of the agency both implicated in criminal affairs, it would be difficult to regain the trust of clients and potential clients. Even without the verdict of the Old Bailey case, Francis Stevens, working with Edgar Cartwright and Charles Henry Simmonds, appeared to have succeeded in causing the ruin of his rival agency, and his former employer's business.

From June to October 1904, the six men who had been charged with conspiracy to pervert the course of justice were on bail, but they would find it hard to live their usual lives – the shadow of the court case hanging over their heads. Henry Slater was a confident man, but even he would have been nervous, his whole life and reputation on the line. He knew that his numerous identities and former careers would again be picked apart in court, his hard-won identity as Britain's most famous private detective exposed again to reveal the ambitious and unscrupulous man underneath.

Chapter 14

A Very Peculiar-Looking Man

On Monday, 17 October 1904, the men finally appeared at the Central Criminal Court to hear the charges against them read out. They were prosecuted by the Solicitor-General Sir Edward Carson, together with Henry Sutton (who would be made a judge the following year), Charles Matthews, Archibald Bodkin, and Guy Stephenson; for the defence, Rufus Isaacs KC and Richard Muir appeared for Henry Slater; William Leycester for George Henry; Charles Gill KC and John Valetta for Osborn; Rollo Graham Campbell for John Pracy and Cyril Broughton Smith; and Forrest Fulton for Frederick Stanley Davies.

Three Plymouth men, Frank Mead, the GWR clerk; John Cleeve, a pub landlord; and pub barman Edward Legg, were all called on to give evidence. What they said showed how the case would focus not only on the character of the detectives, but also on the character of those caught up in their work. Tom Pollard was the key example. It was at John Cleeve's pub, the Golden Fleece, where Fred Davies suggested to Pollard that they should go to Jersey. However, Pollard had rejected the invitation because his clothes were shabby; he was particularly conscious about his boots. It was clear that Pollard was regarded as an oddity by locals in Plymouth; this was a man who had had a good life in the past, but was now reduced to shabby clothing and drinking in pubs with strangers. Mead said that Pollard's clothes generally were odd, with Pollard liking to wear a very long coat – he was 'very peculiar looking; he was not a man one would be likely to forget.' John Cleeve told how he heard Tom turn down the Jersey trip because he had no money, to which Davies had responded, 'Never mind, I will pay all expenses'. Cleeve said this was not an unusual situation: 'Pollard very seldom paid for any drinks – he never had any money.' The men's evidence implied that Pollard was an alcoholic, but it was also clear that Davies had been encouraging him to drink. Edward Legg noted that Pollard and Davies had visited the Bodega Wine Vaults, where he worked. One time, Legg said, 'I refused Davies when he asked for a drink, as Pollard had had enough, and so I told him to take Pollard out – they went away arm in arm – Davies always paid.'[355] Pollard frequently came in prior to meeting Davies, though; he could come in once a day, on his own, and wait to see if anyone would buy him a drink. The local pub landlords and staff always recognised the tall man in the long coat, who never paid for his own drink. In terms of unethical tactics undertaken by Slater's detectives, it's clear that taking advantage of a man on his uppers, with known issues with alcohol, was not their finest hour.

Pollard was, in this initial testimony, seen as a rather sad, lonely figure who was vulnerable to the offers of friendship, drink and money from the London strangers. The detectives had sensed his vulnerability and used it to their advantage. This was never clearer than when Marie Travert gave her evidence, detailing Davies' connivance in explicit detail. Speaking through an interpreter, the Frenchwoman remembered the night in March 1902 when three men appeared at Alexandra Macnamara's house. Marie's testimony clearly showed that it was Davies who was in control of the situation, asking for wine, and persuading Tom Pollard to follow Marie up to her room. It was Davies who had entered Marie's bedroom to see her and Tom still lying in bed. It was Davies who had given both Marie Travert and Marie Leroi money. After Pollard had left, Marie added, Davies went upstairs with her, and the two had sex. Davies paid her for her services not only with Tom, but also with him.

Marie remembered Davies and Pollard because 'we were not in the habit of frequently receiving persons of that kind'. As with individuals in Plymouth, Marie also distinctly remembered Pollard because of how tall he was.[356] Marie Leroi, who gave evidence after her countrywoman, made similar comments. She remembered Pollard as 'a tall dark man' and Davies as 'a man with a big moustache'. She also claimed that there had been another man - 'tall and fair' - who she had sex with in her room, while Marie Travert was with Pollard. This was, apparently, a stranger who Davies and Pollard had met on the boat to Jersey. Davies had somewhat unorthodox, as well as unethical, approaches to his work.

This was not the end of Davies' poor behaviour; in court, there were suggestions that Marie Travert and Alexandra Macnamara had been the victims of intimidation to stop them giving evidence. In January 1904, some men had visited both women and made proposals to them. Marie Travert was not allowed to say what these proposals had been - Charles Gill objected to her being asked questions about them - but it was clear there had been an attempt to 'get at' the two women, and they had been kept under supervision since as a result. The judge stated that if it could be shown that the men who threatened Travert and Macnamara were one or more of the accused, then more questions could be asked. Although it is highly likely that the detectives had indeed tried to keep these witnesses from giving evidence against them, it seems they could not be positively identified. Those threatening the women were able to play on understandable fears: Marie Leroi reported Macnamara as saying she was frightened she would be prosecuted for running a brothel. Ironically, this led to the women all being determined to give truthful evidence, despite Mrs Macnamara's fears, and despite her having been threatened. When faced with solicitors and a court case, they were scared not by the private detectives but by the repercussions of not telling the truth in a court of law.

Again and again, reading the trial records, it is clear how little respect the detectives had for those in the provinces. Pollard, to Davies, was a sad, drunk figure who could be easily taken advantage of. The Jersey women were prostitutes who would do anything for money, and could be threatened to keep quiet afterwards. Davies and his colleagues, conversely, insisted on being seen as 'gentlemen' – Marie Leroi said the only word of English she understood from that evening in March 1902 was 'gentlemen' – 'a word I am forced to know' – and that it sat awkwardly with what they wanted her and Marie Travert to do that evening. Leroi made this explicit: 'I saw what they wanted.'[357]

Shortly after Marie Leroi's evidence, an individual stood to give his own evidence. It was Thomas Pollard. Much of his evidence reinforced the idea of him as a man who was lacking money, friends, and a meaningful life. He had been living with his parents in Plymouth since 13 April 1901, when Kate had made him leave London. He was an easily influenced man, who sat back while others made the decisions that impacted his life. He had not actively wanted to separate from his wife, but she had decided that he should leave. This was a man who had travelled the world, who had been married twice, and been a father – but now, in early middle age, he was reduced to living with his elderly parents, supported by the three shillings a week that his wife sent him as 'personal spending money'. Most of this was spent on tobacco and newspapers.

Pollard's evidence showed his vulnerability. He was an easy target. He had also failed to realise he was being watched, and manipulated, by the detectives until twelve months after the events of Plymouth and Jersey. He was lonely, and thus susceptible to the detectives' attempts to get him to trust them. Cyril Broughton Smith had followed him into a paper shop and started a conversation with him. Smith realised that Pollard was lonely, and could be manipulated, and had fed this information back to Basinghall Street. At this stage, the office had recalled him, concerned about ethics, but they then realised that his idea – to 'persuade' Pollard to commit adultery – was the only option other than failure. Slater's agency prided itself on its 100 per cent success rate in divorce cases – so failure was not a possibility.

Thus, in March 1902, Fred Davies had been dispatched to Devon. He too had casually started a conversation with Tom Pollard - this time in the Golden Fleece pub - claiming to have known him when Pollard had lived in London. Even though Pollard, unsurprisingly, did not recollect Davies at all, the detective persuaded him that this was purely because he had not had a moustache at that time, and so looked different. Davies had bought the men drinks, and Pollard soon believed they were firm friends. Tom Pollard always liked people who bought him drink, and Davies proved always willing to pay. Davies was also willing to go walking with Pollard both round the town and out in the countryside. In return, Tom used his local knowledge to take Davies to the 'prettiest places' in the district, and by the time Davies asked Pollard to go to Jersey with him as he was 'utterly sick of Plymouth', Pollard thoroughly trusted him.[358] Davies buying him new clothing created a sense of obligation. After repeated requests, feeling under pressure, and wanting to please his generous friend, Pollard agreed to go to Jersey. It was like a holiday for him, having all his food and drink paid for by his generous friend (although, Pollard insisted, he was able to buy some 'small items which I had the money to pay for'); cigarettes; games of billiards and ping-pong; and, finally, sex with a prostitute, again paid for by his friend.[359]

Later, Pollard realised the extent of the detectives' scheming - that the many 'accidental' meetings he had with Davies over time were not so spontaneous. He now realised that when Davies gave him excuses about why he was sometimes absent from Plymouth, he was actually back at the Basinghall Street office; and Davies's fake identity seemed now to be suspicious, along with his reasons for why he was sometimes absent from Plymouth, when he was presumably back at the Basinghall Street office. As Pollard told the court, Davies had told him that he travelled, as a result of being in business with a relative, at one point explaining an absence by saying he had been in South Africa on a business trip. Pollard now realised that he had never seen Davies engaged on any business.

At the Old Bailey, Pollard admitted not having defended himself in the divorce case, and blamed his lack of financial resources. He had got as far as consulting solicitors, but was unable to pay for them. Without a solicitor to keep him in touch with what was going on, he relied on the press for information. He had read in the newspaper that the divorce court was due to start hearing Kate's divorce case on a certain date in November, and so came to the Strand on that date, only to learn that it was not being heard then. He then returned to Plymouth, and it was again only from reading the newspaper that he learned that the divorce case had been heard the day before. Another week passed before he wrote to the King's Proctor about the case, and then, a month later, he received the letters advising him to contact Longley's Detective Agency to be given information that would be useful in getting the King's Proctor to intervene.[360] These letters helped Pollard enormously, spelling out exactly what he needed to do, and what he needed to bring with him to a meeting: the divorce citation, any letters and telegrams sent to him by Kate Pollard while he was in Plymouth, a photo of her, and copies of the local Devon papers in which his divorce was reported. From his subsequent meetings with Frederick Murray, the King's Proctor's agent in Plymouth, Pollard met Maud Goodman and Louisa Ford.

Tom's tales of woe, and his reliance on others for money - from his estranged wife and his mother, to strangers such as the detectives - meant the public in the gallery were likely to have been on Kate's side. Men were expected to be responsible, strong, the breadwinners looking after their families. Instead, here was a man admitting to giving away his son without a care; of making his second wife work for a living; of failing to maintain accommodation for her; and of drinking away any spare cash he had. Tom had, at various points, claimed to be unable to work due to long-term paralysis (despite being able to walk to the pawnbroker and the pub), faced losing a financial bequest from his first wife unless he started 'asking after' his eldest son, away in America (he didn't), and a frequent borrower of money from friends and family.

He noted that Kate had evicted him after finding out that he had been drinking in a pub, in the company of their young son, while she was at work. He had then, on 1 February 1901, received a solicitor's letter, stating that Kate had requested a deed of separation unless he started treating her with 'courtesy and respect'.[361] Since arriving in Plymouth, Kate had been sending him money with the intention that he would contribute to his mother's increased expenditure: instead, he had spent the money on things for himself. Eventually, arrangements were made for Kate to pay eight shillings to his mother, Mrs Pollard, and only three directly to Tom, although Tom was able on occasion to 'intercept' his mother's payment and spend it himself? Tom's mother was also abused by him. She wrote to Kate on several occasions to describe her son as 'mad drunk' and to say that despite trying to care for him, he had been calling her 'vile names'.[362]

At the start of June 1902, Tom Pollard had journeyed from Plymouth to London intending to accost Kate. He borrowed more money from his mother to pay for the night train. Tom thought Kate still lived in Forest Gate, where she had been before their marriage. He knew that she wouldn't want to see him, but sent a telegram to where he thought she was living – at her sister's house – to tell her to meet him. He arrived at Paddington at between 6.00 am and 7.00 am, and then got a cab. However, he had no money left to pay for the cabman, and when he reached the house, Kate's sister called the police. Pollard argued that Kate could pay the fare – 'she had my money, I considered, and I had not the money to give him'.[363] Pollard admitted at the Old Bailey that he was drunk at the time. Challenged, he denied that he had picked up a prostitute in the Edgware Road and left her in the cab, but it is evident that others believed he had. After being rejected by Kate's family, Tom had to walk several miles back to central London, turning up at the house of one of his siblings and asking for a loan of twenty-five shillings.

This tale was recounted under cross-examination to make clear that Tom's behaviour both before and during his stay in Plymouth was appalling, and that he had a history of drunkenness, and, possibly, paying for prostitutes. Osborn had asked him about women he had been with in Plymouth, telling him that his firm knew all about it. In response, Pollard had denied any association with women. The court was now being asked to think about who was telling the truth: was it the respectable solicitor, or was it the drunken, penniless man?

The Old Bailey trial report is where Tom Pollard's voice can be heard. It is his account. But it also establishes why the detectives thought it would be easy to catch him *in flagrente delicto* with another woman, and why they might have been surprised to find out that they couldn't, without resorting to underhand methods. Tom was a sad drunk, whose main concern was ensuring that others paid for him to drink and eat – he was essentially unemployable. He also seemed to dislike the women in his life. He was critical of Kate for failing to look after him, and accused his mother of having a habit of lying.[364]

Tom knew he was going to look bad in court, and therefore resorted to half-truths and obfuscations as a means of damage limitation. He was unwilling to admit how much his wife and his mother had done for him, arguing that his mother only cooked for him a little when he was living with her. He took money off these women, even stealing the money his wife gave his mother to help maintain him. He enjoyed the company of the detectives, notably Davies, because they gave him the alcohol, cigars, and dining that he wanted – but women were way down his list of needs and wants. Even when he learned that Kate had sought a divorce, his primary concern was what would happen to him financially.

Pollard had denied sleeping with any women, but then said that his denial only applied to Plymouth. He only admitted having slept with Marie Travert in Jersey when he was formally asked about it.[365] At the end of his cross-examination by Charles Gill, Pollard stressed his concern about the financial implications of the end of his marriage, making clear what his priority was: 'I have lost the weekly allowance.'[366]

Further cross-examinations by Graham Campbell and Forrest Fulton - on behalf of Davies and his fellow detectives - followed, but these were far shorter, and restricted to specific details of certain events. Fulton's cross-examination further emphasised how Pollard would drink with anyone who offered to pay, despite his protestations that he only drank with Davies when Davies forced it on him - something which was hard to believe. Re-examined, he said that the only two Slater's detectives he knew were Fred Davies and Cyril Broughton Smith, and that he obviously had also met Osborn. All three had offered him drink on each occasion he had seen them.[367]

Tom Pollard's testimony was over. He may have implicated the detectives in fabricating evidence, but he also came across as a feeble individual for whom many at the Old Bailey would have had little sympathy. It was something of a character assassination, and showed that it was not just Slater and his men who were in the dock - it was also the man they were accused of manipulating. He appears to have been the opposite of Henry Slater, and thus someone Slater would have had difficulty empathising with. Yet it is hard to believe that Slater would have been completely unaware of the case: it went on for so long, it cost so much money, and his friend Albert Osborn was deeply involved. Henry Slater may have taken a back seat at his agency, but it was still his business, and that business was engaged, for nearly three years, on getting the weak Thomas Pollard to sleep with women for money.

Chapter 15

Plymouth Girls and Private Detectives

It is a measure of how infamous the Slater trial was, how much publicity and interest it had generated, that on 1 November 1904, the court breathlessly noted the presence of a well-known figure who had come to watch events. Maud's evidence had been eagerly awaited, and she had spent the morning in court, before the court broke for lunch. As everybody filed back in, replete, an instantly recognisable man entered. The man was Winston Churchill. At this time, he was a Liberal MP, having defected from the Conservatives nearly seven months earlier. The 29-year-old had been eagerly following the case, and today, he had come in person to see for himself what all the fuss was about, and to see the good-looking Maud Goodman.[368] He was joined on his visit by James Rochfort Maguire, businessman and former Irish MP.[369] Churchill took a seat next to the judge, Justice Darling, and was described in the press afterwards as having been an 'interested spectator in proceedings'.[370]

That afternoon, Churchill listened to Maud, a reluctant witness, as she gave the court a picture of a seedy lifestyle in her area of Plymouth - it was a place where people came and went, where relationships were often fleeting but did not rely on the niceties of marriage. The local women all knew each other, and had friendships, but their loyalty could be bought by wealthier individuals. Maud recounted the story of Emma Smith bringing her back to Minnie Wilson's lodgings at Summerland Place and finding Osborn there. Maud made clear that she had never seen Osborn before. Her testimony stressed Osborn's powers of persuasion, and how he had got her friends to work on her, encouraging her to positively identify Tom Pollard as a man she slept with. As Minnie Wilson had told her, after talking to Osborn, 'You have got to sign the paper. You know the gentleman [Pollard], and it is just as well for you to sign it now as at any other time, because you have got to sign it.'[371] Maud detailed the process of initialling Pollard's photo and signing a statement confirming that she knew him, while in the private bar of the Swan Inn; her statement read that she knew the gentleman whose photograph she had seen, and which she had initialled, 'and he has had intercourse with me, Maud Goodman.'

Maud had been reluctant to sign right up to the point where she eventually did so, in pencil. In her account, she was clear that she had been coerced to sign both by Osborn and her friends. When she was shown the statement in court, she confirmed that the initials on the photograph were written by her, but insisted that the statement had been altered: 'This is not my writing... it is not what I wrote.'[372]

From Maud's testimony, it was apparent that she had been put under pressure by Osborn to confirm that she had slept with Pollard, and that she had been unsure as to whether she had or not. The photo did not make clear Pollard's one significant feature – his height – and without this, she may not have remembered him, even if she had slept with him. In addition, the photograph was fourteen years old, when Tom was not so down on his luck, and she may not have been able to associate it with the shabbier man he now was. Osborn had pressured her; so too did John Pracy. Pracy took her to identify Pollard on the Hoe; Maud had made clear she couldn't identify him from his back, so they walked around the Hoe until he was facing him. In court, Maud remembered, 'I thought he knew me, or at least Louie Ford said he recognised me, and I did not trouble to look whether he did or not... I said to Bray [*sic*] "I suppose he knows me".'[373] After being pushed to do so, she later confirmed to Pracy that Pollard was the man she had taken to Summerland Place and 'he there had intercourse with me.'[374]

This was a young woman living on her own in Plymouth, reliant on the other women she came into contact with – a peripatetic network of women. They were not educated or wealthy, and their lives, although chaotic, had a certain pattern. Then, suddenly, these London men – Osborn and Pracy – had come into their lives, promising money and excitement, and Nellie Bell, Minnie Wilson, and Louie Ford were all swept into their path. They were drawn into helping to get Maud to agree to identify Pollard by the thought of a reward. Maud said she had been 'frightened' by Osborn's push to get her to London to testify, but at the same time, it was a trip to the capital, expenses paid, and she must have been tempted by the novelty of the visit, as well as by the money being offered by Osborn.

She must have thought that trip to London would be the end of the matter, but, of course, it wasn't. Now, Maud was contacted by Frederick Murray, acting for the King's Proctor; on 27 March 1903, she got Maria Congdon's daughter to write a letter to Osborn for her. She wanted Osborn to explain what was going on, noting that Murray had told her a 'different tale' to what Kate Pollard had said in the divorce court, 'so I thought I would write to you as I did not know how to act in seeing Pollard.'[375] In response, Osborn had written a convoluted letter that almost seems designed to further confuse Maud. It said that there was no proof that Murray had been working on the King's Proctor's behalf, and that the latter wouldn't send a solicitor. Osborn even tried to convince Maud that Murray was engaged on some kind of fraud, telling her that there was no Murray listed in the 'Law List as practicing at Plymouth'. Yet Osborn clearly feared that Murray *was* the King's Proctor's representative, as he had claimed, and so still told Maud to stick to 'the truth'. The truth, of course, was what she had been persuaded to sign in the statement drafted by the men.

Osborn also wanted to know what Frederick Murray had told Maud regarding Kate Pollard's evidence in 1902, claiming that

Kate's evidence was about matters 'quite different' to Maud's. It was clear that even at this stage, Osborn was panicking. He made further enquiries, and found out that Frederick Murray really was who he said he was. He asked Maud for more details of what Murray had asked her, and stressed that she should only give the Plymouth solicitor the same information she had provided Osborn with in her signed statement. Unfortunately for Osborn, Maud had then visited Murray's office with Nellie Bell. Murray told Maud to tell the truth, and unlike Osborn, he did not ask her to lie for money. She therefore made clear that she did not recognise Pollard as a client but only as a man who had been pointed out to her at Plymouth Hoe, and that she had never slept with him. Osborn and the Slater detectives had made an error in choosing Maud to persuade. She and her friends might be willing to do a lot of things for money, but they had little or no experience of the legal system. Once it became clear to Maud that she was going to have to deal with the King's Proctor and more court appearances, she became intimidated and questioned what she was doing.

Considerable pressure was also put on Maud by Slater's agency, and this pressure contributed to her change of heart. Joseph McKenna was sent to Plymouth to get her to sign another statement, confirming that she did know Pollard, and she refused point blank. Pracy was then despatched to try to get Maud to sign; he even told her that he had been sent down to Plymouth 'because McKenna could not do anything with me.'[376] On Maud again refusing to sign a statement, Pracy had sent out for some whisky, and Maud proceeded to drink all day, with Pracy coming and going, each time hoping that she was drunk enough to sign. From her examination at the Old Bailey, it appears clear that both Osborn and Pracy tried to coerce Maud to say what they wanted her to say; their behaviour was unethical, particularly Pracy's attempts to get Maud drunk in order to make her more amenable to signing documents that involved her lying. Maud and her friends were perceived to be just a couple of prostitutes whose lives did not matter; they were to be used and discarded for the sake of the Pollard divorce.

Under cross-examination, the most that Maud would admit to is that she slept with a man on or around 3 June 1902 at Summerland Place, but that she did not know his name, and although he looked like Pollard, she wasn't sure if he was. She said that once she had been to Frederick Murray's office, she 'never said that he was the man who slept with me in June - I have no doubt about it now.'[377] All that had happened, she spluttered, was that she had once slept with a gentleman who looked a bit like the man in the photograph she had seen. Maud was clear about the benefits of her lifestyle; she and her friends could decide whether they exposed a man who had slept with them - they didn't trouble themselves about their clients' reputations as 'we can please ourselves'. However, she was not keen to give a client away when it was in relation to a divorce case, rather than a crime. She was also clear that it was not going to be possible to positively identify Pollard as a client, even if he had been: 'I go with different gentlemen at Summerland Place'.[378] The problem with Maud's testimony is that, as had happened throughout the previous two years, she kept changing her mind: about whether she had slept with Pollard, whether a divorce case would influence what she said about a man, and whether she would give a client 'away'.

The cross-examination exposed Maud as someone who might say anything if offered money, or persuaded by friends. However, the overall impression was still one of the detectives, and Osborn, competing to get her story (or their preferred version of her story) by pressurising her and using her friends to get to her. Although Maud did not come off particularly well, she did help to portray both Osborn and Pracy as unethical individuals who were willing to do anything to get a result in a case. Absent from her testimony, though, was mention of any other detectives than Pracy and McKenna, only one of whom was on trial.

Later, it was the turn of three of Slater's former employees to give evidence at the Old Bailey. They had spent much of 1904 explaining their roles and how the agency operated, and now had to do so again. Charles Fielding, Edgar Cartwright and detective Samuel Marrison were the men who were asked to detail their experiences of working for Henry Slater. Charles Fielding described himself as undertaking office work, including copying reports, rather than detective work; as he detailed it, he also inadvertently corroborated Slater's story that he was little involved in the agency by the late 1890s. Fielding had worked for Slater's firm for eight years - from 1895 to 1903. For all of this time, he said, 'I always thought he was the proprietor - [George] Henry...was the manager at the agency.'[379] It was clear to Fielding that George Henry was the man who was in day-to-day charge, and that Slater was a more distant figure - he 'thought' Slater was the agency's owner, but had few dealings with him. Conversely, Albert Osborn was a man so often at Basinghall Street that it was a rare day when the office did not see him. Fielding noted that Osborn came to the office almost every day, but sometimes twice a day, and that he could come 'in and out as he liked'. This was unlike Slater, who between 1900 and 1902 'very seldom came to the office, and then at irregular intervals', sometimes only staying a short time. Even when Slater came to the office, he never arrived before midday.[380]

Although Henry Slater was apparently rarely at his agency, Osborn still had a private telephone line direct to his office. There was a mutual partnership between the two men, to the extent that at Basinghall Street, business cards for Osborn and Osborn were kept on hand, so that they could be given to clients. The private detectives employed by Slater's would help themselves to Albert Osborn's business cards - they knew where they were kept, and what they were for. It stood to reason that a married man or woman seeking the agency's help in shadowing their spouse might be considering divorce, and would therefore need a divorce lawyer. The detectives could therefore help by recommending the Osborn family firm. Likewise, to his clients,

Osborn would recommend using Slater's agency to get evidence of adultery that was needed by the divorce courts.

However, despite the detectives and administrative staff all knowing how close the relationship was between Osborn and Slater, and being aware of the former's frequent visits to their office, they did not keep reliable or consistent reports of such visits. Fielding was asked to go through his call book to track the visits by Osborn and Knowles to the office, but found gaps in the records; on 20 September 1901, for example, he had recorded Osborn visiting, but not Knowles, and he couldn't remember when Knowles had first visited, although he had certainly done so four days later. On 28 September, both men had called but were not recorded as visiting together. Osborn had again visited three times between 3 October and 9 October – but these were just the visits entered by Fielding into his book, and did not represent all visits Osborn had made. Given his 'daily' dropping-in, Fielding admitted that he did not always enter his name in the book. What Fielding's book did make clear was the frequent visits of both Osborn and Knowles from September 1901 until June 1903.

Another job that Fielding undertook during this period was to make out a list of everyone who had called at the office from his call book and hand it to either George Henry or Edgar Cartwright at the end of each day. This would be sent on to Henry Slater with a covering letter detailing what kind of business they had dealt with. Fielding also had to make a copy of each report he received from the agency's detectives, and in the Pollard case, a junior clerk named Bowden, who worked on the third floor of the office – where the back room was staffed by various detectives and clerks who did not have their bases elsewhere in the building – had given him the reports. Fielding made a 'fair copy' of them, but did not see any reports made from Jersey. He knew Davies had been there on the Pollard case, although he didn't know the specifics of what he was doing there, and so he had gone to George Henry and told him that he could not find the relevant reports. Henry responded that 'they must not see daylight.' Fielding was told to send Osborn the copies of the reports, and asked him, 'I understand from Mr Henry that Davies' reports from Jersey with regard to the Pollard case are not required?' to which Osborn apparently responded, 'That is right; there is nothing in *them*.'[381]

In Fielding's account, he had witnessed Osborn and George Henry meeting on the second-floor landing at Basinghall Street, opposite Fielding's office. Fielding told the court that he had overheard the conversation between George Henry and Osborn, where the latter had volunteered to travel to Plymouth and see what he could do for Henry – and Henry's eager affirmative response. It was then that Osborn duly turned up in Devon.[382] Fielding also kept a separate book detailing the movements of the detectives – where they had been sent, over what dates, and where they needed to be (although not always when they returned). Unfortunately, Fielding could abbreviate these details so much that they weren't very useful; although he had recorded that Cyril Broughton Smith was still working in November 1901 and had been sent on a job on 16 November that year, it simply noted his destination as 'Argyll Street', and didn't record the case he was working on.[383] There was, at the time, an Argyle Street [sic] in Plymouth. Like several of the 'ordinary' detectives, Smith was paid on a daily system – men on this system would go to the office each day to see if their services were required, and if they weren't, they would leave, unpaid. Detectives might be employed to make inquiries, or simply to watch people, and Fielding was not sure if Smith was employed just to make inquiries into the Pollard case after he returned from Plymouth.

Fielding's evidence was of a valued office worker at Slater's; despite his police experience, he was not employed as a detective and did not travel with the agency – instead, he was solely based at Basinghall Street and engaged on administrative matters. He was therefore a useful witness in terms of the paperwork that he had assembled recording Hugh Knowles' visits and the frequency with which Albert Osborn attended the office (not to mention his close relationship with Henry Slater). Under cross-examination, he also proved to be a valuable defender of Slater's, as he could detail the desire of Simmonds, Cartwright and Stevens to destroy Henry Slater. He recognised that Slater had suspected him of being in communication with Simmonds' Detective Association, but denied having learned anything of their plans before they left. However, he knew that Simmonds' business was 'started to compete with Slater's; if they could get rid of Slater, I suppose it would be a *very* good thing for Simmonds and Co.'[384] He had seen Simmonds' adverts, which stressed the connection with Slater, and detailed the circulars that Simmonds' agency had sent out, saying that he had one in his possession because Simmonds had sent one to all of Slater's 'representatives' (detectives). The impression Fielding gave is that following the establishment of Simmonds' Detective Association, there was a sense of widespread suspicion at Basinghall Street, with the remaining workers all viewed as being in communication with the men who had left.

Charles Fielding left Slater's employment in July 1903, but had not seen his boss for several months before that; the last time he had seen him, in fact, had been the end of February or start of March that year. From 1901 onwards, the business was being managed by George Henry, Edgar Cartwright and William Hamilton, and Fielding made clear how close Cartwright in particular was to the action; he lived on Basinghall Street - at number thirteen - and had the keys to the office, his first job of the day being to open the office doors, and then to open the morning letters. He was the first, then, to see what reports or letters had come in and therefore to know what was going on. Although Slater was absent, he was sent batches of reports and letters even while he was in Australia, and none were returned to the office as having been undelivered. And what of William Hamilton's role? Fielding did not even know what it was. He was in a senior position, but used to split his time between working in Slater's office, and going out 'on business', and Fielding wasn't sure what he was doing at this time.

In fact, Hamilton had been questioned back in March, where he described himself as one of the managers at the agency - he was of a higher rank than the detectives, but junior to George Henry. He was Slater's most trusted employee, primarily because of his longevity; he had been with Henry Slater from the start. A former commercial traveller, he had moved into inquiry work, working 'for a foreign government'. When Slater's Detective Agency opened in 1885, Hamilton had started work there, and by 1904 had worked there for nineteen years.[385] When Fielding first arrived at Slater's in 1895, Hamilton was seeing clients, but he stopped around 1898, with George Henry taking over responsibility for meeting them. Fielding felt that Hamilton was superior to the likes of Fred Davies, but still didn't know quite what his job was. He was certainly part of Slater's coterie, however, together with Albert Osborn.

Fielding's final comment at the Old Bailey was that he remembered a registered parcel arriving, addressed to George Henry. He opened it in front of Fielding, and it contained a diamond stud and pin, in a case - a present from Hugh Knowles, for a successful commission. The evidence of Edgar Cartwright, who followed Charles Fielding into the stand, emphasised how valuable a client Knowles was to the agency. As the cashier at Slater's, before he moved to become a private detective at the rival Simmonds' agency, he saw the cash coming into the business, and the money being paid out to its staff for their expenses. He had even seen the report George Henry made - in shorthand - after Knowles' initial visit in September 1901. Knowles - not Kate Pollard - was the client, but the man he wanted watching was Tom Pollard, a 'tallish, dark' man with a medium build and a black moustache. His address - his parents' home at Headlands Park - was provided.

On this same day - which Cartwright, referring to his accounts, had noted as being 20 September - payments from Knowles began to be made. By the end of 1901, they already totalled £500, and by August 1902, £1,290. The total sum paid by Knowles to find evidence of Thomas Pollard's alleged adultery, by 2 March 1904, was over £2,000, excluding Osborn's separate charges. Cartwright noticed the handwriting of Cyril Broughton Smith (operating under the pseudonym of Roberts), John Pracy (operating as John Bray), Frederick Davies, and Iles (working as Sargent). Crucially, Cartwright also had a record of the reports he had made for Slater's use while the latter was absent from the office, which included, on 5 December 1901, a record of a call from Mr Knowles. This promised to pay a total of £500 'for which sum he was informed we would carry the thing through'.[386] This was clearly not the case: Knowles would pay far more in total. Cartwright's squirrelling away of copies of these documents and, together with some of the reports submitted by other private detectives (including Smith and Davies), had proved incredibly useful. He had known that they might become weapons with which to discredit his former employer and his famous detective agency, and in the Old Bailey, he was able to do so.

Samuel Marrison's evidence echoed Cartwright's in his description of the reports that detectives were told to write. Marrison was employed as a private detective from 1898 to 1902, but he said that in reality, he was little more than a junior clerk. One of his duties was to take the reports from the second-floor office, and put them into envelopes. Each envelope was labelled with the name of the case it related to. On 22 September 1902, when Edgar Cartwright was dismissed from the agency, Marrison had been ordered to gather all the papers relating to the Pollard case, including the private detectives' reports.[387] Marrison duly collected them all, and took them to the back room on the second floor. George Henry was there with another agency employee, Mr Shayler.[388] Marrison gave the papers to Henry in Shayler's presence. When he made a repeat trip with other papers, he found the two men, joined by Frederick Davies, poring over a heap of the papers, which were now spread out over the table. Later still, he found several papers smouldering in the room's hearth. The remaining papers were then put back in their envelopes, but when Marrison tried to remove them in order to refile them in the general office, Davies told him to leave them.

Originally, in the divorce court and the police court, Marrison had said that it was George Henry who had ordered him to collect the papers. Now, in the Old Bailey, he said he had told an untruth. It was not George Henry, but Henry Slater himself who had ordered him to. Either Marrison was telling an untruth earlier, or he was telling an untruth now. Undoubtedly, memories might be hazy after so much time, and two court cases, but the testimony of many of the witnesses created a cloud of confusion, views and counterviews that made who had done what unclear.

On 29 September, Marrison had received a letter from Cartwright enclosing a business card for the new Simmonds' Detective Association. He handed in his notice the same day, intending to work the week out. Marrison insisted that he had 'always' had some idea of leaving Slater's, and had told George Henry he was leaving to go to America. Now, in court, he insisted that was the truth - he had intended on going to visit his uncle there. But George Henry suspected otherwise, and when he gave his notice in, the manager told him, 'You had better go at once'. Henry's suspicions were correct, as the letter from Cartwright had also contained an invitation for Samuel Marrison to come and work for the new rival agency. On Monday, 6 October, Marrison proved another defector to Simmonds' Detective Association, starting work there on twenty-five shillings a week - a large increase from what he was earning at Slater's. After he gave evidence in the King's Proctor's case at the divorce court, Simmonds gave Marrison a pay rise. Now, at the Old Bailey, Marrison admitted that he had thought it 'might be' a good thing if Cartwright, Stevens, and Simmonds ruined Slater.[389] Few of the witnesses earlier that year had been objective in their testimony. Since then, they had had time to work on their memories and their loyalties.

Chapter 16

The Verdict

Others had come and gone during the previous two weeks, giving their evidence. The police detectives who had arrested the men; the passbook keeper at the London and Westminster Bank, where Slater's account was held; the former Slater's men who Henry Slater had seen as duplicitous traitors for communicating with the men of the rival Simmonds' agency - and, of course, the Plymouth witnesses. The statements of each of the accused men had also been read out: Osborn claimed that he had believed Maud Goodman's statements that she had carnally known Tom Pollard, and had given her ample opportunity to change her views. He had worried about Frederick Murray approaching her because he hadn't known who the Plymouth law clerk was. In fact, he initially believed that Murray represented Simmonds' Detective Association. Fred Davies and George Henry simply said they were innocent, while John Pracy insisted Maud had genuinely believed Pollard to be the man she had slept with. Cyril Broughton Smith, as a temporary employee, admitted foolish tactics designed to make him look good and 'thus improve my position with the agency'.[390] Henry Slater maintained that he was 'paying almost no attention to business' in 1901, and denied knowing anything about anything.

The final man to give evidence in the autumn of 1904 was Frederick Murray. He was taken through the details of his involvement by Charles Gill, from his initial instructions on 5 January 1903, through to Maud's second statement in May, and their noisy trip to London, confirming that he had nothing to do with how the case was conducted. It was then time for Rufus Isaacs, KC, to argue that the only evidence against Henry Slater had come from Samuel Marrison, but that his evidence was not consistent.

Sir Edward Carson, the solicitor-general, was scathing in his view of Slater. He noted that Henry Slater made clear in his press advertisements that he was responsible for the agency, and that it was he who took the firm's profits. His detectives sent him reports and letters about the Pollard case, and that therefore, Slater must have known about it. The amounts of money being paid by Knowles must also have raised suspicions: either Slater was defrauding him – charging far too much money for ordinary sleuthing activities – or he was charging him a lot because he knew his team's work was both dangerous and illegal. In other words, the money being charged was danger money.

It was now Thursday, 3 November 1904. At the Old Bailey, all the parties gathered, tired after being present in court until late the previous evening. There was George Henry, clean shaven and pursed-lipped, he and Cyril Broughton Smith looking keenly at those around them. There was the good-looking John Pracy, and Fred Davies with his oiled hair and thin nose, who, onlookers said, had taken the most eager interest in proceedings. There was Albert Osborn (who, it was said, resembled Cecil Rhodes, the politician who had died two years earlier in Africa), and finally, the imposing Henry Slater: tall and with a heavy build, leaning forwards, and peering at the court over his gold-rimmed glasses. The men were about to learn their fate.

The last person to speak had been Rufus Isaacs, Slater's defence counsel, 'who had argued that his client's case should not be proceeded with'. Could the solicitor-general now convince Justice Darling that a jury was needed? Sir Edward Carson rose to argue that the conspiracy charge covered a span of time – from when the agency had been instructed by Hugh Knowles to make inquiries, up to the time when 'Mrs Pollard's petition for a divorce had been dismissed by the President of the Divorce Division, Sir Francis Jeune'. If Henry Slater had taken part in the conspiracy to 'bolster' the evidence used in the divorce case, Carson argued that he was just as guilty as his detectives. Rufus Isaacs was about to make a comment in response, but the judge stopped him. Slater quickly looked over his gold-rimmed spectacles at Isaacs, while the other men in the dock exchanged glances. There was an audible, excited rustle round the court, for the legal men, defendants, and onlookers all knew that the judge's intervention meant that he was going to let Slater leave the court as a free man.

'My duty is simple,' said Justice Darling, quieting the courtroom again. He explained that although there was much to dislike in terms of Slater's conduct, and that he was probably guilty of neglecting his business, there was not sufficient evidence that Slater had been involved in the Pollard conspiracy to put to a jury.[391] Rufus Isaacs therefore stood up, and formally asked for the jury to return a verdict of 'not guilty' against the man they called Henry Scott. This was done, and Mr Isaacs now turned to leave the court.

Slater had been seated quietly in a corner of the dock. Now, though, a warder opened the gate to the dock, and, realising that he was free again, he stepped down into the court, and on seeing Rufus Isaacs making his way to the exit, he lost his previous cool and reserved demeanour and started shaking. He bounded across the court, ran up the exit steps, and grabbed Isaacs' gown. The latter turned, surprised, to see Slater holding out his hand to him. The two men shook hands - with the detective agency boss wringing his counsel's hands repeatedly before he sank back onto the nearest chair, exhausted. While this was going on, Frederick Davies sat in the dock with tears running down his cheeks.

Slater was immediately a free man, and with his acquittal, the press felt that the main news was written. Even Justice Darling informed the jury that it was probable the case would now end on the next day it sat - there would be less than a day of court left. He was right. On Monday, 7 November, all the remaining men - now without their boss - gathered again in the Central Criminal Court to hear judgement against them. For Albert Osborn, the day was a frustrating one. After all the evidence, all the witnesses, the accounts of his journeys down to Plymouth and his attempts to get written statements from the Devon women, the jury could still not agree between them what his role had been, and the jury members were duly discharged from making a verdict. Osborn was therefore released on bail, to face another trial at the next Sessions. For the men further down the career and social ladder, the jury had no such qualms about what to do. They were all found guilty. George Philip Henry, as the day-to-day manager of Slater's Detective Agency, was sentenced to twelve months in prison. The judge believed that this was probably not the first time he had acted unethically. Then, Frederick Stanley Davies and Cyril Broughton Smith - seen by the judge as the 'tools' of George Henry - were sentenced to six months each. John Pracy received a three-month sentence, his role being considered to be less important than the other two detectives. The four men were led off to serve their sentences, the guilty verdicts covered in an unusually concise way by the British press.[392] Once Henry Slater, the main man, had been freed, much of the impetus to cover the case dissipated; especially so as the inveterate publicist had now gone incredibly quiet.

One might have expected Slater to agree to press interviews now he had been found not guilty - to stress his innocence and to use the verdict to renew his relations with the press. But he realised that this was still the end for him: he had been acquitted, but his detectives hadn't been. The trial had seen his agency's reputation destroyed, and he had been exposed as a man who faked his identity, who had a dark past involving multiple career changes and a desire to ruin his previous employer. His reputation as a man to trust had been shattered. Likewise, how could his agency survive? Slater's Detective Agency had once been seen as the top detective agency not just in London but the UK; it was the place to go to get problems solved. Now, though, it was viewed as a place where criminal activity took place, where detectives would fake evidence where none could be found. It summed up everything that parts of society – from police and press to the public – disliked about the profession, playing into their fears about what private detectives got up to. Judge Darling had commented that the trial had rightly 'stamped out' the agency.[393] Slater's agency was indeed no more; and neither was Henry Slater.

The story was not quite over, though. Kate Pollard still wanted her divorce, but her estranged husband would soon give her the evidence she needed without private detectives having to fake it. Everybody had under-rated Thomas Pollard. He had been dismissed as a lazy layabout – an alcoholic who wanted nothing more than to sponge off his wife, his parents, friends and even strangers – and had come across as a sad, pathetic creature in court. In fact, there was some sympathy for Kate, his long-suffering wife. However, his past – his travels, his prior marriage to an American woman, and his desertion of his first-born son – hinted at a more complex personality.

Back in 1901, the Plymouth census recorded Thomas Pollard's parents as living with a woman named Emma Amelia Toll, together with her widowed father.[394] Thomas had known Emma, and been friends with her – a fact not noted anywhere in the trial. This friendship, at some point, turned into more. By 1905, Thomas was in an established relationship with Emma. He was still legally married; she was single. She became pregnant, but needed to give birth away from everyone they knew in Devon; they were not quite quick enough, for Plymouth locals had spotted that Emma was visibly pregnant. However, one day, she simply disappeared from Plymouth, never to be seen there again. Thomas had engaged rooms at Eastbourne Terrace in Paddington, London, and moved there on 11 May 1905. Three days later, Emma Toll gave birth to a son, Jeffrey, at Queen Charlotte's Lying-In Hospital. Located on the Marylebone Road at the time, this was one of England's oldest maternity homes, having been founded nearly two centuries earlier. Under an assumed name, Emma had her son, but did not register his birth. Within a few days, she returned to the rooms on Eastbourne Terrace.

A month later, on 19 June, Thomas, Emma, and their baby boy left London for Liverpool, staying one night at the Adelphi Hotel and then two nights at the Imperial Hotel on Lime Street. Then, on 22 June, Thomas, Emma, and their baby boarded a steamship, the *Victorian*, at Liverpool docks, bound for Canada. There was excitement aboard the long journey, however. Hugh Knowles, who had been financially supporting Kate since the Old Bailey trial concluded, had engaged another private detective to track Thomas down. This private detective was a very different beast to Henry Slater's tribe, however. John Conquest was a former Metropolitan Police detective inspector, and he got legitimate results. It is through him that we know what Thomas' actions after the trial were.[395]

Conquest traced Thomas Pollard to London, and at Eastbourne Terrace, interviewed the other residents. He discovered that Pollard was still a drinker, and that when drunk, he had happily told these new 'friends' who he really was, that he was the infamous husband who had been talked about in the Slater trial. He had also boasted of having been married three times, with each of his wives giving birth to a son; he did not admit that Emma was not, in fact, his third wife. He and Emma had taken the rooms under the name of Radcliffe, but Conquest needed to find out who 'Mrs Radcliffe' really was. His enquiries in Plymouth discovered that it was Emma Toll - the pregnant woman who had disappeared from the town.

Tom Pollard was served with new divorce papers by the terrier-like John Conquest, while on board the transatlantic ship. He admitted everything; 'You must know I can't resist the suit. Everyone must see I am living with the lady.'[396] Interestingly, Tom was now going by the name of Colonel Radcliffe; like Henry Slater, he liked a title that he was not entitled to, aiming to impress those he came into contact with. His title suggested a status that he did not have, and this is likely to have been the same reason Slater had adopted the rank of captain: it denoted a certain respectability and social clout.

On arrival at their final destination of Montreal, Tom and Emma registered at the Grand Union Hotel as a married couple, before settling at the city's Queens Hotel. Emma then sent a letter home so that her elderly father would know where she was. Tom Pollard then fades from the record, but Emma is known to have remained in Canada. Suffering with tuberculosis from at least 1911, she was admitted to Ontario's Rockwood Hospital, where she died on 27 December 1916. Her occupation was given as housewife, but her marital status as single. Tom Pollard never married her, and nor did he look after his youngest son, who was sent to the local workhouse when his mother became ill.[397]

John Conquest had easily found evidence that Slater's agency had not, but the two images of Thomas Pollard that result conflict with each other. On the one hand, there is the drunken layabout who detectives struggled to get to have sex with a prostitute. This is the man who wandered into pubs looking for strangers to buy him drinks, and who relied on money from his estranged wife to survive. On the other is a man who got his lover pregnant, boasted about being a 'celebrity' in the news to his neighbours, ran to Liverpool with Emma when she was still recovering from the birth of her child, and then fled to Canada with her. How he paid for all of this is not known; how he managed to get not only across the country but across the Atlantic while apparently reliant on drink is equally unknown. It is possible that lawyers succeeded in presenting an image of Thomas Pollard that was something of a fiction, wanting him to be seen as a pathetic fall-guy. Conversely, he could have been cleverer than the detectives realised and was playing them, realising that they were trying to use him and getting them to pay his way. Either way, he succeeded in making Slater's detectives look both amateur and desperate. So too did John Conquest through his dogged shadowing of Pollard and his success in finding believable evidence.

Because of Conquest's evidence, Kate Pollard was more successful with her second divorce petition than her first, gaining her *decree nisi* on 24 April 1906. Perhaps to nobody's surprise, four months later, on 9 August, she entered Paddington Register Office and quietly married her long-time supporter and financial benefactor, Hugh Knowles. Two years later, the couple had a son. The Pollards' son Reginald duly adopted his stepfather's surname, and the Knowles family settled at their homes in Kensington and Brighton. The marriage survived until Hugh's death in 1940; Kate relocated to the Summertown area of Oxford, and died there in 1960.

And what of the other main characters in this story? Going back to December 1904, a month after the Old Bailey trial, the attorney-general entered a *nolte prosequi* (no prosecution) record for Albert Osborn, and he was finally free to continue his life as a solicitor, living with his wife and nephew in Kensington. He died in 1919. George Henry was released from Wormwood Scrubs prison in November 1905, and returned to his wife and son in Southend-on-Sea, taking up work as a builder's collector, collecting payments.

The Slater's detectives had varied fortunes after they were released from Wormwood Scrubs. John Pracy started work as a self-employed confectioner, living in various parts of London, and dying in 1944. Fred Davies may have lived with his brother in north London on his release, surviving until the mid-1950s. Cyril Broughton Smith never married, but on his release from prison lived in west London and worked as a surveyor, corn agent, and commission agent. He died in 1946. Their fortunes after the trial were as varied as the men who had given evidence against them in the case. William Hamilton, who also worked on the Pollard divorce case, continued working as a private enquiry agent but by the time of the 1911 census was in the City of London Union Workhouse Infirmary, where he died of chronic bronchitis and heart failure six months later. Henry Iles became an insurance agent and then an engineering agent in south London. Joseph McKenna was employed at a detective agency run by competitor Herbert Marshall, before moving to work for former detective inspector turned private detective John Sweeney on Regent Street. By 1921, he was the chief inquiry inspector for Pickford's Carriers.

And now for the fortunes of Simmonds' Detective Association and its main players – the men who were keen to ruin Slater, and those who defected to it. Charles Simmonds himself continued to work as a private detective, but by 1921, described himself as an unemployed one. He was a long-time resident of the Chertsey area of Surrey, but may have died in Kent in 1946. Francis Stevens, Slater's nemesis, had established Simmonds' agency with Simmonds and Edgar Cartwright, donating a substantial amount of money towards it. However, from at least 1908, he was a manufacturer's agent for hardware exports, and in the 1930s, described himself as a builder. He died in Hampstead in 1947, aged 86.

Edgar Cartwright had cause to employ Albert Osborn as his solicitor in 1904, when he sought a divorce from one of his wives, Florence, on the grounds of Florence's alleged 'incapacity to consummate the marriage' (something Florence angrily denied). By 1912, he had left Simmonds, and established his own detective agency, Wright's, based at Moorgate in the City of London, with a second office on Oxford Street. This agency, where former Slater's man Samuel Marrison also worked, survived until at least 1940. Cartwright, who lived in Southend and London, died in 1959.[398]

Private detectives were known for their adoption of fake names and identities as part of their job; in fact, in court, there had been questions about whether all the detectives employed by Slater's took on extra identities. John Pracy was John Bray; George Henry was Henry Slater Jr. But so many of the other people in this book also took on different names. Hugh Knowles was born Hugh Kino, and Albert Osborn was born Albert Ochse.[399] Victorian and Edwardian society was, in part, based on a house of cards. It was all about appearance, of the illusion of being someone. In Osborn's and Knowles' cases, their new identities obscured their origins as the children of immigrants to Britain, designed to remove prejudice against them and to enable their families to move up the social ladder. In the detectives' case, their different names both enabled them to carry out investigations without risk of being exposed, differentiating between their work and home identities, and to give the impression of a higher social status. Kate Pollard changed her name on both her marriages, each surname giving her a different status. As a Pollard, she would come to see her name as a reminder of her unemployed husband, but as a Knowles, she would be a respectable, upper middle-class wife and mother.

In adopting these different names and identities, these individuals highlighted the constant flux of their society, and the ability to fake a life and status, even if only for a while before being exposed. They also highlight, though, the link between detective work and the theatrical profession. Some detectives were former actors and actresses – and even Henry Slater himself had been on the amateur stage in his youth.[400] To be a detective involved taking on a role, to immerse oneself in someone else's life, and to 'pass' as a member of someone else's society. You might have to dress differently, adopt a different accent or personality, in order to get someone's trust – or to remain anonymous to them, to not stand out or draw attention to oneself. No wonder that John Pracy was described by one paper, as he stood in court, as 'passing for an actor' in terms of his appearance.[401]

The ultimate actor, with his multiple names and identities, was, of course, the boss – Henry Slater himself. In November 1904, he left the Old Bailey, and in doing so, shed for good his identity as the extrovert, well-known private detective. It was now time for his final role.

Chapter 17

A Final Identity

At the close of his trial, George Tinsley, aka Henry Scott, aka Henry Slater, was theoretically a free man, acquitted of the charges against him and, unlike his colleagues, not destined for prison. At this point in the narrative, he appeared to have been ruined. His agency, and its methods, had been called to account, with the whole private detective industry being attacked by the judge and the press. It was no wonder that Slater's agency disappeared. The name of Henry Slater didn't entirely disappear, though. Two years after the verdict, when Kate Pollard finally got her divorce, she merited a few mentions in the press again. Each mention of her successful divorce linked her again with the detective agency Hugh Knowles had employed.

Henry Slater also lived on through the desire of others to have what they perceived as an exciting life like his. In fact, this had started before the court case, as can be seen in the existence of a Henry Slater in the 1901 census. This was a man living in East Ham, claiming to be a private detective. On an initial view, this looks like it should be the man himself, for there is no other individual on this census claiming to be him. Yet on closer look, key facts differ: this Henry Slater has middle names - George Kenneth - and claims to have been born in America, whereas the real individual, although his birthplace changes over time, never said he was born anywhere other than London.[402] This imposter also turns up in marriage records and the 1911 census, each time adding new elements to his backstory.[403] He is the son of a secret service agent in America; he grows younger on each document; he takes on new partners quickly, each time adding or changing a name. One wife had a fake name and disappeared quickly. Another wife was abandoned to a London workhouse, while a third outlived him, having realised that her husband was an impostor.[404] Henry Slater may have been ruined professionally by his trial, but others continued to want to impersonate him, seeing him as the epitome of glamour and intrigue. Many people equated real-life detectives with fictional ones, imbuing them with the same glamour; some seem to have adopted the persona of Henry Slater to make themselves appear more interesting. The individual mentioned above 'improved' the name, exaggerating it, and creating a new persona from one that George Tinsley had created in the first place. At one point, the occupation claimed by this man changes from private detective to entertainer. One feels that Slater, the former minstrel and glee-singer, would have approved.

Pretending to be Slater after 1904 was made easier by the fact that the real man had gone underground. He had realised that the Slater name was forever tarnished; in addition, it was a pseudonym created for the purpose of running a detective agency - if the agency no longer existed, there was no need for Slater to exist either. His deputy, Henry Slater Junior, was now George Henry again, and would live a quiet retirement in Southend-on-Sea, near Tinsley's own family, but his boss chose not to revert to his birth name. For a year while researching this book, I was unable to find out what had happened to George Tinsley after 1904; his wife Emma was easier to follow, living quietly in Southend until her death in 1939. In 1911, she described herself as married, but in the 1939 register, she called herself a widow. Was this a guess, or did she know that her husband had died at some point within those decades? It was unclear, as was George Tinsley's fate. Then a random local newspaper article published nearly two decades after Emma Tinsley's death, in 1958, suddenly opened up a whole new life. It also proved that Emma had known exactly when her husband had died.

By 1901, George Tinsley, aka Henry Slater, Henry Scott, and Henry Brown, had started a relationship with a woman named Elizabeth Akers. Elizabeth was a labourer's daughter from North Kensington, twenty years younger than Slater. How they met is not known, but the first evidence for them knowing each other can be found in the marriage of Elizabeth's younger sister Alice, which took place in the Wiltshire village of Lydiard Millicent - now a suburb of Swindon - on 14 August 1901. The marriage was witnessed by Elizabeth Akers and a man named Henry Gordon. Henry Gordon cannot be found in any other local records; but the way he wrote his signature is rather similar to the surviving signatures of George Tinsley.[405] It also appears that Francis Stevens was entrusted not only with Henry Slater's real name, but also with the identity of his partner. When Slater went to Australia in January 1902, Stevens was aware that he had travelled with 'his niece, Miss Baker'. This is how the name was recorded in a 1903 newspaper article - but it is surely a mistranscription of 'Miss Akers'.[406] Slater may have pretended she was his niece for the sake of both their reputations, but she was certainly closer to him than this title would suggest.

Henry Gordon was the latest incarnation of Henry Slater, and by 1905, this identity had further developed to become George Henry Gordon - the first names reflecting both his birth name and his famous adopted one. As with his persona of Henry Scott, he claimed to have changed his name by deed poll, but again, there is no proof that he actually did so; he simply thought of a name, and started to be known by it. He did not need to work, as he earned a great deal from his detective work, and had substantial savings to live on.

Henry Slater's last home in England displayed this fortune to the world. In 1921, he is listed, under his final pseudonym, at 3 Haslemere Road in Crouch End. Part of the local conservation area, the road is a quiet, leafy, winding one between Crouch Hill and Crouch End. Number three is a substantial, detached, late Victorian villa, set back from the road and shielded today by trees.[407] It is substantially larger and grander than the terraced villas in which George Tinsley had spent his married life; and in a leafier, more salubrious area than Emma Tinsley's homes in Tottenham. The 1921 census for this address records Elizabeth Akers as the head of household, and 'Henry Gordon' as her lodger; this may have been done for both financial and personal reasons, neither wanting to bring Elizabeth's reputation into disrepute, and Henry still being married. Up until the year of the demise of Slater's agency, a house almost opposite Slater's had been home to Frank Matcham - the theatre architect whose London hotel had been the temporary home of the Plymouth girls brought down to give evidence against Henry Slater's detectives.

In the mid-1920s, the former detective gave his address as 46 Finsbury Square, back in the City of London, a business address that he could only have used for a relatively short period of time, given the presence of other tenants during that decade. The use of that address suggests that 'Gordon' may have continued to have business interests in the city, but there is no proof of what they might have been.[408] They were certainly enough to keep him in a life of some luxury; George Henry Gordon died on 5 December 1926, not in London, but at Hyères, in the South of France, aged 77.[409] He was an elderly man, living his last days in a sunny town facing the Mediterranean. He might not have ever been linked to Henry Slater, if it wasn't for the will he left; a will that also shed light on his hidden childhood, and led to the newspaper article in the 1950s.

George Henry Gordon had left the bulk of his estate to Elizabeth Akers, and she lived off it until 1951, when she died in Salisbury.[410] Under the terms of the will, on Elizabeth Akers' death, several bequests had to be made on Gordon's behalf. These included the continuance of Emma Tinsley's maintenance - which after her death had been paid to one of their daughters - but also several bequests to members of the Park Lane Chapel Sunday School in Chelsea.

A Final Identity 169

These bequests were very specific: one to the harmonium player, one to the girls of the school, one to the boys.[411] It strongly suggests an emotional attachment to the place. George Tinsley presumably used to go to the Sunday school, but it had been a long time ago. He had lost touch with the area of his childhood, and those who worked there, and had failed to realise that in 1913, the Park Lane Chapel had been demolished. It had since been replaced by a new church – St Andrew's.

Now, members of his family argued that given that there was no evidence that there had been a Park Lane Chapel Sunday School, and that the chapel itself no longer existed, they should have the money that Gordon had bequeathed. Representatives from St Andrew's Church, however, felt the church should receive it as the successor to Park Lane Chapel. No link was made between 'GH Gordon', as he was described in the articles, and Henry Slater; memories were short in the press world, and times had moved on, despite 'Gordon's' estranged wife being listed as a Tinsley. The case showed continued differences between family members, for youngest daughter Winifred, and Amy Tinsley's daughter Vera Storrar both made clear that they didn't want to contest the validity of the bequests, whereas older sister Lilian did.[412] In the event, St Andrew's Church was determined to be entitled to the bequests.

Today, the only physical evidence of Henry Slater's existence, outside of press cuttings, lies in north London. In the former St Marylebone Cemetery in East Finchley, halfway along its Central Avenue, are a line of rather impressive headstones, facing the avenue. The last one before a large tree is one topped with a large cross. It reads:

To the very dear memory of George Henry Gordon/Who passed to the higher life/December 5th 1926

And then, below, text is inscribed. The text is not, as one might expect, a Bible verse or two, but the first and last verses from an 1899 poem by the Black American poet Paul Laurence Dunbar, *When all is done*.[413]

The words were ordered to be inscribed by the faithful Elizabeth Akers - whose own cremated remains were buried in the same grave in 1951, and whose name is inscribed on the side of the grave. They remember the man who reinvented himself several times. George Tinsley died, to be replaced by Henry Slater. Henry Slater died, to be replaced by George Henry Gordon, his first names an amalgamation of his previous identities. Each time he wanted to be a different person, he killed off the old one, setting the sun on his previous lives and, like the sun, rising again to start a new day. When he finally died for real, those he left behind must have found it hard to believe that he really had gone this time, and would not return under a different guise. He was a larger-than-life character whom other people's lives revolved around, the centre of life for Emma Tinsley and Elizabeth Akers, and the detectives who worked for him at his Basinghall Street agency.

For two years, I sought to find out what had happened to Henry Slater at the end of his trial. His apparent disappearance into nowhere seemed improbable; and although I could guess at him changing his identity again, without the 1958 press article detailing the problems with his 32-year-old will, he would have remained impossible to find. In a way, it feels a let-down. This was a story about a showman, an extroverted character who refused to stay a humble clerk, but who instead became a man of many trades. He was a private detective who achieved fame (and later infamy) through his innovative use of publicity tactics. Yet he was also a man largely estranged from his family, separated from his wife, living a quiet life in London and France. However, mystery remains. It's still not clear why Gordon insisted that his will wasn't read for eleven months after his death, and nor do I know what else he did for the quarter century after his agency closed.

Even his final years as a detective agency boss are shrouded in doubt and intrigue. He was living not just a double life - one involving his wife and children, the other involving the Akers family – but a multiple one, as Henry Slater, Henry Scott, George Tinsley, Captain Brown, and George Henry Gordon. During the course of the King's Proctor's case at the divorce court, Sir Edward Carson had commented that he hoped the case might help establish who Henry Slater was, because there were so many identities held by the man in charge.[414] But had the case – which occupied the attention of the Edwardian press and public for most of 1904 – really established who Slater really was?

He was a man who was also a juggler, keeping all these identities going. By the Edwardian era, he was maintaining at least two homes for himself, one for his family, and perhaps a fourth already with Elizabeth Akers; he claimed that for periods he was away in Australia, when there are no passenger records for individuals of around the right age under any of his adopted names. Was he really away, or was he closeted with his friend Elizabeth, living a quiet life away from the shenanigans of his detectives? From this distance of history, it is impossible to know the real story behind his later years, or his motivation for this constant shifting of his own personal reality.

I discovered his final identity, and his final resting place. I knelt in the Central Avenue of the cemetery at East Finchley one cold December day to photograph the grave I had been looking for – but despite this, and my searching, his origins remain cloudy. The 12-year-old living with his grandfather at the coffee-shop in Chelsea back in 1861 emerged from nowhere. His parents still can't be found, nor the reason his birth wasn't registered and nor a baptism recorded. George Tinsley's birth and childhood were not preserved for prosperity, although Henry Slater later ensured that his career would be. It's still not clear how he met Elizabeth Akers, nor what exactly their relationship was – whether it was a master-servant one, a friendship, or a sexual relationship – but the archives suggest that he found himself part of the Akers family, and embraced that. As with much of Henry Slater's life, the sequence in which events happened, and why he adopted a whole raft of identities, is impossible to decipher without him being able to tell us, but it does point to an individual who was never satisfied with who he was, and despite his fame, wanted the anonymity of a pseudonym... or four.[415]

The man with several identities found more than one family for himself, and more than one career; but it is as the private detective that Henry Slater achieved fame, and although his doubtful legacy might have been the request by judges for there to be a form of registration and standards for private detectives to abide by in future, he showed how for the Victorian man, anything was possible - with a bit of creativity, determination, and an inquisitive mind. Nearly a century and a half since his heyday, I hope my own inquisitiveness and detection work in tracking him down would make Henry Slater proud.

Bibliography

Books

Abelson, Elaine S, *When Ladies Go A-Thieving: Middle-Class Shoplifters in the Victorian Department Store* (OUP, Oxford, 1989)

Begg, Paul and Bennett, John, *Jack the Ripper: The Forgotten Victims* (Yale University Press, 2014)

Darby, Nell, *Sister Sleuths: Female Detectives in Britain* (Pen & Sword, Barnsley, 2021)

Froëst, Frank, *The Grell Mystery* (WM Collins & Son, 1913, rpt 2015)

Gray, Drew, *London's Shadows: The Dark Side of the Victorian City* (Bloomsbury, London, 2013)

Hayhurst, Alan, *Staffordshire Murders* (The History Press, Stroud, 2008)

Kesselman, Bryan, *'Paddington' Pollaky, Private Detective: The Mysterious Life and Times of the Real Sherlock Holmes* (The History Press, Stroud, 2015)

Pinkerton, Allan, *The Expressman and the Detective* (WB Keen, Cooke & Co, Chicago, 1874)

Shpayer-Makov, Haia, *The Making of a Policeman: a social history of a labour force in metropolitan London 1829-1914* (Ashgate, Farnham, 2002)

Shpayer-Makov, Haia, *The Ascent of the Detective: Police Sleuths in Victorian and Edwardian England* (OUP, Oxford, 2012)

Slinn, Judy, *A History of Freshfields* (Freshfields, London, 1984)

Stapleton, Susannah, *The Adventures of Maud West, Lady Detective* (Picador, London, 2019)

Articles and reports

Abelson, Elaine S., 'The Invention of Kleptomania', *Signs*, 15:1 (Autumn 1989), pp.123-143

Anon., 'London Borough of Haringey: Conservation Area No 5 Crouch End: Conservation Area Character Appraisal, Appendix 1' (2010) (www.haringey.gov.uk/sites/haringeygovuk/files/crouch_end_character_appraisal_web_viewing_compress_0.pdf)

Anon., 'Old Manor Hospital', ArtCare (n.d.), https://salisburyhealthcarehistory.uk/old-manor-hospital/

Black, Erin, 'Damnation Alley: Plymouth's forgotten street of brothels and sin', *Plymouth Herald*, 21 September 2019

Bolton, Diane K., Croot, Patricia E.C. and Hicks, M.A., 'Chiswick: Growth', in T.F.T. Baker and C.R. Elrington (eds), A History of the County of Middlesex: Volume 7: Acton, Chiswick, Ealing and Brentford, West Twyford, Willesden (London, 1982), *British History Online* (www.british-history.ac.uk/vch/middx/vol7/pp54-68)

Caldwell-Smith, Peter, 'Annual Report on the Health, Sanitary Condition, etc of the borough, for the year 1914' (Metropolitan Borough of Wandsworth) (https://wellcomelibrary.org/moh/report/b18250828/204#?c=0&m=0&s=0&cv=204&z=-1.6322%2C0.5292%2C4.2645%2C1.6802)

Calinescu, Dan, 'Dickens' Short-Hand Writer's Business Card (1830)', *Victorian Web* (www.victorianweb.org/authors/dickens/gallery/109.html)

Chittick, Kathryn, 'Dickens and Parliamentary Reporting in the 1830s', *Victorian Periodicals Review*, 21:4 (1988)

Clegg, Gill, 'Housing Schemes', *Gill Clegg's Chiswick History Web Pages* (Brentford and Chiswick Local History Society, n.d.) (https://brentfordandchiswicklhs.org.uk/search-discover/chiswick-history-homepage/housing-schemes/)

Croot, Patricia E.C. (ed), 'Settlement and building: from 1680 to 1865, Little Chelsea, Sandy End and World's End', A History of the County of Middlesex: Volume 12: Chelsea, *British History Online* (www.british-history.ac.uk/vch/mddx/vol12/pp61-66)

Donald, Robert, 'The Wool Exchange at Work', *Good Words, Volume 39* (January 1898), pp.814-818

Enss, Chris, 'Wild Women of the West: Hattie Lawton', *Cowgirl* magazine (5 July 2017), at https://cowgirlmagazine.com/hattie-lawton-wild-women-wednesday/

Flaherty, Anne (ed), 'The District Line Celebrates 150th Anniversary', *ChiswickW4* (29 January 2019) (www.chiswickw4.com)

Higgs, Michelle, 'Making Ends Meet - The Role of the Victorian Pawnbrokers', 9 January 2014 (http://visitvictorianengland.blogspot.com/2014/01/making-ends-meet-role-of-victorian.html)

Lloyd, Matthew, 'Theatres and Halls in Plymouth', *ArthurLloyd.co.uk* (www.arthurlloyd.co.uk)

Lloyd, Matthew, 'Theatres and Halls in Jersey', *ArthurLloyd.co.uk* (www.arthurlloyd.co.uk)

Hallett, Christine, 'The Attempt to Understand Puerperal Fever in the Eighteenth and Early Nineteenth Centuries: The Influence of Inflammation Theory', *Medical History* 49(1) (2005), pp.1-28

Musgrove, F., 'Middle-class education and employment in the nineteenth century', *Economic History Review*, 12:1 (1959)

Picard, Liza, 'Education in Victorian Britain', British Library (2009) (www.bl.uk/victorian-britain/articles/education-in-victorian-britain)

Picard, Liza, 'The Victorian Middle Classes', British Library (2009) (www.bl.uk/victorian/britain/articles/the-victorian-middle-classes)

Powell, W.R. (ed), 'West Ham: Transport and postal services', A History of the County of Essex: Volume 6 (London, 1973), pp.61-63. *British History Online* (www.british-history.ac.uk/vch/essex/vol6/pp61-63)

Rushton, Steve, 'Notting Dale reveals Britain's slide back toward Victorian levels of inequality', *Occupy.com*, 24 July 2017 (www.occupy.com/article/notting-dale-reveals-britain-s-slide-back-toward-victorian-levels-inequality#sthash.qPAXoeWF.dpbs)

Savage, Gail L, 'The operation of the 1857 Divorce Act, 1860-1910, a research note', *Journal of Social History*, 16:4 (1983)

Schneider, Wendie Ellen, 'Secrets and Lies: The Queen's Proctor and Judicial Investigation of Party-Controlling Narratives', *Law & Social Inquiry*, 27:3 (2002)

Sheppard HW (ed), 'The Potteries and the Bramley Road area and the Rise of the Housing Problem in North Kensington', Survey of London: Volume 37, Northern Kensington (London County Council, 1973), pp.340-355. *British History Online* (www.british-history.ac.uk/survey-london/vol37/pp340-355)

Walford, Edward, 'Chelsea', in Old and New London: Volume 5 (London, 1878), pp.50-70. *British History Online* (www.british-history.ac.uk/old-new-london/vol5/pp50-70)

Walkowitz, Judith R and Walkowitz, Daniel J, "We are not beasts of the field": Prostitution and the poor in Plymouth and Southampton under the Contagious Diseases Act', *Feminist Studies*, 1: 3/4 (Winter-Spring 1973)

Wallop, Harry, 'Victorian England: a nation of coffee drinkers', *The Telegraph*, 15 July 2010 (www.telegraph.co.uk/news/uknews/7892631/Victorian-England-a-nation-of-coffee-drinkers.html)

Theses

Pointon, Vivien F.T., 'Mid-Victorian Plymouth: A Social Geography' (PhD thesis, Polytechnic South West, 1989), https://core.ac.uk/download/pdf/29817146.pdf

Websites

Ancestry (www.ancestry.co.uk)
ArthurLloyd.co.uk (www.arthurlloyd.co.uk)
British Museum (www.britishmuseum.org)
British Newspaper Archive (www.britishnewspaperarchive.co.uk)
Capital Punishment UK (www.capitalpunishmentuk.org)
ChiswickW4 (www.chiswickw4.com)
Freshfields (www.freshfields.com/en-gb/about-us/our-history/)
General Register Office (www.gro.gov.uk)
Her Majesty's Courts Service, 'Royal Courts of Justice Visitors Guides' (www.hmcourts-service.gov.uk/infoabout/rcj/history.htm)
Library of Congress (www.loc.gov)
London Picture Archive (www.londonpicturearchive.org)
Old Bailey Proceedings Online (www.oldbaileyonline.org)
Pinkerton (www.pinkerton.com)
Probate Search (https://probatesearch.service.gov.uk)

Silchester Residents' Association, 'Notting Dale History' (www.silchesterestate.org/about-us/notting-dale-history)
TheGenealogist (www.thegenealogist.co.uk)
The National Archives (www.nationalarchives.gov.uk)
Victorian London (www.victorianlondon.org)
Victorian Web (www.victorianweb.org)
Wellcome Library (www.wellcomelibrary.org)
Whistler Paintings (www.whistlerpaintings.gla.ac.uk)
Wright State University (www.libraries.wright.edu)

Notes

Much of the Old Bailey trial coverage is taken from Old Bailey Proceedings Online (www.oldbaileyonline.org), October 1904, trial of Henry Scott (55), otherwise Henry Slater; George Philip Henry; Albert Osborn, John Pracey [sic] (32), otherwise John Bray; Frederick Stanley Davies (39); Cyril Broughton Smith (35) (t19041017-788).

Newspaper reports have been taken from newspapers at the British Newspaper Archive and The Times Digital Archive. Divorce records from The National Archives have been accessed via Ancestry (www.ancestry.co.uk). Freemasonry and probate records have also been accessed via Ancestry with the latter also accessed via https://probatesearch.service.gov.uk. Census records have been accessed via Ancestry and TheGenealogist (www.thegenealogist.co.uk).

Preface

1. *Westminster Gazette*, 13 February 1893.

Introduction

2. Her Majesty's Courts Service, 'Royal Courts of Justice Visitors Guide', www.hmcourts-service.gov.uk/infoabout/rcj/history.htm.
3. Wendie Ellen Schneider, 'Secrets and Lies: The Queen's Proctor and Judicial Investigation of Party-Controlled Narratives', *Law & Social Inquiry*, 27:3 (2002), p.449.
4. Questions taken from the trial reports in the *Dundee Courier*, 31 March 1904, p.5; *Daily Telegraph*, 31 March 1904, p.4; and *St James's Gazette*, 31 March 1904, p.14.

Chapter 1: When Kate Met Tom... and Hugh

5. W.R. Powell (ed), 'West Ham: Transport and postal services', A History of the County of Essex: Volume 6 (London, 1973), pp.61-63. *British History Online* (www.british-history.ac.uk/vch/essex/vol6/pp61-63).
6. Both the 1871 and 1881 censuses give Henry's birthplace as Bow, East London, but baptism records for Layston, Hertfordshire (Buntingford being within the parish of Layston at that time) show that Henry John Sampson, son of William Carter and Maria Sampson, was baptised there on 28 August 1831. Henry's father, William, was a tailor born and bred in Buntingford, although sometime between 1841 and 1849 he would have himself moved to London; initially to Mile End, before moving to Bermondsey by 1851. By 1858, he had returned to Buntingford, although he would later again move to London - the 1891 census records the octogenarian William and Maria Sampson living in Walthamstow.
7. The 1871 census for Church Row, Southwark, records the presence of a daughter, Harriett A Sampson, aged 11 months and born in Portslade. This is likely to have been Jessie Hannah, various permutations of her name being recorded in the archives.
8. Some accounts state that she was born in the Brighton area, like her brother Frank and sister Jessie, but the 1871 census records the family as living back in London. Given that they were, at that time, living in Church Row, part of the parish of St Olive Horsleydown - and that Kate's birthplace is given in other sources as Horsleydown - it seems likely that the family had permanently returned to the greater London area by this point, although it doesn't explain why Kate's birth was registered in the Brighton district.
9. Fowell Street and its surrounding roads were demolished under a slum clearance order to build the Lancaster West Estate. This was designed in the early 1960s, and at the centre of it was Grenfell Tower, which caught fire in 2017.
10. Steve Rushton, 'Notting Dale reveals Britain's slide back toward Victorian levels of inequality', Occupy.com (24 July 2017), www.occupy.com/article/notting-dale-reveals-britain-s-slide-back-toward-victorian-levels-inequality#sthash.qPAXoeWF.dpbs.

11. Silchester Residents' Association, 'Notting Dale History', www.silchesterestate.org.uk/about-us/notting-dale-history/.
12. St Francis was presumably the St Francis of Assisi school on Pottery Lane, although I've been unable to ascertain when this school, which still exists, was open; British History merely records that it is 'of unknown date'. Both it and the associated church were designed to cater for the poorer residents of the area, which included a substantial Irish Catholic community H.W. Sheppard (ed), 'The Potteries and the Bramley Road area and the Rise of the Housing Problem in North Kensington', *Survey of London: Volume 37, Northern Kensington* (London County Council, 1973), pp.340-355, at *British History Online* (www.british-history.ac.uk/survey-london/vol37/pp340-355).
13. The 1911 census for 55 Ridley Road shows that at this time, the house comprised five rooms, including the kitchen and downstairs living area. In 1891, Henry was absent from home, but when present, he was one of five people living there: he and Jane, daughters Jessie and Kate, and two male boarders.
14. *London Evening Standard*, 25 April 1906, p.9.
15. *The Sun* (New York), 30 December 1887, p.1; *South Wales Echo*, 20 January 1888, p.2.
16. Christine Hallett, 'The Attempt to Understand Puerperal Fever in the Eighteenth and Early Nineteenth Centuries: The Influence of Inflammation Theory', *Medical History* 49(1), pp.1-28 (2005).
17. Information taken from the death certificate of Leslie Hepburn Pollard (died 12 July 1890 and registered 14 July 1890 in the Superintendent Registrar's District of Lewisham; Registrar's Sub-District of Lee) and the birth certificate of Leslie Buckler Pollard (born 3 July 1890 and registered 14 July 1890 in the Superintendent Registrar's District of Lewisham; Registrar's Sub-District of Lee). Accessed from the General Register Office website (www.gro.gov.uk).
18. At another time, the couple lived at Bedford Place in Bloomsbury, but I have not been able to ascertain when exactly this was.
19. Baptisms of Leslie Hepburn Buckler Pollard, son of Thomas Pollard of 11 Chippenham Road, wine merchant, and Leslie Hepburn Buckler, and Reginald Pollard, son of Thomas Pollard of 11 Chippenham

Road, wine merchant, and Kate Pollard, at St Peter's, Paddington, both on 4 January 1894 (www.ancestry.co.uk). Little Leslie's name was registered as Leslie Buckler Pollard, but he was baptised with his mother's full name.

20. 'Mrs Charles Julius Kino/Knowles (nee Louisa Essinger)' at 'The Paintings of James McNeill Whistler: A Catalogue Raisonné' (www.whistlerpaintings.gla.ac.uk/catalogue/names/result/?nid=KnowMrs&filter=all) and 'Charles Julius Knowles' at The British Museum (www.britishmuseum.org/collection/term/BIOG34011).

21. 1881 census for 3 Edinburgh Terrace, Kensington. The 1891 census records Hugh and three younger siblings at home at '7 The Terrace' in Kensington; although their parents are absent, they have the governess, parlourmaid, housemaid, nurse and kitchenmaid present to keep an eye on them.

22. The estate of Charles Julius Knowles of 17 Kensington Gore and Glebe House Sherborne Lane. Reported in *Daily Telegraph* of 23 March 1900. Charles was listed as formerly being of the Wood Street Clothing and Woollen Warehouse Company, promoter of the City and Westminster Properties (Limited) and of the London Woollen Company (Limited).

23. 1901 census for 46 Hampton Road, Forest Gate, East Ham. Jane and her two daughters are both listed by the surname Sampson Dale on the census return. Birth records show that Evelina Sampson's birth was registered in the Royston district of Hertfordshire in April-June 1890 (she was born at Buntingford on 12 April 1890); her older sister was registered as Janet Sampson in July-September 1886 in the Islington district.

24. On her marriage, at Holy Trinity, Paddington, on 27 March 1908, Evelina Sampson Dale listed 'Henry Dale, gentleman' as her father (her mother, Jane, was a witness). The 1891 census records mother and daughter as Jeannie S Dale [sic] and Eveline S Dale [sic].

25. Baptised as Jeannie Louisa, Kate's sister preferred to use her mother's name, Jane. In 1891, she used the name Jeannie Sampson Dale, claiming to be married, and in 1901 was Jane Sampson Dale.

In 1911, she recorded herself on the census as Jane Dale, widow. However, there is no record of a marriage between Jane and a Mr Dale - Henry or otherwise - even though, in 1920, when she married Brazilian journalist Dr José Carlos Rodrigues, she gave her name as Jane Sampson Dale. When Jane placed a remembrance notice in the papers for her husband and elder daughter, Janet, who died in 1938, she stated that Evelina was Dr Rodrigues' daughter, and gave Janet's name as Lady Janet Rodrigues Garthwaite. Janet was the divorced wife of Sir Wlliam Garthwaite, but the use of Rodrigues again implied that Rodrigues was her maiden name and thus her father's name, when it was her stepfather. Neither daughter would have grown up with that surname, as Jeannie did not marry José Carlos until they were adults.
26. Gail L Savage, 'The operation of the 1857 Divorce Act, 1860-1910, a research note', *Journal of Social History*, 16:4 (1983), p.104.

Chapter 2: The World of the Private Detective

27. In *The Expressman and the Detective* (1874), Pinkerton makes this clear, for example, at page 16.
28. Even the Pinkerton's website is non-committal on the subject of when it was established, preferring to simply say that it occurred in the '1850s' ('Our History', www.pinkerton.com/our-difference/history). The Library of Congress gives the date as 'circa 1850' but its deposited Pinkertons files only date from 1853 (family directors file) and 1857-1861 (administration and criminal cases) (www.loc.gov/item/mm75036301/). Much of the Pinkerton agency's early history is known largely through the memoirs of Allan Pinkerton himself, and therefore have to be treated with caution, as he was prone to hyperbole; in particular, the extent to which Kate Warne was involved with the mission to protect Lincoln is derived from Pinkerton's account, written after her death. It is probable that his account is tinged with both grief at her loss, and a desire to illustrate his innovative use of female detectives by stressing her role in the case.

29. See, for example, Chris Enss, 'Wild Women of the West: Hattie Lawton', *Cowgirl* magazine (5 July 2017), at https://cowgirlmagazine.com/hattie-lawton-wild-women-wednesday/.
30. Charles Frederick Field was born in 1803 in Chelsea. He was a police inspector by the time of his marriage to Jane Chambers in July 1841, and retired in 1852. However, in all the censuses after his retirement, he lists himself as a retired police inspector, a more respectable job title than that of private inquiry agent, although some records list both a residential address (Stanley Villas) and an office address (Eldon Chambers) for him, which would be unusual for a completely retired man. (1860 London Royal Blue Book, 1861 census for 5 Stanley Villas, Chelsea; 1871 census for 5 Stanley Villas, Chelsea). Charles Field died on 27 September 1874, his entry in the National Probate Calendar describing him as 'late Chief Inspector of the Detective Police of the Metropolis' (National Probate Calendar for 17 October 1874, on Ancestry).
31. *Northern Daily Times*, 11 December 1858, p.2.
32. Alan Hayhurst, *Staffordshire Murders* (The History Press), pp.15-36.
33. *Leeds Intelligencer*, 25 October 1856, p.2, citing *Globe*, 11 June 1856. Field claimed in this advert to have agents working for him in New York - Mr C Hays and Mr R Stokeley - who were both described as 'independent detective police'.
34. Richard Clark, '1837-1868 Public executions', Capital Punishment UK at www.capitalpunishmentuk.org/1837.html. Charles Field would continue working as a private detective and formed partnerships with various individuals working in related fields. In March 1866, a bankruptcy hearing took place involving Charles Henry Nicholls, who was described as a 'bill broker' of Kensington Crescent and Devereux Court, Strand (the latter, of course, being Charles Field's detective office). Nicholls states that he had been in partnership with Field for 'several years' until July 1865, and that his debts were not from this partnership (*London Evening Standard*, 10 March 1866, p.7).
35. *Hereford Journal*, 11 April 1855, p.4.
36. *Northern Daily Times*, 11 December 1858, p.2.

37. *Northern Daily Times*, 11 December 1858, p.2. The case turned out to be a protracted one; it first resulted in Evans bringing an action for criminal conversation against Robinson, which he lost. There was next a trial without payment of costs, which Evans won, gaining him £500 in damages. Evans then 'promoted' a suit in the Court of Arches against his wife, with a view to gaining divorce via an Act of Parliament against his wife. He was unsuccessful. Robinson then found himself charged with perjury for claiming he had not had an 'improper' relationship with Mrs Evans, but the jury refused to return a verdict, and he was discharged. Finally, once the Matrimonial Causes Act had come into effect, Evans petitioned for a divorce, and was successful. The marriage had lasted far longer than Evans' attempts to end it - the couple had married in Cheltenham in 1850, but separated within six months.
38. Bryan Kesselman, *'Paddington' Pollaky, Private Detective: The Mysterious Life and Times of the Real Sherlock Holmes* (The History Press, 2015), p.19, p.106.
39. See Bryan Kesselman, *'Paddington' Pollaky, Private Detective* (History Press, 2015) for more details on Pollaky's life and career.
40. See, for example, the *Sporting Times* of 19 October 1929 and *Belfast Telegraph* of 19 March 1938. Pollaky died at Brighton in 1918.
41. *Manchester Courier*, 1 July 1869, p.3.
42. *Manchester Evening News*, 13 October 1876, p.2.
43. *Truth*, 8 February 1877, p.30.
44. The number of individuals describing themselves as private detectives or private inquiry agents in the census similarly increases between 1881 and the early twentieth century. Relying on the census, however, underestimates the number of private detectives there were likely to be in operation - some, for whatever reason, did not state it as their profession on the census, preferring to keep their work undercover, or combining the job with another one when finances dictated.
45. This is discussed at length in Haia Shpayer-Makov's *The Ascent of the Detective: Police Sleuths in Victorian and Edwardian England* (OUP, 2012). See, for example, page 226.
46. Elaine S. Abelson looks at this phenomenon in *When Ladies Go A-Thieving: Middle-Class Shoplifters in the Victorian Department*

Store, (OUP, 1989) and 'The Invention of Kleptomania' (*Signs*, 15:1 (Autumn 1989), pp.123-143).

47. It is tempting to see part of this – the growing number of private detectives in London – as a reflection of public disenchantment with the police in the aftermath of its failure to identify or capture Jack the Ripper in 1888, but it is not that simple; some police detectives had simply served their twenty years with the police and retired, rather than making a choice to leave early and become private detectives.

48. All advertised in the *London Evening Standard* of 31 July 1886, p.1. Alfred Knowles was still working in 1891, when he described himself as a 'confidential agent', still based at 79 Euston Road. He was a Londoner born and bred, and was born in 1846. George Trace (born in Devon in 1847) was listed as a police constable in the 1871 census for 33 Bow Street, Covent Garden, and by 1881, had become an inspector (1881 census for 31 Mckerrell Road, Camberwell). Uriah Cooke exaggerated his police career for kudos, claiming to have been a police detective and son of Chief Inspector George Clark; he had actually only been a constable, and was actually a labourer's son.

49. Crime historians have discussed the views about whether Martha Tabram and Emma Elizabeth Smith, for example, were victims of the Whitechapel murderer, noting that these views have varied. Some police detectives at the time – such as Detective Constable Walter Dew and Inspector Frederick Abberline – assumed that Tabram and Smith were earlier victims of the Ripper, listing Mary Ann Nichols as his third victim, whereas others disagreed (see Paul Begg and John Bennett, *Jack the Ripper: The Forgotten Victims* (Yale University Press, 2014), pp.3-4, pp.19-20, p.35, p.63; Drew Gray, *London's Shadows: The Dark Side of the Victorian City* (Bloomsbury, 2013), pp.31-32). The belief by the likes of Abberline that Smith and Tabram could also be Ripper victims reflects some assumptions in the press at the same time; when Elizabeth Stride was murdered in the autumn of 1888, some press reports suggested that Tabram might have been murdered by the same person as Emma Elizabeth Smith, Mary Ann Nichols and Annie Chapman (*Dundee Courier*, 2 October 1888, p.3). Later in 1888, and again in 1889, London newspapers explicitly listed

Smith and Tabram as two of 'Jack the Ripper's victims' (*Reynolds's Newspaper*, 11 November 1888, p.5; *London Evening News*, 17 July 1889, p.3 and 18 July 1889, p.3). This served the purpose of creating a panic about a mass murderer who had killed several women over a longer stretch of time, as well as highlighting the failure of the police (both City of London and Metropolitan) in solving any of these cases.
50. *The Times*, 11 October 1888.
51. It has been noted that Victorian police officers were 'largely drawn from the ranks of the working classes', and this helps explain why some private detectives were similarly of working-class origin, when so many had been former policemen. However, by the late nineteenth century, private detectives were equally likely to have come from the ranks of lower middle-class clerks (Gray, *London's Shadows*, p.227, citing Haia Shpayer-Makov, *The Making of a Policeman: a social history of a labour force in metropolitan London 1829-1914* (Ashgate, 2002)).
52. My own research into the backgrounds of London-based individuals who described themselves as either private detectives or private inquiry agents between 1870 and 1911 (using the censuses of 1891-1911, press advertisements and publicly available birth, marriage, and death information).

Chapter 3: The Office on Basinghall Street

53. Today, the road lies between Moorgate and Bank underground stations; Bank, however, only opened in 1900.
54. A painting by John Philipps Emslie of 68-69 Basinghall Street, from 1883, shows this style of building. It can be seen in the London Picture Archive, record no 1053 (www.londonpicturearchive.org.uk).
55. 'Wool Exchange, 22-26 Basinghall Street', record no 38120, at the London Picture Archive (www.londonpicturearchive.org.uk).
56. Robert Donald, 'The Wool Exchange at Work', *Historical Periodical* (January 1898), p.814.
57. *Gloucestershire Echo*, 16 September 1885, p.2. It is possible that earlier adverts exist in editions of newspapers that have not, as yet,

been digitised; much of the material here is derived from those publications that have, at time of writing, been digitised for this period within the British Newspaper Archive. In September 1885, Slater advertised primarily in Gloucestershire (in the *Gloucestershire Echo* and *Cheltenham Chronicle*), with one advert surviving for the *London Evening Standard*, and one for the *Norfolk Chronicle*.

58. *London Evening Standard*, 29 July 1902, p.1.
59. *London Evening Standard*, 30 July 1886, p.8, *Retford and Worksop Herald*, 11 July 1891, p.1, as just two examples.
60. *London Evening Standard*, 28 September 1887, p.1.
61. Wireless telegraphy developed over the late 1880s and 1890s. In the UK, the National Telephone Company started in 1881, being taken over by the General Post Office in 1912. Henry Slater advertised both NTC and GPO telephone numbers in his adverts: with the NTC, his number was 302 Bank, and with the GPO, 302 Central.
62. *Dundee Evening Telegraph*, 11 November 1904, p.2.
63. *Ibid.*
64. 'The Diamond Cut Diamond' was also the name of an eighteenth-century farce by WH Murray that was still being performed in 1887; it's tempting to see the press story about the trial as seeing the latter as a similar kind of farce - but there is no evidence that this was the case.
65. The trial of the individuals took place in November 1886 at the Old Bailey. James Palmer and four others had been accused of robbing diamond merchant Julius Tabak of 300 diamonds worth a total of £1,400, but the evidence hinged on the testimony of a convict named Donato Denunzio, and his daughter Elena. Adolphe Weiner received a sentence of seven years; Leon Weiner, Daniel Jacoby and Samuel Scanland five years each; and James Palmer ten years. (Old Bailey Proceedings, November 1886, trial of Adolphe Weiner (43), Leon Weiner (34), Daniel Jacoby (24), James Palmer (29), Samuel Scanland (43) (t18861025-1047).)
66. There is substantial news coverage of the trial in the press, and a long account on Old Bailey Online, but there is no mention either of Slater or Moser in any of these.

67. In the list of detectives placing adverts in the *London Evening Standard* of 13 December 1887, Moser's advert was directly beneath two placed by Slater. At this point, Moser was based at 31 Southampton Street. In early 1893, he moved to Arundel Street.
68. *The Times*, 21 January 1897, p.16.
69. TNA J77/437/3331 (divorce petition of Edward James Clarendon Williamson, 1889); TNA J77/447/3639 (divorce petition of Harriet Ellen Moser, 1890); TNA J77/484/14738 (divorce petition of Maurice Moser, 1891).
70. Moser's complex relationship with Antonia served to distract him from his agency work, and Slater was able to gain the upper hand - but only for a short time, and Moser's agency continued to operate. Unlike Slater's, though, Moser's agency was smaller, with a limited number of office staff. Those he had, though, he taught well. When his 'wife' Antonia (they never legally married) launched her own detective agency, aided by her daughter Margaret, she would show how much she had learned from her soon to be ex-partner by placing her own similar press adverts.
71. In this case, Slater gave the job of watching Antonia Moser to one of his own female detectives, Louisa Sangster (*Daily Telegraph*, 26 July 1890, p.3; *The Times*, 22 July 1890, p.3; *Derby Daily Telegraph*, 22 July 1890, p.4).
72. *The Times*, 22 July 1890; *Jersey Independent*, 26 July 1890; *Daily Telegraph*, 26 July 1890, p.3; *Derby Daily Telegraph*, 22 July 1890, p.4. In the divorce petition itself, it is possible to see what Louisa Sangster had done on behalf of her employer, Henry Slater, as it is stated that Antonia Williamson had committed adultery at 3 Garrick Street, Covent Garden, on several occasions between November 1889 and January 1890, and at 4 Sussex Mansions, Maiden Lane between January and February 1890. You can imagine the female detective skulking outside both these properties - very near each other and near Moser's detective offices at Southampton Street - and monitoring Antonia and Moser's comings and goings (TNA J77/437/3331, divorce court file, appellant Edward James Clarendon Williamson, respondent Charlotte Antonia Williamson, co-respondent Maurice Moser).

73. *Brighton Gazette*, 25 May 1889, p.1.
74. *London and Provincial Entr'acte*, 15 October 1887, p.5.
75. The absence of women does not mean they were not employed; however, research I have conducted into female detectives suggests that they tended to be named less than men, and were less evident in press and archival documents as they tended to work on a shorter-term basis than men, perhaps only for a few months before working in another area, or marrying or engaging in family commitments.
76. *Buckingham Advertiser and Free Press*, 24 December 1892, p.2; *Cork Daily Herald*, 6 December 1892, p.3.
77. *Sunderland Daily Echo*, 1 December 1892, p.3.
78. *London Evening Standard*, 31 December 1892, p.1. The Press Association stated that the case would 'in all probability put an end to the missing word competition' (*Preston Herald*, 14 December 1892, p.5).
79. Another advertisement was more of a calculated risk. In 1891, Slater had featured in a newspaper advert for St Jacob's Oil, stating that he had suffered from rheumatism since 1888, which had caused him 'excruciating pain'. It was only the application of St Jacob's Oil that had relieved his discomfort, he said (*Hull Daily Mail*, 5 November 1891, p.2). On the one hand, this advert offered Slater another chance to get his name out there to readers who might study adverts for ailments but not those expressly for the services of private detectives. On the other, it associated him with illness and physical frailty - even if the point of the advert was to highlight the success of 'St Jacob's Oil' in making him physically active again, the association with infirmity and rheumatism still remained. For Slater, however, the chance to highlight his name and business - complete with full address - was too good an opportunity to miss.
80. *Buffalo Evening News*, New York, 26 June 1891, p.7.
81. *Westminster Gazette*, 13 February 1893, p.9.
82. *Surrey Mirror*, 21 June 1895, p.4.
83. *Westminster Gazette*, 13 February 1893, p.9. The following excerpts from the interview are all from this source, which was subsequently reprinted as far afield as Australia, where it appeared in the *Sydney Morning Herald* of 6 May 1893, p.4.

84. *Westminster Gazette*, 13 February 1893, p.9.
85. The final advert for Slater's at 27 Basinghall Street was on 29 September 1894; on 1 October 1894, it advertised in the *Evening Standard*, giving the new address of 1 Basinghall Street (*London Evening Standard*, 1 October 1894, p.2). As 1 October was a Monday, it seems that Slater's staff moved from one office to another over the weekend of 29-30 September.
86. *Daily Telegraph*, 2 July 1902, p.16.
87. *Dundee Courier*, 31 March 1904, p.5.
88. Maurice Moser and Henry Slater both advertised in the 11 January 1893 issue of the *London Evening Standard* (p.1). Slater started one of the eight adverts he placed in this issue with 'Slater's Detectives (male and female) for secret watchings…' whereas Moser stated: 'Agents in every city in the world, staff of detectives (including ladies) in every station of life'.

Chapter 4: Changing Direction

89. *Morning Post*, 31 March 1904, p.8.
90. Freemasonry Registers on Ancestry. They record that Henry Scott, age 48, of Clarendon Mansions, Brighton, was initiated into the Kent Lodge on 13 October 1897. He was passed 10 November 1897, and raised 8 December 1897.
91. *The London Gazette*, 31 October 1933, p.7078. For more on Maud West's identity, see Susannah Stapleton, *The Adventures of Maud West, Lady Detective* (Picador, 2019), pp.238-241.
92. As Henry Scott, Slater was said at various points to be living at Mount Street, Mayfair; Palace Street in Westminster; and Palace Court Mansions in Bayswater, as well as having his Brighton base.
93. *Belfast News-letter*, 6 June 1904, p.5.
94. *London Evening Standard*, 31 March 1904, p.2.
95. *Daily Telegraph*, 23 March 1904, p.7.
96. *Daily Telegraph*, 2 July 1902, p.6.
97. I cannot find a record of Slater leaving Britain or arriving in Australia in ship passenger records for the time, but given that he was using

more than one pseudonym at the time, it is possible that he travelled under a false name, or with incorrect details.
98. *Sydney Morning Herald*, 29 May 1902, p.11.
99. *Chard and Ilminster News*, 31 March 1900, p.3.
100. This is interesting, given both the real identity of Henry Slater and what would happen to him in later years, as this book shows later.
101. *Taunton Courier*, 4 April 1900.
102. *The Times*, 20 April 1894, p.1.
103. In an arena where hyperbole was prevalent, it is refreshing to see that Attwood's claim of longevity, made regularly at the turn of the century, was based in fact. In 1902, he claimed to have been established nineteen years, and, in fact, it was nearer twenty, for he was advertising his 'private inquiry office' at 6 Catherine Street as early as July 1882 (*Daily Telegraph and Courier*, 18 July 1882, p.8).
104. *Daily Telegraph*, 2 July 1902, p.16.
105. 20 Moorgate Street [*sic*], the address given as the offices of Barclays' Detectives, was described as uninhabited in the 1901 census. Numbers 22, 24 and 26 were similarly uninhabited, which may suggest business offices that were only inhabited during the working day, with staff returning to their home addresses when the business was closed. However, no individual named Barclay(s) and claiming to be either a detective or a private inquiry agent can be found in the 1901 census. The name may have been used only for professional purposes, as seems to have been common, or there was still sufficient stigma to the title of private detective that some individuals preferred not to describe themselves thus in the census returns.
106. *Morning Post*, 30 April 1901, p.1.
107. The earliest surviving advert for cycling lady detectives at Slater's is in the *Evening Standard* of 26 May 1895.
108. *London and Provincial Entr'acte*, 18 October 1902, p.12.
109. The letter was received by Captain Frank Douglas-Pennant in September 1901, and was warning him that his wife Maud had been sleeping with two other officers, at least one of whom was with Douglas-Pennant in the King's Royal Rifles. She admitted the first affair; her second lover was tricked into admitting his role. Douglas-Pennant gained his

divorce, remarried, and died in 1967 aged 101; Maud Douglas-Pennant never remarried.

110. *London Evening Standard*, 1 May 1895, p.2. The lady in question was referred to as 'Mrs A O'B Clifford' in the coverage of the court case, and her former husband as 'Mr Schofield'. Records show that she was born Annetta Smith, and had married Charles John Schofield in Kensington on 4 February 1891 (BMD records). Her divorce petition against John Charles Schofield was filed on 4 February 1891 - her twelfth wedding anniversary - with the decree nisi being granted on 8 February 1892 and the final decree on 9 August 1892. The divorce petition states that Annetta sought a divorce on the grounds of repeated adultery with different women, and cruelty - and also alleged that her husband had given her a sexually transmitted disease - something he strenuously denied (TNA J77/465). After divorcing John Schofield, Annetta married Isidore Clifford in the district of St George Hanover Square, in the March quarter of 1893 (1a 685). Hence her being described in court as Mrs Clifford. Annetta would petition for a divorce from Isidore Clifford in 1901; he counter-petitioned, alleging that she had committed adultery with George or Gordon Ware-Warburg (TNA J77/713/1688; TNA J77/727/2102; TNA J77/722/1953).

111. *London Evening Standard*, 16 February 1899, p.6. Mrs Smith was Catherine Eleanor (nee Pung), who married Fred John Smith in Lambeth in the December quarter of 1883 (1d 908). She had originally filed for divorce from her husband on 25 June 1898, and her final decree was granted on 15 February 1899 (TNA J77/644/19646).

112. This is evident in Catherine Eleanor Smith's case, as her divorce solicitors were Osborn and Osborn; Kate Pollard's solicitors were also Albert Osborn's firm.

Chapter 5: Finding Evidence

113. *Cork Examiner*, 28 October 1904, p.8.
114. A woman could only divorce her husband if she could prove adultery and one other cause, such as physical violence or desertion. The

system was a patriarchal and misogynistic one - it was easier for men to obtain a divorce, as they only had to prove adultery, without any other reason, whereas women had to show two causes. The King's Proctor noted that Kate had also claimed that she had had to 'seek protection' at her brother's house due to violence on the part of Thomas Pollard - this claim of violence was necessary in conjunction with the adultery claims in order to gain her divorce (*Pollard v Pollard: The King's Proctor Showing Cause: Plea of the King's Proctor*, J77/756/3018/11, The National Archives).
115. *Westminster Gazette*, 24 March 1904, p.7.
116. *Ibid.*
117. *Ibid.*
118. Judith R Walkowitz and Daniel J Walkowitz, '"We are not beasts of the field": Prostitution and the poor in Plymouth and Southampton under the Contagious Diseases Acts', *Feminist Studies*, 1: 3/4 (Winter-Spring 1973), p.73.
119. Erin Black, 'Damnation Alley: Plymouth's forgotten street of brothels and sin', *Plymouth Herald*, 21 September 2019, at www.plymouthherald.co.uk/news/history/damnation-alley-plymouths-forgotten-street-3329633.
120. *Ibid.*; Vivien F.T. Pointon, 'Mid-Victorian Plymouth: A Social Geography' (PhD thesis, Polytechnic South West, 1989, via https://core.ac.uk/download/pdf/29817146.pdf), p.342.
121. Matthew Lloyd, 'Theatres and Halls in Plymouth', *ArthurLloyd.co.uk* at www.arthurlloyd.co.uk/Plymouth.htm, accessed 29 March 2023. The theatre was demolished in 1937, and the new Theatre Royal, in a different location, only dates from the early 1980s.
122. *St James's Gazette*, 27 April 1904, p.13.
123. In court, Edgar Cartwright detailed this telegram, and said it was sent to Smith on 13 November 1901. (*The Times*, 14 May 1904, p.5).
124. The King's Proctor stated that Davies worked in Plymouth from 26 February until 10 March, but newspapers later state the 11th; he was first able to make Pollard's acquaintance on 1 March. (TNA J/3018/11, p.213).
125. *Aberdeen Press and Journal*, 18 March 1904, p.6; *Manchester Courier*, 5 November 1904, p.19.

126. Marie Travert later claimed that there had been three men in Jersey – the 'tall and dark' Pollard; the shorter and fairer Davies; and a third man who 'acted as a valet to the other two'. Yet Davies claimed to be posing as a valet, so it's not clear whether there were genuinely three men, or whether the court reporter who recorded this had confused the mention of the valet, and assumed there were three (*The Times*, 14 May 1904, p.5). However, as this book notes, elsewhere, there was mention of a third man who Davies had befriended, so this may simply be a case of confused reporting.

127. This was the latest incarnation of the town's theatre and opera house; the Theatre Royal had existed since 1828, but had a chequered history before being destroyed in a fire in 1899. Lillie Langtry opened the new theatre and opera house on 9 July 1900 (Matthew Lloyd, 'Theatres and Halls in Jersey', *ArthurLloyd.co.uk* at www.arthurlloyd.co.uk/Jersey.htm).

128. The hotel book-keeper, Alice Bradbrook, later gave evidence that Pollard and Davies had stayed at the Star from 11 to 17 March. Pollard's bill for the week was £1 17s 1d, and Davies's was £2 13s 8d. Davies paid both men's bills (*The Times*, 14 May 1904, p.5).

129. The boarding house keeper is only named as 'Mrs Macnamara' in press reports, but the 1901 census for Jersey shows only one person of that name there – Alexandra McNamara [*sic*], b1849 St Helier, who was running a lodging house at 7 Hilary Street, St Helier. She was described as married, but had no husband present. At that time, she had a lodger named Marie Tremers [*sic*], who, given the inconsistency with which some census enumerators recorded 'foreign' names, is likely to have been the same Marie Travert referred to in reports as seducing Pollard at the lodging house. Marie Tremers was single, from Caen in France, and was 26 years old in 1901. She was described as a servant – either for Mrs McNamara or another household. The King's Proctor plea in 1903 also states that the boarding house where Pollard stayed was at 7 Hilary Street (TNA J/3018/11. p210). By May 1904, Marie had returned to Caen (*The Times*, 14 May 1904, p.5).

130. *The Times*, 14 May 1904, p.5.

131. *Ibid*.

132. *Nottingham Evening Post*, 25 October 1904, p.5.
133. 'On one occasion on the receipt of a telegram, [George] Henry said that Davies had been successful. Davies's visit to Plymouth and his trip with Pollard to Jersey cost £34.' (*The Times*, 14 May 1904, p.5).
134. It was Tom Pollard who was shown the photograph later in court, and who confirmed that it had originally been a photograph of him and his wife together (Old Bailey Online, t19041017-788). Other reports claim that Osborn was the man who showed the photograph to Maud Goodman and Louisa Ford, but it's likely that he commissioned Iles to do so.
135. *Westminster Gazette*, 24 March 1904, p.7.
136. Although it's not possible to ascertain that the Maud Goodman was the same woman I've identified through parish records and census returns, it seems likely that she is the same. She was a local woman, living in the right area, young and susceptible - needing to earn money by whatever means. She stayed single throughout the protracted affair, but finally married in Plymouth in 1907. With her husband, she moved over the county border into Cornwall, where she was still living in 1921.
137. Although few details of Maud and Louisa were given in press or trial reports, Louisa described herself as a widow when in court in March 1904, and the presence of a widow of this name still living in Summerland Place in 1911 means that this is likely to be the same woman (*Northern Whig*, 25 March 1904, p.7).
138. Charles Ford's death was not registered in England or Wales, and it is likely that he died at sea.
139. In 1911, Louisa and her son Frank were still listed as living at 8 Summerland Place; Louisa's occupation was given as general servant, and she and Frank, who was then 10 years old, shared a single room in the house.
140. *Western Evening Herald*, 9 July 1904, p.3.
141. *Echo*, 18 March 1904, p.3. Alexander Thomas, a retired naval storekeeper, died on 8 March 1904, two years after Pollard checked on him.
142. Conversation taken from the *Daily Mirror*, 9 May 1904, p.5 and *Evening Echo* (Cork), 2 November 1904, p.4.

143. *Morning Post*, 19 March 1904, p.8.
144. *Ibid.* Edgar Cartwright later said that Pracy only continued to observe or watch Pollard until 23 June 1902, but this doesn't correlate with other reports (*St James's Gazette*, 16 May 1904, p.13).
145. In court, it was stated that this sum had been spent between 27 September 1901 and 26 March 1902 (*The Times*, 14 May 1904, p.5).

Chapter 6. The Honey Trap

146. It's not 100 per cent clear where the girls were staying; most reports say number three Summerland Place, but Nellie Bell, who lived at that address, was described as living there but said Maud merely 'frequented the house'. A few reports have Maud at number eight or even number nine.
147. The 1901 census records Minnie Wilson, Florence Simpson, Eliza Jope, Emma Gulley, Catherine Flowers, and Emily Jane Testor as the keepers of lodging houses between three and nine Summerland Place.
148. Emma Smith was a witness in the subsequent court case, and in early November 1904 was found unconscious and bleeding in Newcastle Street, Plymouth, having been the victim of an assault. Her attack made a mere paragraph in the papers, and it was not clear whether the assault was random, or whether, conversely, Emma had been the victim of a targeted attack. (*Dundee Courier*, 4 November 1904, p.7).
149. It is also possible that the differing accounts in the newspapers means that some errors may have crept in, particularly when newspapers were not that careful in copying accounts in other publications. By 1911, most of the 1901 residents of Summerland Place had moved on, except for Louisa Ford; there was a shop at number one, but most of the other houses up to number nine had multiple families or individuals living in one or two rooms in each house. The men were largely labourers, working on the docks and roads, or working in the hospitality industry; women claimed to be charwomen, laundry workers and servants. I use the word 'claim' as Maud admitted to

resorting to prostitution, yet she and her friends commonly claimed to be servants when asked. They might well have worked as such and only supplemented their income with occasional prostitution, but conversely, they may have worked as prostitutes usually, but said they were servants to preserve an element of respectability to their lives. Other residents may have done likewise; therefore, their descriptions of their work cannot always be trusted.
150. *Northern Whig*, 25 March 1904, p.7.
151. *Echo*, 18 March 1904, p.3.
152. *Ibid.*
153. *Belfast News-letter*, 14 June 1904, p.10.
154. *Sheffield Daily Telegraph*, 8 June 1904, p.8.
155. *Dundee Courier*, 22 April 1904, p.6.
156. Osborn later gave evidence that the divorce petition had been drawn up by his clerk on 14 July, and filed on 15 July, before being sent to Slater's on 17 July. However, the petition states that it was filed on 14 July (TNA J77/756/3018; *Dundee Evening Telegraph*, 23 March 1904, p.5).
157. Louisa Ford referred to Maud this night as being 'a little girl in red' (*Northern Whig*, 25 March 1904, p.7).
158. *Northern Whig*, 25 March 1904, p.7.
159. *Birmingham Mail*, 18 June 1904, p.3.
160. *Western Times*, 19 March 1904, p.4.
161. *Yorkshire Evening Post*, 18 March 1904, p.6.
162. *Westminster Gazette*, 18 March 1904, p.7.
163. In court, Maud stated that she didn't want to come to London for the trial, but that Pracy had told her she had to. She had all her expenses paid, and was given an additional £4.
164. *Birmingham Mail*, 18 June 1904, p.3.
165. *Dundee Evening Telegraph*, 23 March 1904, p.5.
166. This hotel was short-lived; in 1910, the *Westminster Gazette* stated that London County Council had 'practically completed arrangements' to demolish it and replaced it with the 'French Palace', a permanent exhibition of French arts, with a theatre in one of its wings (*Westminster Gazette*, 29 July 1910, p.9). In 1913, it was reported

that children had 'slipped past the housebreakers who are razing Matcham's Hotel' in order to gather coltsfoot flowers (*Westminster Gazette*, 28 February 1913, p.4).
167. *St James's Gazette*, 16 May 1904, p.13.
168. *Coventry Evening Telegraph*, 16 March 1904, p.3.
169. *Birmingham Mail*, 18 June 1904, p.3.

Chapter 7: The Agency Burns

170. *Daily News*, 6 March 1903, p.9. Francis Stevens had married Emily Gertrude Henson in Bristol when he was 19; she was 20, and six months pregnant. The marriage seems to have failed very quickly and they went their separate ways. Their son, Marmion, was brought up by a series of caretakers in London and Oxfordshire. In 1892, at Christ Church, Greenwich, Emily bigamously married Thomas Edward Simpson, a licensed victualler, claiming to be a spinster. When Stevens petitioned for a divorce in March 1899, he cited Simpson as co-respondent. Private detectives appear to have been able to track Emily's movements up to 1899, but although they knew she was living 'as man and wife' with Simpson, nobody appears to have been able to find out that she had actually committed bigamy – there is no mention of it in the divorce petition or in newspapers of this time (TNA J77/664/197; marriage of Francis William Stevens and Emily Gertrude Henson, Bristol, September 1880 (vol 6a p127); birth of Marmion Frank Stevens, December 1880 Wandsworth (vol 1d page 696) and his birth date of 27 November 1880, as recorded in the 1939 Register for Chipping Norton; marriage at Christ Church, Greenwich, on 7 February 1892, between Emily Gertrude Henson, 30, and Thomas Edward Simpson, 27, via Ancestry).
171. The 1881 census for Ashton Court, Long Ashton, Somerset lists 'William Stevens' as footman to John G[reville] Smith, baronet; the Clifton Society, 8 January 1891, notes that 'Mr Stevens', coachman and valet to Sir Greville Smyth [sic] had given a present to Sir Greville's stepdaughter on her marriage. Although baptised as Francis William Stevens at Twerton, Somerset, on 28 December 1860, Stevens seems

to have used the name William in his prior jobs, and was known interchangeably as Francis and William while at Slater's.
172. Francis's first son by his second wife was even named after his former employer – Greville Thomas Scott Stevens was baptised at St Cuthbert's, Hampstead, on 25 February 1901 (via www.ancestry.co.uk).
173. *Daily Mirror*, 10 June 1904, p.5.
174. *Ibid*.
175. Francis Stevens married Elizabeth Hannah Lancaster in Surrey a month after his final decree was issued (the final decree was issued on 22 January 1900; Francis and Elizabeth married on 21 February 1900 – TNA J/77/664/197, marriages for Christ Church, Mortlake, via Ancestry).
176. *Liverpool Evening Express*, 6 March 1903, p.6.
177. *Ibid*.
178. *London Daily News*, 6 March 1903, p.9.
179. *Daily Telegraph*, 21 April 1904, p.7.
180. Thomas Craig would not last long at Simmonds before moving on to Longley's Detective Agency at Holborn. Longley's was established in 1901, allegedly by another former Slater's detective. I have been unable to ascertain the exact identity of 'Mr Longley'.
181. *Daily Telegraph and Courier*, 21 April 1904, p.7.
182. *Staffordshire Sentinel*, 16 March 1904, p.3.
183. *Daily Telegraph*, 21 April 1904, p.7.
184. *Heywood Advertiser*, 18 March 1904, p.2.
185. *Aberdeen Press & Journal*, 17 March 1904, p.6.
186. Charles Fielding ultimately left Slater's on 25 July 1903 (*Daily Telegraph*, 23 March 1904, p.7).
187. *Globe*, 2 November 1904, p.2.
188. *London Evening Standard*, 5 March 1903, p.1.
189. *London Evening Standard*, 3 October 1902, p.1.
190. *Daily Telegraph and Courier*, 2 July 1902, p.16.
191. *Liverpool Weekly Courier*, 7 March 1903, p.6.
192. See, for example, adverts in the *Evening Standard* of 5 March 1903, p.1 and 6 March 1903, p.1.

193. *Belfast Telegraph*, 6 March 1903, p.4.
194. *Sheffield Daily Telegraph*, 6 March 1903, p.3.
195. *London Evening Standard*, 13 October 1902, p.1; *Daily Telegraph*, 23 April 1904, p.16.
196. *Daily Telegraph*, 23 April 1904, p.16.
197. *Edinburgh Evening News*, 6 June 1904, p.3.
198. Thomas Harvey Pritchard, head passbook keeper at the Lothbury branch of the bank, would later give evidence about this account, noting the agency paid in between £1,000 and £2,000 per month in 1901 (Trial of Henry Scott et al, t19041017-788, Old Bailey Online, www.oldbaileyonline.org).
199. *Edinburgh Evening News*, 6 June 1904, p.3.
200. *Ibid*.
201. See note 180 regarding Mr Longley's identity. In addition it is possible that 'Mr Longley' of Longley's agency may not have existed, and actually be one of Slater's men working under a pseudonym.
202. Thomas Pollard's evidence at the Old Bailey, Old Bailey Online, t19041017-788.
203. *St James's Gazette*, 10 June 1904, p.13.
204. Thomas Craig had left back in July 1902, followed by Marrison on 29 September 1902, according to the *St James's Gazette* of 16 May 1904, p.13.
205. *Daily Telegraph & Courier*, 16 May 1904, p.7.
206. *The Times*, 14 May 1904, p.5.
207. *St James's Gazette*, 16 May 1904, p.13.
208. TNA J77/799/4325; *London Echo*, 6 December 1904, p.3. Iles had to give evidence at the subsequent divorce case, which took place in December 1904, after Slater's had disbanded following the trial of Slater and several of his detectives. Iles continued working for Slater's until the end, but had to give evidence in this case over a year after working on it.
209. *Forest Hill & Sydenham Examiner*, 12 June 1903, p.3; TNA J77/776/3611.
210. *Daily Telegraph*, 16 June 1904, p.5.
211. TNA J77/1793/4126, divorce between Ethel Hyde Ryan and Charles Montgomerie Ryan.

212. TNA J77/1793/4126, divorce between Ethel Hyde Ryan and Charles Montgomerie Ryan. Ethel would remain married but separated until her husband's death in 1935, after which point she gave her status as single.
213. Murray is referred to in various terms, including as a solicitor. The 1901 census for 42 Portland Square, Plymouth, records him as 'solicitor's clerk', but by 1911, and now living at 12 Leigham Terrace, he was a solicitor.
214. *Aberdeen Press & Journal*, 2 November 1904, p.6.
215. *Birmingham Mail*, 18 June 1904, p.3.
216. *Ibid*.
217. *Ibid*.
218. *London Evening Standard*, 26 December 1903, p.1.
219. *Ibid*.
220. *London Evening Standard*, 14 December 1903, p.1.

Chapter 8. At the Divorce Court

221. TNA J3018/11, *Pollard v Pollard: The King's Proctor Shewing Cause: Plea of the King's Proctor.*
222. *Edinburgh Evening News*, 16 March 1904, p.5; TNA J3018/11, *Pollard v Pollard: The King's Proctor Shewing Cause.*
223. TNA J3018/11, *Pollard v Pollard: The King's Proctor Shewing Cause*, p.212.
224. TNA J3018/16, p.215.
225. *Nottingham Journal*, 23 January 1904, p.3.
226. *Ibid.*; *Aberdeen Press and Journal*, 23 January 1904, p.6.
227. *Cheshire Daily Echo*, 25 March 1904, p.3.
228. *Ibid*.
229. *Eastern Evening News*, 18 March 1904, p.3.
230. *Cheshire Daily Echo*, 25 March 1904, p.3.
231. This was commented on in the divorce court ('Did they appear to be on intimate terms?' - 'Yes; they addressed each other by their Christian names.' - *Daily Telegraph*, 23 March 1904, p.7).

232. Fielding was asked by Sir Edward Clarke how many detectives Slater's agency was employing at the time he worked there, and responded 'about thirty' (*Daily Telegraph*, 23 March 1904, p.7).
233. The Whiteside case may be a reference to the decision by William Southey Whiteside, of Madras, to divorce his wife Maria Charlotte after over thirty years of marriage. The couple had been separated since 1872, when Maria returned to England with their children for their education; she was without William for at least seven years, and he alleged that in his absence, she had developed a relationship with an artist named Luigi Meo. The divorce petition was filed in 1891, but a divorce was not granted until 1893. Whiteside died seven years later. (TNA J77/481/4639). The reference to Colonel Hill may relate to the libel case brought against Colonel Sir Edward Stock Hill, MP for Bristol South, by Welsh accountant Arthur H Roberts in 1890. Hill admitted writing comments about Roberts in a letter to Roberts' father David, a fellow Freemason, but claimed that he hadn't published the letter to a wider audience and therefore hadn't committed libel. Arthur Roberts, a member of his father's accountancy firm Roberts & Sons, had sought £5,000 in damages, and although the jury at Glamorganshire Assizes found in his favour, he was awarded only £700 (*Morning Post*, 31 March 1890; *York Herald*, 1 April 1890). There is no direct evidence of Slater's Detective Agency being involved in this case, but there are no other obvious cases involving a Colonel Hill from this period. The link to Freemasonry - brought up during the case - is interesting given Henry Slater's own membership of the Freemasons.
234. Sir Edward Clarke (1841-1931) had been solicitor-general between 1886 and 1892; Sir Edward Carson (1854-1935) became solicitor-general in 1900.
235. *Daily Telegraph*, 23 March 1904, p.7.
236. *Ibid.*
237. In July 1902, an advert for Longley claimed that he had been successful 'for the past seven years', i.e. since around 1895. It is unlikely he would have considered his work at Slater's within this seven-year period, so, if true rather than an embellishment of it, it suggests he established

his own agency at around the same time that Hamilton thought Slater had started to step back (*Daily Telegraph*, 2 July 1902, p.16).
238. *Morning Post*, 31 March 1904, p.8.

Chapter 9. Will the Real Henry Slater Please Stand Up?

239. The difficulties that Maud West's adoption of a different name cause for researchers is implied by Susannah Stapleton's book *The Adventures of Maud West, Lady Detective* (Picador, 2019), pp.62-63.
240. *Daily Mirror*, 17 March 1904, p.6.
241. Bryan Kesselman, *'Paddington' Pollaky, Private Detective* (The History Press, 2015).
242. 1861 census for 1 Albion Place, Chelsea.
243. Marriage of Richard Elliott, eating house keeper, and Elizabeth Fromont, widow, at Paddington Parish Church on 5 April 1847. Richard gave his father's details as William Elliott, labourer; Elizabeth was the daughter of Richard Hurry, farmer. The witness at their wedding were relations of Elizabeth's - William Gillespie and his wife Elizabeth (nee Hurry).
244. Elizabeth Elliott, aged 67, died in Chelsea in 1858, and was buried at Brompton Cemetery on 15 December that year. Richard Elliott, widower and waiter, married Sarah Eyles, spinster, at Islington Parish Church on 30 December 1861. Richard stated that his father was William Elliott, farmer; Sarah was the daughter of John Eyles, builder. The witnesses at this wedding were butcher John Dunville and his wife Mary Ann; Mary Ann may well have been a relative or old friend of Sarah's, as both were from Wiltshire villages. Sarah was, before her marriage, a servant, and she was nearly thirty years younger than Richard Elliott.
245. Richard Elliott's parentage is also unknown. Although there are Elliott baptisms in the Lambourn parish registers, there are none for a Richard Elliott. He may have been born in Lambourn and baptised elsewhere, but no obvious record for him can be found in the environs of Lambourn or in London. He claimed his father was

named William Elliott, and was a farmer; but although a William Elliott can be found in Lambourn at the time of Richard's birth, and had several children baptised there, Richard was not one of them.

246. The 1871 census for Chelsea records Richard Elliott as living at 349 Fulham Road and being a coffee-shop keeper. He lived there with wife Sarah. Both he and his second wife Elizabeth were buried at Brompton Cemetery, but I have been unable to locate what happened to third wife Sarah after Richard's death.

247. Edward Walford, 'Chelsea', in *Old and New London: Volume 5* (London, 1878), pp.50-70, at *British History Online* (www.british-history.ac.uk/old-new-london/vol5/pp50-70).

248. Due to this rebuilding and infilling, by the time George Tinsley was living at Albion Place, the area of Little Chelsea was 'beginning to lose its separateness and becoming just part of the development of Fulham Road' ('Settlement and building: from 1680 to 1865, Little Chelsea, Sandy End and World's End', in Patricia E C Croot (ed), *A History of the County of Middlesex: Volume 12, Chelsea*, at *British History Online* (www.british-history.ac.uk/vch/middx/vol12/pp61-66).

249. *Leisure Hour, 1863*, included in Lee Jackson's *Dictionary of Victorian London* at www.victorianlondon.org/food/coffeerooms.htm.

250. John Timbs, *Curiosities of London* (1867), included in Lee Jackson's *Dictionary of Victorian London* at www.victorianlondon.org/food/coffeerooms.htm.

251. Harry Wallop, 'Victorian England: a nation of coffee drinkers', *The Telegraph*, 15 July 2010, accessed at www.telegraph.co.uk/news/uknews/7892631/Victorian-England-a-nation-of-coffee-drinkers.html.

252. The Factory Act of 1833 had ordered employers to provide part-time education to under 13s, but this was 'easily ignored' according to Liza Picard. There is no evidence either that George Tinsley came from a family where he would have needed to work in a factory, although of course, we only have his own account of his origins and the relatively few census returns that record his existence to go on (Liza Picard, 'Education in Victorian Britain', British Library (2009) (www.bl.uk/victorian-britain/articles/education-in-victorian-britain).

253. F. Musgrove, 'Middle-class education and employment in the nineteenth century', *Economic History Review*, 12:1 (1959), p.99.
254. Liza Picard, 'The Victorian Middle Classes', British Library (2009) (www.bl.uk/victorian-britain/articles/the-victorian-middle-classes).
255. F. Musgrove, 'Middle class education and employment in the nineteenth century', *Economic History Review*, 12:1 (1959), p.102.
256. *Ibid.*
257. Michelle Higgs, 'Making Ends Meet - The Role of the Victorian Pawnbrokers', 9 January 2014, at http://visitvictorianengland.blogspot.com/2014/01/making-ends-meet-role-of-victorian.html.
258. *The London Quarterly Review*, January 1883, p.66.
259. *Ibid.*
260. *Ibid.*
261. It is hard to track George's career, not only because he changed profession several times, and the newspapers did not always report the dialogue in court entirely accurately, but also because there is another George Tinsley in the archives whose career is rather similar to the future Henry Slater's. This other George Tinsley was born c.1852 in Cheshunt, Hertfordshire, and by 1871 was working as a pawnbroker's assistant. His employer was George Pockett, whose shop was based at 18 Liquor Pond Street in St Andrew Holborn, Liberty above the Bars, in the City of London. This was a large establishment: George Pockett actually owned or leased 16, 17 and 18 Liquor Pond Street; at number 16 was the boarding house for his assistants (several boys in their late teens and early twenties), run by a female housekeeper; at number 17 was his warehouse; while the shop was at number 18. In addition to his assistants, Pockett was helped by his own children, including George, John and Henry Pockett. George Tinsley was living at 16 Liquor Pond Street in 1861, as a pawnbroker's assistant, and was still working for Pockett ten years later when he had to give evidence in a burglary trial (*Middlesex County Times*, 11 November 1871, p.3). George subsequently worked as a pawnbroker's manager, a furniture dealer and a commercial traveller selling jewellery, showing that taking on various careers during one's lifetime was fairly common during the Victorian era, as well as in our own. However, this George Tinsley is

not the same as the future Henry Slater: he is well documented in the censuses, and was childless, being married to Rosina Mary Rogers in 1880, and there is no evidence of him ever having worked as a private detective (neither does he disappear following the 1904 trial, but is listed in the 1911 census for Finchley).

262. Judy Slinn, *A History of Freshfields* (Freshfields, 1984), pp.43-44.
263. Histories of the company give its address as Fleet Street, but contemporary newspaper advertisements make clear that between 1868 and at least 1873, the company was still based at 5 Bank Buildings, Lothbury. Henry Freshfield, son of James William, had been born at New Bank Buildings, Lothbury on 2 February 1814, and baptised at the parish church of St Margaret two months later (baptisms for St Margaret, Lothbury, 13 April 1814, on Ancestry).
264. '1871: Building Global Trade', at www.freshfields.com/en-gb/about-us/our-history/.
265. Marriage of Henry William Hirsch and Eliza Mary Cartwright, St Mary's Battersea, 26 August 1871.
266. Marriage of Eliza Nixon and William Cartwright, All Saints Fulham, 30 June 1850.
267. Emma's age, as given on the 1861 and 1871 censuses and her marriage, suggests a year of birth of 1849; however, the birth of Emma Elizabeth Cartwright was registered in the June quarter of 1848 in St James, Westminster (vol 1, page 100), and the 1851 census clearly states that she was 3 years old at that time (1851 census for Cubitt's Cottages, Wandsworth, on Ancestry. Cubitt's Cottages, named for Thomas Cubitt, would have been quite new homes at this time, although by 1914, the Medical Officer of Health reported that there were cases of 'domestic overcrowding' here, with tenants taking in lodgers to keep themselves afloat economically - Peter Caldwell-Smith, 'Annual Report on the Health, Sanitary Condition, etc of the borough', p.189, at https://wellcomelibrary.org/moh/report/b18250828/204#?c=0&m =0&s=0&cv=204&z=-1.6322%2C0.5292%2C4.2645%2C1.6802.
268. Edith Elliott Tinsley was baptised on 19 February 1871 at St Anne's, Wandsworth, her father described as a solicitor's clerk living in Wandsworth. The 1871 census, taken on 2 April, records the family

living at 4 Falcon Grove, Battersea, with George, 22, listed as a solicitor's clerk. Baby Edith is listed there as a 3-month-old baby, suggesting a birth date of January, with her baptism taking place when she was around a month old.
269. Dan Calinescu, 'Dickens' Short-Hand Writer's Business Card (1830)', at www.victorianweb.org/authors/dickens/gallery/109.html; Kathryn Chittick, 'Dickens and Parliamentary Reporting in the 1830s', *Victorian Periodicals Review*, 21:4 (1988), p.151.
270. *Sheffield Daily Telegraph*, 31 March 1904, p.12.
271. *South London Chronicle*, 2 January 1875.
272. *South London Chronicle*, 12 December 1874, p.5 and 27 March 1875, p.4.
273. An advert in the *Illustrated London News* of 2 July 1859 (p.2) advertises 'new song, *The Timid Little Maid*, by the Composer of *A Young Lady's No*...This arch and captivating song will be an immense favourite, the pun on beau and tie in the second verse is exceedingly happy and will tell well when sung'.
274. *South London Chronicle*, 27 March 1875, p.4.
275. *South London Chronicle*, 3 April 1875, p.4.
276. *South London Chronicle*, 24 April 1875, p.5.
277. Diane K. Bolton, Patricia E.C. Croot and M.A. Hicks, 'Chiswick: Growth', in T.F.T. Baker and C.R. Elrington (eds), A History of the County of Middlesex: Volume 7, Acton, Chiswick, Ealing and Brentford, West Twyford, Willesden (London, 1982), pp.54-68, *British History Online* (www.british-history.ac.uk/vch/middx/vol7/pp54-68).
278. Gill Clegg, 'Housing Schemes', Brentford and Chiswick Local History Society (https://brentfordandchiswicklhs.org.uk/search-discover/chiswick-history-homepage/housing-schemes/); Flaherty, Anne (ed), 'The District Line Celebrates 150th Anniversary', *ChiswickW4* (29 January 2019) (www.chiswickw4.com/).

Chapter 10. Dubious Tactics

279. 1841 census for 2 York Street West, Stepney; 1851 census for Portland Villa, Aston, Birmingham; 1861 census for White Hall Road,

Woodford, Essex. He would later describe himself as a financier and a gentleman (1891 and 1901 censuses for 44 Sydenham Road, Croydon; 1911 census for 7 Cottage Road, Eastbourne).

280. Henry Salter closed his business down in 1882. He died in Eastbourne in 1911, aged 89.
281. *Morning Leader*, 31 March 1904, p.5.
282. *Ally Sloper's Half Holiday*, 18 October 1890, p.7.
283. I believe Harry is erroneously listed as Harry J. Sheppard, born in Wellington, Shropshire, who is listed as living with a Wandsworth-born corn factor at Francis Street, 1 Edinburgh Mansions, Westminster, and working as a solicitor. Three years before this article appeared, in 1887, an advert appeared in the *Daily Telegraph* from a 'G. Shepherd' of West Kensington Park. This advert appealed for George Tinsley, 'who, when last heard of, was living at Battersea', to contact him, and he would 'greatly oblige'. I have been unable to find a Shepherd living at the address given in the advert. Although such an advert would normally mean there was something advantageous to Tinsley being offered, given others' complaints, it is possible that this was a cover, or a trick to get Tinsley to get in touch. Much as I would like to think that 'G. Shepherd' was a Sheppard undercover, there is no evidence for this (*Daily Telegraph*, 11 March 1887, p.8).
284. *Morning Leader*, 31 March 1904, p.5.
285. *Daily Telegraph*, 31 March 1904, p.4; *Morning Post*, 31 March 1904, p.8.
286. *Weekly Dispatch*, 23 November 1890, p.10. There are cases involving Perryman in the press and in Old Bailey accounts as well as The National Archives' MEPO files, covering at least 1891 to 1907.
287. The house was advertised in 1896 as being for sale. It was described as currently let to tenants at the 'low' rent of £35 per year, although it's not known if this was the same rent that the Tinsleys paid for it - in 1894, it had been advertised at £40 per annum (*Marylebone Mercury*, 21 February 1896, p.4; *The Era*, 21 July 1894, p.24).

288. Details of the house are taken from an advert its owner, G.H. Chirgwin, placed in 1894, when he sought to let it while he was engaged at the Alhambra in Brighton (*The Era*, 21 July 1894, p.24).
289. Emma had been in a dog-cart with a friend and a servant, travelling along Ford's Grove Lane one Saturday afternoon. They collided with a large bakery van and all three in the dog-cart were thrown out. Emma was severely shaken, and needed medical help; the doctor who attended her found that she hadn't broken any bones, but that she was 'suffering from the effects of a severe shock to the system' (*Middlesex Gazette*, 27 September 1890, p.3).
290. *London Evening Standard*, 9 December 1892, p.6.
291. *Ibid*.
292. *Ibid*.
293. *Ibid*.
294. *Birmingham Daily Gazette*, 9 December 1892, p.6.
295. George Tinsley's solicitor was Henry Kisch; Chirgwin, as stated, defended himself, but had failed to appear earlier so the case was found in Tinsley's favour in his absence. The men then appeared at the Under-Sheriff's Court in order for damages to be assessed; it was this assessment that prompted all the newspaper reports of the case - there are none for earlier stages of it.
296. One theatrical newspaper, for example, covered the case stating that Chirgwin had made a visit to the house by 'sending his coachman over the wall. He intends next time to get in through the keyhole.' (*Music Hall & Theatre Review*, 9 December 1892, p.9).
297. George was absent from Chirgwin Villa at the time of the 1891 census, although Emma and their daughters were all living there (1891 census for Chirgwin Villa, Harringay Road, Tottenham). Press accounts of the Chirgwin incident give the address as Park Street; Park Street turns into Harringay Road, so the villa may have been on the bend where the two roads meet. Emma was described in this census as married, but living on her own means; neither of her older daughters - Lilian, then aged 18, and Amy, then 16 - were working, suggesting that they were being maintained by George Tinsley, whether or not

he was living there. George Tinsley cannot be found in the 1891 census, under any of his known names or addresses.

Chapter 11. Before the Chief Magistrate

298. *Daily Mirror*, 22 April 1904, p.3.
299. *Evening Star*, 21 April 1904, p.3.
300. *Evening Echo* (Cork), 23 April 1904, p.3.
301. Frank Froëst, a Scotland Yard detective with over twenty years' experience, was promoted to chief of the Criminal Investigation Department in 1906. He would later also become an author, writing *The Grell Mystery* in 1913. In a 2015 introduction to the book, Tony Medawar describes the blue-eyed, 'genial' Froëst as 'once the most famous policeman in the world' (Tony Medawar, 'Introduction', *The Grell Mystery* (Collins, 1913 rpt 2015, p.v)
302. *Beverley and East Riding Recorder*, 30 April 1904, p.2.
303. Carlin would rise to become detective superintendent, and was regarded as one of the 'Big Five' at Scotland Yard. He retired in 1927 and died three years later (*Nottingham Journal*, 29 September 1930, p.3).
304. *Beverley and East Riding Recorder*, 30 April 1904, p.2.
305. *Ibid.*
306. *Evening Echo* (Cork), 23 April 1904, p.3.
307. *Beverley and East Riding Recorder*, 30 April 1904, p.2. It states that he was arrested the same day as Slater, but it's not wholly clear whether he was arrested at 1.45 on Friday morning, or whether it was actually early on Saturday morning.
308. The men's outfits and sitting positions were described by the *Daily Mirror* (25 April 1904, p.3). However, it didn't bother to describe John Pracy at all, seemingly regarding him as the least interesting and important figure. It had justified its description of Davies by saying that he was 'the central figure in the "Jersey incident"'.
309. *Daily Telegraph & Courier*, 25 April 1904, p.11.
310. *Beverley and East Riding Recorder*, 30 April 1904, p.2.
311. *Morning Post*, 26 April 1904, p.4.
312. *Morning Leader*, 26 April 1904, p.3.
313. *Morning Post*, 26 April 1904, p.4.

314. *Exeter and Plymouth Gazette*, 27 April 1904, p.6.
315. The detective is described under various names in the press; however, Brown seems to be the more commonly used name, and there was definitely a Metropolitan Police detective-sergeant of this name at the time.
316. The *Sheffield Daily Telegraph* of 27 April 1904 gave Smith's address as 5 Featherstone Buildings, where William Hamilton was based. However, other sources state that he gave Longley's office address – number three.
317. *Hampshire Telegraph*, 30 April 1904, p.7.
318. *Ibid.*
319. *Daily Mirror*, 27 April 1904, p.3.
320. *Ibid.*
321. *Newcastle Chronicle*, 30 April 1904, p.14; *Newcastle Evening Chronicle*, 30 April 1904, p.6.
322. *East Anglian Daily Times*, 2 May 1904, p.6.
323. *Newcastle Evening Chronicle*, 30 April 1904, p.6.
324. *East Anglian Daily Times*, 2 May 1904, p.6.
325. *Ibid.*
326. *Western Chronicle*, 6 May 1904, p.6.
327. *Dundee Evening Telegraph*, 7 May 1904, p.4. Cyril Broughton Smith was likely to have actually been living in west London at the time; he was from Kensington, and would later be living in Hammersmith. There's no evidence of him living outside of this part of London, although the 1911 census records him visiting friends in Solihull.
328. *Dundee Evening Telegraph*, 7 May 1904, p.4.
329. Fielding listed five individual detectives working for Slater by their surnames, in addition to the men in the dock. These were Iles, McKenna, King, Bush, and Britain. Bush may have been the retired Metropolitan Police detective inspector George William Bush, who would have been around 50 at the time; he would have been one of Fielding's colleagues in the police with both men retiring around the same time. Joseph McKenna has already been mentioned; he would later work for Sweeney's detective agency on Regent Street. Henry James Iles, again mentioned earlier, later found work as an insurance agent. I have not been able to identify either Britain or King with any certainty.

Chapter 12. Cartwright's Revenge

330. Accounts vary; *The Times* of 6 June 1904, p.3, for example, states that Edgar Cartwright started at Slater's as an office boy. The salaries specified are consistent across press reports, however.
331. *Nottingham Evening Post*, 4 June 1904, p.5.
332. *South Wales Daily News*, 6 June 1904, p.3.
333. *Liverpool Mercury*, 16 May 1904, p.8.
334. *Newcastle Daily Chronicle*, 6 June 1904, p.8.
335. *Montgomeryshire Echo*, 28 May 1904, p.2.
336. *London Evening Standard*, 16 May 1904, p.2.
337. This was a common epithet for Maud Goodman among the detectives; John Pracy had originally reported that Maud was 'very troublesome indeed' (*London Echo*, 14 May 1904, p.3).
338. *Daily Telegraph*, 16 May 1904, p.7; *Montgomeryshire Echo*, 28 May 1904, p.2; the latter was a very late account of proceedings on 14 May, despite it referring in its first paragraph to proceedings 'on Saturday', which to many of its readers would have meant the previous Saturday to publication, i.e. 21 May.
339. *Daily Telegraph*, 16 May 1904, p.7.
340. Old Bailey Proceedings Online (www.oldbaileyonline.org, version 8.0), October 1904, trial of Henry Scott, otherwise Henry Slater, George Philip Henry, Albert Osborn, John Pracy, otherwise John Bray, Frederick Stanley Davies, Cyril Broughton Smith (t19041017-788).
341. *Daily Telegraph*, 16 May 1904, p.7.
342. *Newcastle Daily Chronicle*, 6 June 1904, p.8.
343. *Daily Telegraph & Courier*, 7 June 1904, p.7.
344. *Ibid*.
345. Given this class influence, it might be expected that the detectives would be more deferential towards Osborn, but this was not the case – in court, Cartwright was rebuked for accusing Osborn of having committed perjury in the slander case ('Mr Osborn gave evidence against him [Stevens], but he committed perjury. He was not there.' – *Daily Telegraph & Courier*, 7 June 1904, p.7). It may be that this 'respect' was not given because Osborn was seen as being so close to

Slater; yet Osborn had also adopted a false identity of another kind. As noted elsewhere in this book, his father was a German immigrant who had changed his children's surname when they were younger, albeit informally, from Ochse to Osborn.

346. *Daily Telegraph & Courier*, 7 June 1904, p.7.
347. *Daily Telegraph & Courier*, 10 June 1904, p.6.

Chapter 13. Off to the Old Bailey

348. *Morning Post*, 13 July 1904, p.5.
349. *Reynolds's Newspaper*, 10 July 1904, p.1.
350. *Ibid.*
351. *Morning Post*, 13 July 1904, p.5.
352. *Ibid.*
353. *Ibid.*
354. *Devizes and Wilts Advertiser*, 11 June 1903, p.2; *Devizes and Wilts Advertiser*, 18 June 1903, p.2.

Chapter 14. A Very Peculiar-Looking Man

355. All comments here are taken from Old Bailey Proceedings Online (www.oldbaileyonline.org, version 8.0), October 1904, trial of Henry Scott, otherwise Henry Slater, George Philip Henry, Albert Osborn, John Pracy, otherwise John Bray, Frederick Stanley Davies, Cyril Broughton Smith (t19041017-788).
356. In the Old Bailey trial transcript, Marie details how she was approached by a solicitor named Hawksford, acting as the King's Proctor's agent on Jersey, to make a statement following the King's Proctor's intervention in the Pollard divorce case (this would have been either Cyril Hawksford, or his father Francis, both of whom were solicitors based at St Saviour on the island). By this time, she had found a job – which sounds like a servant's position – in Trouville, France, and she had to return to the Channel Islands. By the time of the Old Bailey trial, Marie Travert had also had to

make four visits to London in connection with the case. Although her hotel accommodation and expenses were paid, it's clear that the case caused a lot of disturbance for these women, involving stressful meetings with solicitors, cross-examinations and extensive travel. Marie Travert, like Louie Ford, was also a mother, and people had to be found to look after their children while they gave evidence. In Marie's case, Mrs Macnamara stepped in to look after her daughter.

357. Between Marie's and Pollard's evidence, a short statement was made by John Barrett, a Post Office clerk, detailing payments Edgar Cartwright had made to Fred Davies at Plymouth and Jersey; the evidence of the defendants that had been given in the divorce court when the King's Proctor had intervened were read out. The clerk was John Charles Barrett, who worked in the GPO Money Orders Department. He stated that Cartwright - giving his name as Edgar Wright - had gone to the Lothbury Post Office to make out several money orders to Frederick Davies between 12 and 20 March 1902. These were for various amounts of £2, £4, and £5.

358. Old Bailey Proceedings Online (www.oldbaileyonline.org, version 8.0), October 1904, trial of Henry Scott, otherwise Henry Slater, George Philip Henry, Albert Osborn, John Pracy, otherwise John Bray, Frederick Stanley Davies, Cyril Broughton Smith (t19041017-788).

359. *Ibid.*

360. Cyril Broughton Smith had given Longley's business address - 3 Featherstone Buildings, Holborn - as his home address when initially arrested, and this was later stated to be a 'fake address'. It may not have been his home address, but it was not a fake one.

361. Old Bailey Proceedings Online (www.oldbaileyonline.org, version 8.0), October 1904, trial of Henry Scott, otherwise Henry Slater, George Philip Henry, Albert Osborn, John Pracy, otherwise John Bray, Frederick Stanley Davies, Cyril Broughton Smith (t19041017-788).

362. *Ibid.*

363. *Ibid.*

364. *Ibid.*

365. He tried to state that he volunteered the information before being asked, but could not 'swear that', and it is more believable that he only admitted it as a result of being asked.

366. Old Bailey Proceedings Online (www.oldbaileyonline.org, version 8.0), October 1904, trial of Henry Scott, otherwise Henry Slater, George Philip Henry, Albert Osborn, John Pracy, otherwise John Bray, Frederick Stanley Davies, Cyril Broughton Smith (t19041017-788).
367. *Ibid.*

Chapter 15. Plymouth Girls and Private Detectives

368. *Morning Leader*, 2 November 1904, p.3; *Jersey Evening Post*, 2 November 1904, p.4.
369. He is described in the press simply as 'Rochfort Maguire', and there were several individuals of this name; however, given the presence of Churchill, this is likely to be a reference to James Rochfort Maguire (1855-1925). Churchill would, a couple of years later, become under-secretary of state for the Colonial Office, dealing with southern Africa, and Rochfort Maguire was associated with the British South Africa Company.
370. *St James's Gazette*, 2 November 1904, p.14.
371. Old Bailey Proceedings Online (www.oldbaileyonline.org, version 8.0), October 1904, trial of Henry Scott, otherwise Henry Slater, George Philip Henry, Albert Osborn, John Pracy, otherwise John Bray, Frederick Stanley Davies, Cyril Broughton Smith (t19041017-788).
372. *Ibid.*
373. *Ibid.*
374. *Ibid.*
375. *Ibid.*
376. *Ibid.*
377. *Ibid.*
378. *Ibid.*
379. *Ibid.*
380. *Ibid.*
381. *Ibid.*
382. *Ibid.*
383. Cyril Broughton Smith was still working for Slater's into 1902, but Fielding did not record when Broughton Smith left the company.

384. Old Bailey Proceedings Online (www.oldbaileyonline.org, version 8.0), October 1904, trial of Henry Scott, otherwise Henry Slater, George Philip Henry, Albert Osborn, John Pracy, otherwise John Bray, Frederick Stanley Davies, Cyril Broughton Smith (t19041017-788).
385. *Dundee Courier*, 31 March 1904.
386. Old Bailey Proceedings Online (www.oldbaileyonline.org, version 8.0), October 1904, trial of Henry Scott, otherwise Henry Slater, George Philip Henry, Albert Osborn, John Pracy, otherwise John Bray, Frederick Stanley Davies, Cyril Broughton Smith (t19041017-788).
387. Marrison said that one of the other two cases was the 'Woods case' and the third was 'the Kitchen case; it was an old case that had been put away.' He later said that the Kitchen case dated from around five years before he had started work for Slater, which would put it at around 1893. As the bulk of most private detectives' work was in divorce cases, these two cases might, like the Pollard cases, be commissions where Slater's detectives were under pressure to find evidence relating to adultery. However, a divorce case in the name of Kitchen can't be located for the right time. There are, though, two for the time period when Slater's agency was operational: one is the divorce petition of John Kitchen, who accused his wife of adultery (TNA J77/410/2473, 1888), and the second is a divorce petition from Eliza Mary Briggs against her husband Richard Briggs, who was also known as Richard Kitchen Briggs (TNA J77/650/19829, 1898). The latter case involved painter Richard Briggs, who had married Eliza Mary at Bootle in 1890, and who deserted his wife eleven months later. He was next heard of by her after he 'married' a woman in Clitheroe in 1896. He was then convicted of bigamy at Manchester in 1897 and sentenced to eighteen months in prison. This seems unlikely to have been a case involving Slater. The earlier case, however, involved John Kitchen, who married widow Charlotte Louisa Horner at Brentford in 1878. He petitioned for divorce on 23 August 1888, was granted a decree nisi on 6 December that year and a final decree on 23 July 1889. Charlotte then married Irishman John Mond - the man she had been accused of committing adultery with. However, it seems that the evidence here was clearcut, and Slater's

agency were unlikely to have needed to concoct anything in order for the divorce to proceed – so it's not certain that this was the case the agency was involved in.

388. I have been unable to find out who Shayler was; he is only referred to as 'Mr Shayler' in the Old Bailey Online record of the trial, and press coverage does not expand on his name. Shayler was not called on to give evidence.

389. Old Bailey Proceedings Online (www.oldbaileyonline.org, version 8.0), October 1904, trial of Henry Scott, otherwise Henry Slater, George Philip Henry, Albert Osborn, John Pracy, otherwise John Bray, Frederick Stanley Davies, Cyril Broughton Smith (t19041017-788).

Chapter 16. The Verdict

390. Old Bailey Proceedings Online (www.oldbaileyonline.org, version 8.0), October 1904, trial of Henry Scott, otherwise Henry Slater, George Philip Henry, Albert Osborn, John Pracy, otherwise John Bray, Frederick Stanley Davies, Cyril Broughton Smith (t19041017-788).

391. *Ibid.*

392. *Bingley Chronicle*, 11 November 1904, p.3; *The People*, 13 November 1904, p.15.

393. *The People*, 13 November 1904, p.15.

394. Emma was from Quethiock in Cornwall; she was born and raised on the farm run by her father Ambrose. Only after her mother's death in 1891 did Ambrose relocate to Plymouth, together with Emma. After she left England, he lived alone in Saltash, dying there in 1914.

395. John Conquest was a detective inspector who, like many others in the Metropolitan Police, became a private detective once he retired from the force. Many police detectives were still fairly young when they retired, and so, protected somewhat by their police pension, they could afford to start a new business. In the 1911 census, John Conquest, by now aged 61 and living with his family in Forest Hill, south London, described his occupation as 'police pensioner and private inquiries'.

396. *Empire News & The Umpire*, 29 April 1906, p.7.

397. 'Emma Radcliffe' was an inmate of Rockwood Hospital at the time of the 1911 Canadian census (accessed via www.familysearch.org); the same census has 5-year-old Jeffery [sic] Radcliffe in the Kingston, Ontario workhouse. If this is Thomas and Emma's son, then he was never retrieved by his father. In 1921, he was under the care of clergy in Kingston. Thomas Pollard had three sons by three different women, and did not bring any of them up.
398. The fortunes of the detectives have been ascertained by looking at the censuses for 1911 and 1921 and the 1939 register, as well as by looking at newspaper adverts in the British Newspaper Archive (www.britishnewspaperarchive.co.uk).
399. Hugh Charles Kino was born in June 1875 (BMDs for St George Hanover Square, vol 1a, page 330); Albert Ochse was born in December 1866 (BMDs for Strand, vol 1b, page 547). Both were born in London.
400. I cover this link between acting and private detective work in more detail in my previous book, *Sister Sleuths: Female Detectives in Britain* (Pen & Sword, 2021).
401. *Empire News & The Umpire*, 30 October 1904, p.6.

Chapter 17. A Final Identity

402. 1901 census for 71 Gipsy Lane, East Ham. 'George GK Slater', private detective, gave his place of birth as St Louis, America, but stated that he was a British subject.
403. Henry George Kenneth Ricardo Slater, son of Henry George Slater (deceased), Secret Service agent (USA), married Bruna Cose at Lambeth on 23 March 1906. Don Henry George Kenneth O'Connor Ricardo, son of George Ricardo, American Secret Service detective, married Gertrude Prudhoe at Paddington on 1 June 1911. I believe these individuals to be the same person. 'H Ricardo, born USA, actor' is on the 1911 census for 28 Paddington Green, living with Gertrude, who is listed as 'M Ricardo, actress' (they were not married at this point).
404. 'Maryan Slater', the wife listed in the 1901 census, cannot be located elsewhere; Bruna Cose was abandoned to the workhouse by her

husband. Gertrude Prudhoe was the lucky woman who managed to divorce her husband and remarry (Ancestry records shows that 'Bruna Ricardo Slater' was admitted to the Strood Workhouse on 23 October 1908 after being deserted by her husband; marriage of Gertrude M Ricardo and Charles H Blinkhorn in Wainford RD, December 1937 (vol 4a page 3025)).

405. The marriage of Alice Rebecca Akers and Bernard James Wheeler, Lydiard Millicent, 14 August 1901 (via Ancestry). Alice and Elizabeth's father, Philip Akers, was from Finstock in Oxfordshire, but had lived in London since at least 1865. He died in Kensington in 1889, leaving his widow, also named Elizabeth (nee Carter), to bring up their five children. She died in 1916. I have studied Elizabeth Akers' family, and there is no evidence of her being George Tinsley's niece. However, 'niece' was sometimes used as a euphemism for a relationship between an older man and younger woman.

406. Stevens mentioned Slater's trip, and his companion, during his evidence in his slander suit. It was to show Slater's closeness with his colleague, with Stevens detailing Slater's frequent 'kind' letters to him, sent from Australia (*Daily News* (London), 6 March 1903, p.9).

407. Number three is separated from its neighbours by a large, modern block of flats. This replaced an earlier villa, but there is no evidence that the house numbers were changed as a result of this. The local Conservation Area Character Appraisal suggests that today's 3 Haslemere Road is the same house that Henry Gordon was living in during the early 1920s anon, *London Borough of Haringey: Conservation Area No 5 Crouch End: Conservation Area Character Appraisal, Appendix 1* (2010), p.83.

408. One possibility is that during the First World War One, he may have tried to work as a musical agent; there is a George Henry Gordon listed in a 1915 Post Office Directory as such, based at 17 Shaftesbury Avenue. This was the base of the 'OK' Combine Slide Agency, which let people hire musical slides for six shillings a week. The slides were projected from magic lanterns onto a wall, and let the audience sing along to songs being played by a piano, gramophone or other instrument – so like an early karaoke. This would fit with Gordon,

its proprietor, as being George Tinsley – the man who had been a former amateur actor and member of the Wandsworth Choral Glee Union had a keen interest in singing and performance. I have found thirteen adverts for the agency, all of which date from 1915-1916. For a brief period, the manager of the agency was RE Davies – possibly one Richard Edwin Davies. The company adverts follow those of Slater's Detective Agency in repeating the same word or phrase on each line, and grabbing the reader's attention with novel aspects of the business.

409. Gordon's address at the time of his death was 13 Avenue des Îles d'or, Hyères (Ancestry, National Probate Calendar, 8 December 1926).

410. In 1939, Elizabeth Akers was living at 30 Cholmeley Crescent, Hornsey. At the time of her death, she was at the Old Manor Hospital in Salisbury – a mental health facility previously known as the Fisherton Asylum (Anon, *Old Manor Hospital*, ArtCare at https://salisburyhealthcarehistory.uk/old-manor-hospital/).

411. *Westminster and Pimlico News*, 31 January 1958, p.3.

412. The daughters' names were given as Lilian May Goddard and Winifred Maud Roe, and the granddaughter as Vera Winifred Stoddart or Stoddard (both versions of the name were published within a single article). The case was covered in the Westminster and *Pimlico News* of 31 January 1958, p.3, and the *Chelsea News & General Advertiser* of 31 January 1958, p.3, the articles being identical. Vera, nee Butler, was the daughter of Amy Tinsley and her husband Charles Butler; although listed as her mother's personal representative, she was there because her mother had died seven years earlier (BMD deaths: Amy Eva Daisy Butler died Aldershot, March 1951 (vol 6b, page 23). Vera's married name was actually Storrar, so both versions in the press were incorrect. Of the other two daughters, Lilian May Tinsley had married William Goddard in 1893; Winifred Tinsley had married John Roe in 1921. At the time of the High Court case, Vera was 52, Winifred was 67, and Lilian 84.

413. *When All Is Done* was published as part of the collection Lyrics of the Hearthside by Dodd, Mead and Company in 1899. Paul Laurence Dunbar (1872-1906) was an Ohio-born poet whose parents had been

slaves in pre-Civil War Kentucky. He wrote much of his work in a Negro dialect, although *When All Is Done* is in standard English. Dunbar died of tuberculosis at the age of 33, sixteen months after the end of the Slater's Detective Agency case at the Old Bailey (this information on Dunbar is from www.libraries.wright.edu/special/dunbar/explore/lyrics-hearthside).

414. Sir Edward Carson, KC, solicitor-general, opening the case against Henry Slater at the first hearing of the case of *Pollard v Pollard (King's Proctor intervening)* at the Divorce Division of the High Court of Justice, 16 March 1904. Carson noted that 'there were apparently a number of people associated with that agency [Slater's], and who the chief person was it was difficult to ascertain'. He then listed a number of names, all of which were George Tinsley's pseudonyms (London *Echo*, 16 March 1904, p.3; *Morning Post*, 17 March 1904, p.6).

415. Given that George Tinsley maintained contact with his wife, Emma, providing her with regular maintenance, it is possible that on starting a relationship of some kind with Elizabeth Akers, and still being officially married, he took on the name of Henry Gordon to avoid embarrassing Emma - nobody would know the truth if he was living a new life under a different name. However, he certainly could not remain Henry Slater given the ignominy that the Old Bailey case gave him under this identity, regardless of the fact that he had been acquitted of the charges.

Index

1939 Register, 166, 198, 218, 220

Abberline, Frederick, 185
Abelson, Elaine, 23, 173, 184
Adultery, 12-4, 26, 32, 46-9, 57, 61, 63, 67, 73-4, 76, 81, 85-6, 112, 117, 128-9, 137, 149, 153, 188, 192-3, 216
Advertising, 16, 27, 34-5, 37-8, 41, 44, 46, 48, 70, 78, 119, 125, 191
Akers, Elizabeth, 167-71, 219-21
Ally Sloper's Half Holiday, 107, 208
America (United States of), 4, 7, 35, 36, 139, 154, 159, 165, 170, 219
See also Baltimore, Maryland
American Independence Day, 6
Arrests, 112-4, 116-7, 130, 155, 210, 214
Attwood, Henry George *see* Attwood's Private Detective Office
Attwood's Private Detective Office, 44, 191

Baltimore, 4
See also Maryland
Bank of England, 33
Barclay's Detectives, 44, 191
Barclay, John *see* Barclay's Detectives
Basinghall Street:
  1 Basinghall Street, 28, 37, 119, 131, 190

14 Basinghall Street, 151
27 Basinghall Street, 35, 37, 190
History, 28-9, 186
Instructions from, 53, 62
Legitimacy of location, 28, 43
Office move, 37, 190
Relationships at, 122, 148-9, 151, 170
Slater's room, 41, 48
Staff duties at, 74, 84-5, 124, 127, 129-30, 137-8, 150
Thefts from, 66, 72
Visits to, 49, 64, 71, 112, 150
See also Slander
See also Slater, Henry
Battersea, 97-9, 101, 107, 109, 206, 207-8
Battersea Burial Board, 102
Bayswater, 42, 111, 190
Bell, Nellie, 58, 62, 77, 82, 145-6, 196
Bex, Walter, 113
Bodkin, Archibald Henry, 134
Bow, 179
Bow Street, 185
Bow Street Police Court, x, 113-4, 116-9, 124-5, 127-9, 131
Blackmail, 22, 24, 30, 71
Bray, John *see* Pracy, John
Brighton, 39-42, 46, 111, 162, 179, 184, 189-90, 209

Broughton Smith, Cyril:
  Appearance, 51, 124, 156
  Changing account, 117
  Corruption allegations, 85
  'Daily system', 123, 132, 155
  Different charges, 128
  Disloyalty, 118
  Fake address, 117, 211, 214
  Later life, 162
  Pseudonym, 153
  Sentence, 158
  Solicitor, 134
  Work for Longley's, 73
  Work in Plymouth, 121, 137, 142, 150
  Written reports, 66, 119, 124, 153
  See also Bow Street Police Court
  See also Old Bailey

Borough, 2
Bowden, Mr, 149
Brachygraphy *see* Shorthand
Brixton Prison, 115-6
Brompton, 91, 203-4
Brown, Alexander, 4
Brown, Captain Henry, v, 40, 90, 106, 167, 171
See also Slater, Henry
Brown, Detective Sergeant 117, 211
Buckler, Bessie, 7
Buckler, Clara, 4
Buckler, Leslie Hepburn *see* Pollard, Leslie Hepburn
Buntingford, 2, 179, 181
Burchell, James, 110
Burgess's Detective Agency, 44-5
Burgess, William *see* Burgess's Detective Agency
Bushy Park, 47

Canada, 160-1
Carlin, Francis, 113-4, 210
Carson, Sir Edward, xiii, xiv, 82-3, 86, 89, 105-8, 112, 134, 156-7, 171, 202, 221
Cartwright, Edgar:
  Comments on Slater's involvement, 41, 121
  Court rebuke, 212
  Friendships, 85
  Involvement with Simmonds' agency, 66-8, 72-4, 86, 122-8, 130, 132, 151, 154
  Later life, 163
  Position at Slater's agency, 33, 87, 121-2, 148-9, 152-3, 212, 214
  Stealing, 66-7, 72, 124
  See also Wright's Detective Agency
Cartwright, Eliza (Emma's mother), 98-9, 206
Cartwright, Eliza (Emma's sister), 98, 206
Cartwright, Emma Elizabeth *see* Tinsley, Emma
Cartwright, Florence, 163
Cartwright, William, 99, 206
Central Criminal Court *see* Old Bailey
Census, 2, 184-6, 190, 194-6, 198, 201, 203-4, 206-11, 217-8
See also 1939 Register
Chelsea, 93-4, 109, 116, 168, 171, 174, 176, 183, 203-4, 220
  Royal Borough of Kensington and, 3
Chertsey, 163
Chicago Exhibition, 35-6, 38
China, 4

Chirgwin, George Henry, 109-11, 209
Chiswick, 103-4, 174-5, 207
Cholera, 3
Chorus girls, 50-1, 67, 117
Churchill, Winston, 143, 215
City of London, 1, 28, 30, 44-5, 48, 66, 68, 97, 99, 101, 103, 162-3, 168, 205
City of London Police, 186
Clarendon Mansions, 39-40, 190
Clarke, Sir Edward, 82, 86, 202
Class, 1-3, 10, 14, 17-8, 20, 22-3, 31, 43, 62, 71, 94-6, 99-100, 126, 164, 186, 212
Cleeve, John, 134-5
Cobbe, Frances Power, 25-6
Collins, Alfred, 43
Congdon, Maria, 58, 62, 145
Conquest, John, 160-1, 217
Cook, John, 18
Cooke, Uriah, 24, 185
Copiapó, 98
Cornwall, x, 6, 50, 195, 217
Court of Appeal *see* Royal Courts of Justice
Court of Wills, Wives and Wrecks, The (nickname) *see* Royal Courts of Justice
Court of Probate *see* Royal Courts of Justice
Court for Divorce and Matrimonial Causes *see* Royal Courts of Justice
See also Divorce Court
Craig, Thomas, 66, 73-4, 85-6, 88, 122, 199-200
Cross, J.G. *see* shorthand

Crouch End, 167, 174, 219
Crouch Hill, 167
Cuffe, Hamilton, 5th Earl Desart and King's Proctor:
  Attending court, 119
  Comment on Pollard marriage, 193
  Conclusion of his case, 112
  Identity, xiii
  Impact of case, 146, 171
  Information given to, 74, 125-6, 139
  Intervention, 67, 74, 78, 86-7, 118, 129, 213-4
  Role, xiii
  Rumours regarding investigation, 75, 121
  Setting down of cause, 81-3
  Statements to, 88, 154
  Subsequent charges, 128
  See also Murray, Frederick
139, 145-6, 154, 171, 193-4, 213-4
Cycling detectives, 46, 48, 132, 191
Dale, Evelina, 11-2, 181-2
Dale, Henry, 12, 181-2
Dale, Jane Sampson *see* Sampson, Jane
Dale, Janet, 11, 181-2
Darrell, Mr and Mrs, 48
Darling, Charles, 1st Baron, 143, 156-7, 159
Davies, Frederick Stanley,
  Agency letters, 53
  Appearance, 114, 124, 136, 156, 194
  Arrest, 112-3
  Background, 51, 115, 124
  Befriending Tom Pollard, 51-3, 56, 84-5, 134-8, 142, 193, 195, 210

Charges, 118, 128
Emotion, 157
Expression of innocence, 155
Later life, 162
Spending, 54, 138, 141, 194, 214
Sacked, 87
Role at Slater's, 87, 119, 123-4, 149-50, 152-4
Sentence, 158
Solicitor, 134
Sureties, 116
See also Bow Street Police Court
Dickens, Charles, 3, 100
De Rutzen, Sir Albert, 114-6, 128-9
decree nisi, 13, 15, 63, 67, 76, 81, 161, 192, 216
See also divorce
Devon, 11, 50, 57, 60, 62, 74, 77, 83-84, 104, 138-9, 150, 158-9, 185
See also Devonport
See also Plymouth
Devonport, 50, 54-55
Divorce see Adultery; see Divorce Court; see Matrimonial Causes Act
Divorce Court, x-xii, 44, 67, 81, 84, 87, 90-1, 107, 112, 128-9, 131, 145, 149, 154, 156, 171, 201, 214, 221
Dunbar, Paul Laurence, 170, 220-1

East Finchley, 169, 171
East Indian Railway Company, 98
Eccles, Dr Albert, 55
Education, 26, 94-6, 202, 204
Elections, 30
Edward VII, 35

Elliott, Edith Maria (*nee* Barber) *see* West, Maud
Elliott, Elizabeth (*nee* Fromont), 92, 94, 203-4
Elliott, Evelyn (Maud West Jr), 90
Elliott, Sarah, 94, 203-4
Elliott, Richard, 92-4, 99, 203-4
Evans, Omwell Lloyd, 19

Featherstone Buildings, 73, 117, 211, 214
Female detectives, 21, 24-5, 30, 32-3, 38, 40, 45-46, 68, 70-1, 90, 122, 132, 190-1, 203
See also Moser, Antonia
See also Sangster, Louisa
See also Warne, Kate
See also West, Maud
Field, Charles, 18-20, 24, 33, 183
Fielding, Charles:
    Call book, 149
    Communication with Simmonds's agency, 68, 85, 122
    Description of Hamilton's role, 151-2
    Duties, 42, 56, 84, 148-50
    Exaggeration of evidence, 119
    Naming of colleagues, 202, 211, 215
    Police detective, 33
    Sacked, 68, 85, 151, 199
    Seeing present from Hugh Knowles, 152
    Starting at Slater's, 41, 152
Ford, Louisa 'Louie', 54-5, 60, 62, 82-3, 139, 144-5, 196-7, 214
Forest Gate, 1-3, 6, 11, 140, 181
Forrester, Andrew, 21
Fouché, Joseph, 32-3

Fraud, 18-9, 22, 24, 26, 30, 36, 43, 45, 47, 65, 73, 105, 145, 156
Freemasonry, 39-40, 178, 190, 202
Freshfield, James William, 97-8
Freshfields solicitors, 97-100, 107-8, 206
Froëst, Frank, 113, 210
Fulton, [James] Forrest, 134, 142
Fuzhou *see* China

Gaboriau, Emile, 21
Gill, Charles Frederick, 114-5, 128, 130, 134, 136, 141, 155
Gloucestershire, 19, 187
Goddard, Lilian May *see* Tinsley, Lilian May
'Golden Age' of detection, 23
Goodman, Maud:
  Background, 54, 195
  Court appearance, 83, 143-7
  Description, 63, 67, 197, 212
  Detectives' views on her, 63, 67, 84, 155
  False evidence, 74, 81, 118
  Friendships, 54-5, 58
  Named in divorce petition, 61
  Meetings with Osborn, 59-60, 62, 87, 119, 129, 195
  Meetings with Pracy, 61, 146
  Meetings with Murray, 77, 145-6
  Meeting with McKenna, 78, 146
  Meeting with Tom Pollard, 139
  Payments by Slater's, 66, 75, 123
  Reluctance to go to court, 82
  Reputation, 130
  Visit to London, 62-3
See also Prostitution

See also Sex
See also Summerland Place
Gordon, George Henry, 167-71, 219-21
See also Slater, Henry
See also Tinsley, George
Gordon-Cumming, Sir William, 35
Graham Campbell, Rollo, 116, 134, 142
Great Western Railway (GWR), 52, 134
Gunpowder Alley, 29
Gurney, Thomas *see* shorthand

Hamilton, William, 41, 43, 47, 73, 85, 87, 151-2, 162, 203, 211
Hammersmith, 103, 211
Harringay, 109
Harris, Henry, 22
Henry, George Philip
  Appearance at Bow Street, 116, 118, 128
  Appearance at Old Bailey, 134
  Arrest, 112, 114
  Communication with Osborn, 56
  Deflecting blame, 122
  Drafting adverts, 79
  Fear of being found out, 75
  Friendship with Slater, 68
  Instructions to detectives, 51, 54, 81, 84-6, 153-4, 195
  Later life, 162
  Office, 37
  Personal appearance, 156
  Proposal of Pollard strategy, 50, 88
  Protestation of innocence, 155
  Pseudonym, 40-1, 163
  Role at Slater's, xiii, 39, 41-2, 67, 71, 75-7, 87, 123, 130, 132, 148-52
  Sentence, 158

See also Bow Street Police Court
See also Old Bailey
High Court of Admiralty *see* Royal Courts of Justice
Holmes, Sherlock, 23, 64, 70
Hyères, 168, 220

Isaacs, Rufus, 134, 155-7
Iles, Henry James, 40, 50-1, 54, 59, 75-6, 122, 153, 162, 195, 200, 211
Inland Revenue 72-3, 126

'Jack the Ripper' see Whitechapel Murders
Jersey, 52-4, 56, 75, 81, 84-5, 87, 129, 134, 136-8, 141, 149-50, 194-5, 210, 213-4
Jeune, Sir Francis, 87, 156

Kennedy, Henry, 43-4
Kennington, 2, 44
Kensington, 2-3, 8, 42, 91, 93, 111, 113, 162, 167, 181, 192, 208, 211, 219
King's Proctor *see* Cuffe, Hamilton, 5th Earl Desart
Kino, Charles Julius *see* Knowles, Charles Julius
Kino, Hugh Charles *see* Knowles, Hugh Charles
Kleptomania, 23
Knightsbridge, 91
Knowles, Alfred, 24, 185
Knowles, Charles Julius, 8, 181
Knowles, Hugh Charles:
    Background, 8, 163

Children, 162
Death, 162
Death of father, 9
Funding investigations, 52, 57, 67, 119, 153, 165
Marriage, 162
Obtaining photograph, 54
Presents for detectives, 152
Relationship with Kate Pollard, 8-9, 11, 118
Slater's knowledge of him, 88, 129
Suggestion of divorce, 12
Visits to Slater's agency, 48-9, 86, 149, 151
Wealth, 9-10, 160
Knowles, Kenneth Guy Jack Charles, 162
Knowles, Reginald Skerrett *see* Pollard, Reginald Skerrett

Lawton, Hattie, 17
Lee *see* Lewisham
Lee, William, 52
Legg, Edward, 134-5
Legros, Alphonse, 8
Leroi, Marie, 52-3, 135-7
Lewisham, 5, 180
Leycester, William Hamilton, 134
Liverpool, 160-1
London and Westminster Bank, 72, 155, 200
Longley's Detective Agency, 73-4, 117-8, 124, 139, 199, 211, 214
Longley, Mr, 73-4, 87, 199-200, 202
Lugano, 76
Lydiard Millicent, 167, 219

McKenna, Joseph, 33, 62-3, 78, 146-7, 162, 211
Macnamara, Alexandra, 52-3, 135-6, 194, 214
Maggie's Secret (song), 102
Maguire, James Rochfort, 143, 215
Marrison, Samuel Thomas, 33, 74, 123, 148, 153-4, 156, 163, 200, 216
Marshall, Herbert, 162
Maryland, 5, 7
See also Baltimore
Marquess of Queensberry, xiii, xiv
Marylebone, 91, 159
Matcham's Hotel, 62
Matcham, Frank, 168, 198
Matrimonial Causes Act, xii, 14, 18, 21, 46, 184
Matthews, Charles, 119, 134
Mead, Frank, 52, 134
Memoirs, 17, 24, 31-2, 182
Messrs Watts, Ward and Anthony, 77
See also Murray, Frederick
Metropolitan Police see police
Mile End, 2, 179
Missing Word scandal, 34
Mortgage broking, 100, 105-106
See also Salter, Henry
'Monsieur Lecoq', 21
Moon, Alfred, 104
Monte Carlo, 35
Moser, Antonia see Williamson, Antonia
Moser, Harriet, 32
Moser, Maurice, 24, 31-2, 38, 190
Muir, Richard David, 114-5, 126, 128, 134

Murray, Frederick William, 77-8, 83, 139, 145-7, 155, 201
Myers, Solomon, 114

National Bank of New Zealand, 98
Notting Dale see Kensington

Ochse, Albert see Osborn, Albert
Old Bailey, x, 128-9, 131-2, 139-42, 146, 148, 152-4, 156, 160, 162, 164, 178, 187, 208, 213, 217, 221
Osborn, Albert:
  Advice to Maud Goodman, 77-8
  Appearance, 156
  Complicity, 81, 85-6, 88, 112-3, 118-9, 123, 129, 141-7, 195
  Family, 48, 162
  Friends, 115
  Identity, 163, 213, 218
  Law firm, 13, 48, 76, 148, 153, 163, 192, 197
  Wealth, 115, 124, 126
  Parsimoniousness, 83
  Relationship with George Henry, 56, 84, 150
  Relationship with Henry Slater, xiii, 13, 67-8, 130, 148-9, 151-2
  Reputation, 74-5, 82, 130, 212
  Statement in court, 155
  Visits to Plymouth, 54-7, 59-62, 65, 87, 122, 142-3
See also Bow Street
See also Old Bailey
Osborn and Osborn, see Osborn, Albert
Oxford, 162

Paddington, 7, 63, 83, 91-2, 140, 159, 162, 181, 218
Palace Court Mansions, 42, 111, 113
Palmer, William, 18-19
Palmistry, 64
Panama Canal scandal, 34
Pawnbroking, 96-7, 139
Peek, Sir Henry, 102
Perryman, Charles Wilbraham, 108, 208
Petitions *see* Divorce
Phrenology, 64
Pinkerton, Allan, 17, 182
Pitman's shorthand, *see* Shorthand
Pollaky, Ignatius 'Paddington', 20, 38, 92
Pollard, Elizabeth Wilcocks, *nee* Grigg (Tom's mother), 12, 40, 49, 137, 139-41, 152, 159
Pollard, Kate:
  Birth, 2, 179
  Changing name, 164
  Death, 162
  Employment, 7
  Engaging Osborn and Osborn, 48, 55, 63, 81, 86, 192
  Engaging Slater's Agency, 12, 49, 84
  First divorce petition/decree, 13, 15, 61, 63, 67, 74, 112, 139, 141, 193
  Judicial separation, 129
  Informal separation, 11, 137, 140
  Marriage to Hugh Knowles, 162
  Marriage to Tom Pollard, 2, 6, 7-11, 28, 49, 54, 141, 181
  Motherhood, 7
  Relationship with Hugh Knowles, 8-9, 12, 118

  Second divorce petition/decree, 15, 159-62, 165
  Under investigation, 67, 81-2, 145-6
  Upbringing, 2-3
Pollard, Leslie Buckler (son), 5-8, 10, 180-1
Pollard, Leslie Hepburn (*nee* Buckler), 4-5, 180
Pollard, Reginald Skerrett (later Knowles), 7-8, 162, 180
Pollard, Thomas ('Tom'):
  Adultery allegations, 12, 49-51, 61-2, 67, 77-8, 81, 85-6, 112, 117-8, 134-5, 142, 153, 155, 161
  Appearance, 134-5, 152
  Background, 3, 67
  Boastfulness, 160
  Drinking, 7, 9, 12, 49-50, 53, 75, 85, 87, 129-30, 138, 140-1, 159-61
  Employment, 3-5
  First marriage, 4
  Fatherhood, 5, 7, 159-61, 218
  Letters from Mr Longley, 73-4
  Loneliness, 50, 137
  Overseas travel, 4, 6
  Photograph, 54, 59-60, 144
  Pseudonym, 159-60
  Relationship with Emma Toll, 159-60
  Relationship with Fred Davies, 52-53
  Unemployment/destitution, 10, 15, 49, 63, 130, 137, 139
  Widowed, 5-6
  See also Pollard, Kate
  See also Prostitution
Pollard, Thomas (Tom's father), 12, 49, 137, 152, 159

Polmear, John Henry, 104
Portslade, 2, 179
Plymouth:
   Assault, 196
   Detectives' work, 51-7, 61-2, 64-5, 70-1, 75, 81-7, 117, 121-2, 129, 138-9, 146, 150, 158
   History, 50, 58, 143, 145, 150, 159
   Hoe, 58, 61, 78, 83, 144, 146
   Pollard home, 11, 49, 137, 140
   Toll enquiries, 159-60
   Train to London, 63
See also Goodman, Maud
See also Murray, Frederick
See also Pollard, Thomas ('Tom')
See also Prostitution
See also Summerland Place
Plymouth Blitz, 58
Pracy, John:
   Arrest, 112-3
   Background, 115
   Ethics, 147
   Later life, 162
   Looks, 156, 164, 210
   Use of pseudonym, 40, 118, 153, 163
   Shadowing, 53-4, 57, 196
   Identifying Tom Pollard, 61, 144-5
   Chaperoning Maud, 62
   Loyalty, 84, 155
   Mentioning payments to Maud, 75, 123
   Pressurising Maud, 82-3, 146, 197
   Sentenced, 158
   Sureties, 116
   Solicitor, 114, 134
See also Bow Street Police Court
See also Old Bailey

Radcliffe, Colonel *see* Pollard, Thomas
Radcliffe, Jeffrey, 159-60
Radcliffe, Mrs *see* Toll, Emma Amelia
Rhodes, Cecil, 156
Robinson, Robert Ansley, 19, 184
Roe, Winifred Maud *see* Tinsley, Winifred Maud
Rugeley Poisoner, The *see* Palmer, William
Russia, 8

Sampson, Jane (daughter; Jane Dale), 11, 181-2
Sampson, Jessie, 2, 3, 11, 179
Sangster, Louisa, 32, 37, 188
See also Female detectives
Scherer, Wendel, 92
Scotland, x, 1
Scotland Yard, 36, 113-4, 210
Scott, Captain Henry *see* Slater, Henry
Seymour, Henry *see* Slater, Henry
Septicaemia, puerperal, 5
Sex, xii, 13, 15, 49, 52, 54, 58-9, 67, 89, 118, 135-6, 138, 161, 171
See also Adultery
See also Prostitution
'Shadowing', xiii, 13, 18, 20-1, 30, 32, 49, 61, 76, 79, 85, 122, 124, 148, 161
Shepherd's Bush, 10-1
Sheppard, Harry H., 107-9, 127, 208
Sheppard, Hobart, 107
Shorthand, 99-101, 109, 152
Simmonds, Charles Henry, 33, 66, 68-72, 74, 85-6, 122, 126, 132, 151, 154, 163

Index 231

Simmonds' Detective Association, 66, 68, 86, 87, 106, 151, 154-5, 163
See also Simmonds, Charles Henry
Slander, 35, 66, 69-74, 77, 124-6, 130, 212, 219
Slater's Detective Agency:
  Cases:
    Clifford, Annetta O'Brien case (1895), 47, 192
    Colonel Hill case (1890), 86, 202
    Douglas-Pennant case (1901), 192-3
    Ryan, Major case (1903), 76-77
    Smith, Catherine case (1899), 47-8, 192
    Whiteside case (1891), 86, 202
    Wilcox, John case (1903), 76-7
    Wright, Richard case (1903), 75-6
  See also Moser, Maurice
  Commissioned by Hugh Knowles, 12-3, 15, 49
  Competitors, 44-5
  See also Attwood's Private Detective Office
  See also Barclay's Detectives
  See also Burgess's Detective Agency
  See also Simmonds' Detective Association
  See also Moser, Maurice
  Fees, 55, 57
  Office see Basinghall Street
  Solicitors see Osborn, Albert
  Tactics, 19, 26-7, 29-33, 35, 38, 46, 79-80
  See also *Missing Word* scandal

Slater, Henry:
  At the Divorce Court, x, xii-xiv, 88-9
  Arrest, 112-3
  Amateur dramatics, 100-1
  See also Wandsworth Choral Glee Union
  Banking, 72
  Becoming a detective, 105-6
  Birth, 91
  Childhood, 92-5
  Copycats, 43-4, 70, 165-6, 218
  Early career:
    Jeweller's assistant, 97
    Pawnbroker's assistant, 96-7
    Shorthand writer/tutor, 99-1
    Solicitor's clerk, 97-99
  End of detective career, 159
  Enemies, 68, 107-9
  See also Stevens, Francis William
  See also Sheppard, Harry H.
  Family see Elliott, Richard; Tinsley, Amy Eva Daisy; Tinsley, Edith Elliott; Tinsley, Emma Elizabeth; Tinsley, Lilian May; Tinsley Winifred Maud
  Fatherhood, 99, 101
  Friendships, 64-5, 78
  See also Slander
  See also Stevens, Francis William
  Legal action, 47
  See also Slander
  Marriage, 98
  Old Bailey trial see Old Bailey
  Parentage, 92
  Personality, 125

Press interviews, 35-7
Pseudonyms, 39, 90-1,106-8, 127, 160, 171-2
See also Brown, Captain Henry
See also Gordon, George Henry
See also Scott, Captain Henry
Relationship with Elizabeth Akers *see* Akers, Elizabeth
Semi-retirement: 39-41, 67, 71, 121, 148, 155
See also Freemasonry
Separation, 111
Travel to Australia, 42, 167
See also Tinsley, George
Slater, Henry, Junior *see* Henry, George Philip
Smith, Emma, 58, 143, 196
Smith, Emma Elizabeth, 185
Smyth, Sir John Greville, 64, 198
South Africa, 47-8, 76, 138, 156, 215
South Kensington, *see* Kensington
Southend-on-Sea, 114, 116, 162-3, 166
Southwark, 2, 179
Spitalfields, 29
Stephenson, Guy, 114, 134
Stevens, Emily, 64, 198
Stevens, Francis William:
  Accused of fraud, 65, 125
  Children, 199
  Divorce, 65, 198
  Enmity towards Slater, 66-70, 73-4, 121, 127-8, 130, 132, 151, 154
  Friendship with Slater, 55, 64, 79, 90, 126, 167, 219
  Funding Simmonds' Detective Association, 66, 72, 106
  Involvement with Pollard case, 56-7, 59-60, 65
  Keeping secrets, 71
  Later life, 163
  Leaving Slater's, 66
  Loyalty of colleagues, 125-6
  Manager at Slater's, 55, 122
  Previous jobs, 33, 64
  Suing Slater, 69-70, 77, 124, 212
  Theft of financial information, 72, 125
  Theft of Pollard papers, 66
  See also Simmonds' Detective Association
  See also Slander
Summerland Place, 54-5, 58-9, 77-8, 143-4, 147, 195-6
See also Goodman, Maud
Sutton, Henry, 134
Sweeney, John, 163, 211
Swindon, 167

Teddington Hall, 48
Telegram *see* telegraphy
Telegraphy. 30, 35, 38, 46, 51, 74, 83, 85, 115, 139-40, 187, 193, 195
Telephony, 30, 56, 148, 187
'Theatreland', 24, 28, 30, 44
Thomas, Alexander, 195
Timid Little Maid, The (song), 102
Tinsley, Amy Eva Daisy (later Butler), 101, 169, 209, 220
Tinsley, Edith Elliott, 99, 101, 206
Tinsley, Emma Elizabeth (*nee* Cartwright), 98-101, 103-4, 109-11, 166-170, 206, 209, 220-1

Tinsley, Lilian May (later Goddard), 101, 169, 209, 220
Tinsley, Winifred Maud (later Roe), 109, 169, 220
Tinsley, George, 91-4, 97-111, 127, 165-71, 204-10, 219-21
See also Slater, Henry
Toll, Ambrose, 159, 217
Toll, Emma Amelia, 159-60, 217
Tottenham, 1, 109, 111, 168, 209
Trace, George, 24, 185
Transport, 1, 46, 83
Travert, Marie, 52-3, 75, 130, 135-7, 141, 194, 213-4
Turnham Green, 103

Valetta, John Paul, 114, 134
Victorian (ship), 160

Wandsworth, 101-2, 206, 208
Wandsworth Choral Glee Union, 102-3, 220
Wanstead Flats, 1

Ward, George Washington, 4
Warne, Kate, 17-8, 21, 182
See also Female detectives
Watney, Daniel, 102
Weeks, Arthur, 33
West Ham, 2, 6
West, Maud, 40, 90, 190, 203
See also Female detectives
Whistler, James MacNeill, 8
Whitechapel Murders, 25, 185-6
Wilde, Oscar, xiii-xiv
Williamson, Antonia, 32
See also Female detectives
See also Moser, Maurice
Williamson, Edward, 32
Wilson, Minnie, 54-5, 59-60, 143-5, 196
Wilton Hotel, Pimlico, 76
Wood Green, 113
World War 2 see Plymouth Blitz
Wormwood Scrubs, 162
Wright's detective agency see Cartwright, Edgar